Wilderness Journeys

OFFROAD MOZAMBIQUE • BOTSWANA • NAMIBIA • LESOTHO • SOUTH AFRICA

Willie & Sandra Olivier

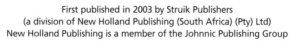

First published in 2003 by Struik Publishers
(a division of New Holland Publishing (South Africa) (Pty) Ltd)
New Holland Publishing is a member of the Johnnic Publishing Group

Garfield House
86–88 Edgware Road
W2 2EA London
United Kingdom
www.newhollandpublishers.com

Cornelis Struik House
80 McKenzie Street
Cape Town 8001
South Africa
www.struik.co.za

14 Aquatic Drive
Frenchs Forest, NSW 2086
Australia

218 Lake Road
Northcote, Auckland
New Zealand

Copyright © in published edition 2003: Struik Publishers
Copyright © in text 2003: Willie and Sandra Olivier
Copyright © in maps 2003: Struik Publishers
Copyright © in photographs 2003: as listed below

ISBN 1 86872 777 7

1 3 5 7 9 10 8 6 4 2

Publishing Manager: Dominique le Roux
Commissioning Manager: Annlerie van Rooyen
Managing Editor: Lesley Hay-Whitton
Cover and Concept Design: Alison Day
Design: Illana Fridkin
Editors: Neill Hurford and Amanda Chapman
Cartographer: John Hall
Proofreader: Christine Grant
Indexer: Mary Lennox

Reproduction by Hirt & Carter Cape (Pty) Ltd
Printed and bound in Hong Kong by Sing Cheong Printing Company Limited

All rights reserved. No part of this publication may be reproduced, stored in a retrieval system, or transmitted, in any form or by any means, electronic, mechanical, photocopying, recording or otherwise, without the prior written permission of the copyright owner/s.

Copyright © in photographs Willie and Sandra Olivier 2003, with the exception of the following: Front cover Mitsubishi Motors (repeated on even pages from 4–10 and 194–210); pages 6–7 Lanz von Hörsten/Struik Image Library; pages 12–13 (main picture, and repeated on back cover, top) Getaway/Patrick Wagner/Photo Access; picture repeated on even pages from 12–32 Getaway/David Roger/Photo Access; 34–35 (main picture, and repeated on back cover, second from top) Getaway/Patrick Wagner/Photo Access; picture repeated on even pages from 98–144 Geoff Dalglish; 146–147 (main picture, and repeated on back cover, second from bottom) Getaway/Justin Fox/Photo Access; 166–167 (main picture, and repeated on back cover, bottom) Jéan du Plessis; 194–195 Hein von Hörsten/Struik Image Library

DISCLAIMER
While every effort has been made to ensure accuracy, the authors and the publisher will not be liable for any inconvenience or loss, resulting from possible inaccuracies. Information such as telephone numbers, e-mail addresses, roads and tracks could have changed since the authors researched the routes, and the publisher would appreciate updated information. Please write to: The Editor, *Wilderness Journeys*, PO Box 1144, Cape Town, 8000 or e-mail updates@struik.co.za.

Visit us at **www.struik.co.za**
Log on to our photographic website **www.imagesofafrica.co.za**
for an African experience.

ACKNOWLEDGEMENTS

For more than two decades we have been privileged to explore many of the beautiful and remote corners of southern Africa both on foot and by four-wheel drive vehicle. Each of these trips was inevitably a journey of discovery for us, giving us a better understanding of the intricate ways of nature.

With this book we wish to share with you some of the enjoyment we have had in the wilds, in the hope that it will help to make your own wilderness journeys enjoyable and memorable.

We would like to say thank you to our friends who joined us on our travels from time to time. A special word of thanks to Louis Wessels who had to stand in for Sandra on a number of occasions as 'note and distance taker'.

Our thanks also go to Annlerie van Rooyen who, as the former publishing manager of Struik's travel books, commissioned us, and to her successor, Dominique le Roux, for her enthusiasm and ideas. We also owe our gratitude to managing editor Lesley Hay-Whitton for her understanding, editors Neill Hurford and Amanda Chapman, designers Illana Fridkin and Alison Day, and cartographer John Hall, who all contributed to turning an idea into a book.

Willie and Sandra Olivier
April 2003

CONTENTS

INTRODUCTION 8

MAP OF THE REGION 10

MOZAMBIQUE 12
    Overview 14
    Maputo Elephant Reserve 18
    Vilankulo to Punda Maria 24
    Gorongosa National Park 30

BOTSWANA 34
    Overview 36
    Gemsbok Wilderness Trail 40
    Mabuasehube 46
    Khutse Game Reserve 50
    Central Kalahari Game Reserve 55
    Makgadikgadi Pans 61
    Makgadikgadi 66
    Nxai Pan 71
    Moremi Game Reserve 77
    Chobe National Park 83
    Tsodilo Hills & Gcwihaba Cave 91

NAMIBIA 98
    Overview 100
    Saddle Hill Guided 4x4 Trail 104
    Conception Expedition 109
    Naukluft 4x4 Trail 114
    Kaokoveld 120
    Nyae Nyae 129
    Khaudum Game Park 134
    North-Eastern Parks 139

LESOTHO 146
    Overview 148
    The Mountain Road & Roof of Africa 152
    Trans-Maloti 158

SOUTH AFRICA 166
- Overview 168
- Karoo 4x4 Trail 172
- Riemvasmaak 177
- Richtersveld National Park 183
- Baviaanskloof 190

THE BASICS 194
- Vehicles, accessories and equipment 196
  - The vehicle 196
    - The basics of 4x4 driving 196
    - Where to get help choosing a 4x4 196
    - Tyres 196
  - Accessories 196
  - The equipment 197
- Driving in difficult terrain 197
  - In sand 197
  - On dunes 197
  - Over rocky terrain 197
  - In mud 198
  - Through rivers 198
  - In elephant country 198
- Maps and navigation 198
- Diseases and other dangers 199
- Enhancing your experience 199
- Bush etiquette 199
- Packing lists 200
  - Essentials 200
  - Camping equipment 200
  - Clothing 200
  - Personal 201
  - Miscellaneous 201
  - Vehicle spares, tools and equipment 201

ESSENTIAL READING 202

INDEX 206

The vast desert landscape of the Richtersveld in South Africa's remote north-west.

INTRODUCTION

Our passion for wild places dates back to the early 1980s when we first hiked many thousands of kilometres on trails throughout southern Africa. The occasional 4x4 journey to the remote parts of Lesotho, the Richtersveld and Moremi Game Reserve introduced us to another way to experience the wilds, but it was our move to Namibia in 1985 that spurred us on to explore the country's remote corners and off-the-beaten-track routes.

With dangerously little mechanical knowledge, only the most basic equipment and often no maps to guide us, but loads of enthusiasm and a strong sense of adventure, we made use of every opportunity to explore the country. As we became familiar with the local tracks and trails, it was only natural that the distant peaks, wide-open spaces and game-rich plains of the wildernesses beyond Namibia's borders would lure us. The rewards have always been great and the memories are indelible.

Although not many of southern Africa's wild places are as remote and isolated as they were two decades ago, there are still many destinations where you can leave the beaten track. This book is not really meant to be a guide to trails; it is rather intended to assist the exploration of those areas that we feel still represent the quintessential spirit of Africa. They include the shimmering lakes of southern Mozambique, some of Africa's top game-viewing destinations in Botswana, the windswept dunes of the Namib Desert, the snow-capped peaks of Lesotho's Malotis and the mountain desert of the Richtersveld.

It is our fervent hope that, while you are reading of the thrilling places on this subcontinent that you can reach in your 4x4, you will enjoy your journey through the pages of this book with us.

We travel to 26 wilderness areas in five southern Africa countries. The countries have been arranged in geographical order, and each section is preceded by a brief description of the country and its main features. The people, animals and birds, routes, facilities, and booking details, where appropriate, follow.

Most of the chapters focus on a particular area. We describe these in geographical sequence (generally from south to north, enabling us to link adjoining areas more easily). In a few instances, where the experience is essentially the journey itself, a tour is described.

We've given distances in the routes section as accurately as possible, but odometer readings can vary, depending on tyres, detours around obstacles and other factors. As it is impossible to describe all the subsidiary tracks, we have focused on the main tracks only. You should derive some comfort from the knowledge that most of the major tracks in southern Africa's wilderness areas are now either signposted or indicated on up-to-date maps.

Distances have been measured either from and back to a central point of departure on the most likely approach routes, or between two destinations. In some cases the distances from the nearest major towns to the point of departure are also provided to assist with planning. Distances are approximate, but generous allowances have been made for game-viewing drives and short detours. Actual distances will depend on the duration of your visit and the frequency of game/scenic drives.

Although we visited most of the areas described here in late 2002 and early 2003 to ensure that the information was as up-to-date as possible, some tracks, infrastructure and signposting might have changed.

Willie and Sandra Olivier

WILLIE AND SANDRA OLIVIER have covered vast areas throughout southern Africa, exploring the region both by road and on foot. They are the authors of *Exploring the Natural Wonders of South Africa*, *Overland through Southern Africa*, the highly successful *Touring in South Africa* and, recently released, *Hiking Trails of South Africa*. Willie is also a freelance lecturer in journalism, specialising in political reporting.

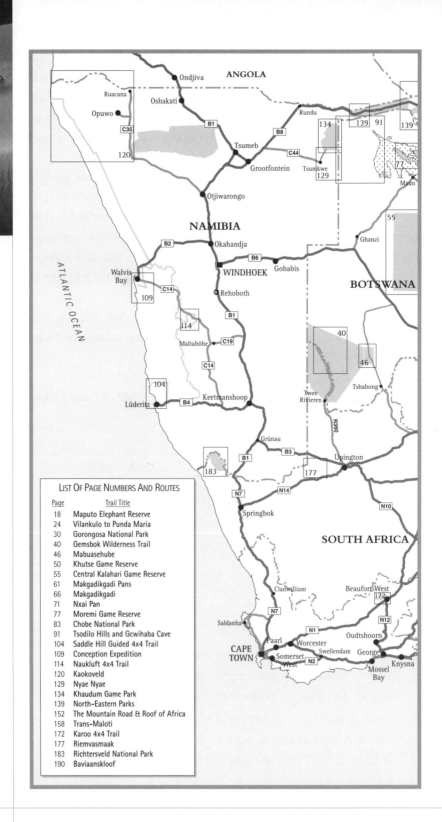

LIST OF PAGE NUMBERS AND ROUTES

Page	Trail Title
18	Maputo Elephant Reserve
24	Vilankulo to Punda Maria
30	Gorongosa National Park
40	Gemsbok Wilderness Trail
46	Mabuasehube
50	Khutse Game Reserve
55	Central Kalahari Game Reserve
61	Makgadikgadi Pans
66	Makgadikgadi
71	Nxai Pan
77	Moremi Game Reserve
83	Chobe National Park
91	Tsodilo Hills and Gcwihaba Cave
104	Saddle Hill Guided 4x4 Trail
109	Conception Expedition
114	Naukluft 4x4 Trail
120	Kaokoveld
129	Nyae Nyae
134	Khaudum Game Park
139	North-Eastern Parks
152	The Mountain Road & Roof of Africa
158	Trans-Maloti
172	Karoo 4x4 Trail
177	Riemvasmaak
183	Richtersveld National Park
190	Baviaanskloof

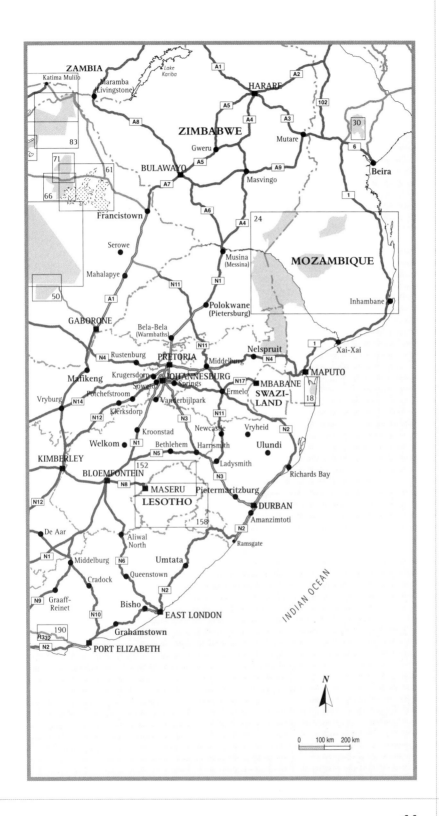

Main picture: A sand dune near Ponta Malongane, Southern Mozambique.
Inset picture: Near Inhambane, southern Mozambique.

Mozambique

MOZAMBIQUE

Delicious prawns, expanses of unspoiled beaches washed by the crystal-clear waters of the warm Indian Ocean, pristine coral reefs and endless expanses of bush come to mind when you mention Mozambique. In just over a decade since the brutal civil war came to an end, Mozambique has recovered remarkably and is once again a popular destination for South African holidaymakers.

Coastal plains cover 44% of the country and are especially dominant in the southern provinces of Maputo, Inhambane and Gaza, as well as Sofa and coastal Zambezia provinces in the centre. Mixed woodlands are characteristic, except in the dry west where they are replaced by mopane and acacia savanna.

Mozambique's four national parks and reserves provide protection to about 12% of the country's surface. But the game-rich parks and reserves served as the larder for both sides during the civil war that raged for nearly two decades. As well-known conservationist Paul Dutton put it: 'The war came to an end when there was no more game left.' So the major attraction of these parks is not game-viewing but rather the wild atmosphere and the birding possibilities.

Environmental degradation is a cause for serious concern in Mozambique and deforestation and slash-and-burn agricultural practices are widespread. The fact is that Mozambique is one of the poorest countries in the world and everywhere you will see people trying to sell something – charcoal, wooden poles, chipped rock, live chickens or mangoes.

Mozambique's climate is tropical. Coastal Mozambique is humid while the interior is dry. The summer months (November to April) are hot with average daily temperatures in the upper 20s. Winters are moderate and pleasant with daily temperatures seldom dropping below 20°C. Most of the rain falls between December and March during violent thunderstorms. Rainfall measurements decrease from between 800 and 1 000 mm along the coast to below 400 mm at Pafuri. Floods have ravaged large parts of Mozambique in recent years.

Mozambique gained independence in 1975 after an 11-year armed struggle against Portuguese colonialism. Socialist economic policies adopted by the Frelimo government wrecked the economy and a civil war led by the South African-backed Renamo rebel movement brought further misery to the country and its people. Peace was concluded in 1992 and the first democratic elections were held two years later. Since 1994 Mozambique has seen a major economic upswing and billions of US dollars have flowed into the country as investment.

It will take years to rebuild the country, and many visitors are shocked when they reach the outskirts of Maputo and see the chaotic informal markets. The Maputo of today is a very different place from the Lourenço Marques that many South Africans remember from the early 1970s. Years of civil war brought the city to a virtual standstill, but its rejuvenation over the last decade has seen Maputo slowly regaining its former splendour.

Bear in mind that poverty is rife throughout the country and wages are in most cases shockingly low. Despite years of misery Mozambicans are amongst the most friendly and pleasant people you could encounter anywhere.

Overview

The road infrastructure has improved enormously, and from Maputo northwards the main highway is fully tarred and generally in good condition. All major towns are accessible by gravel road but in the remote rural areas there are still many tracks that can be explored.

While English is increasingly spoken and understood, Portuguese is the official language, and you might have difficulty in communicating with people outside popular resort areas. Learning a few useful phrases or keeping a small dictionary handy will make your visit easier and more fun.

BORDER POSTS AND FORMALITIES

Arriving at a Mozambican border post for the first time can be quite confusing as there are several formalities, and officials speak only Portuguese. Operators at Ressano Garcia claiming to be employed by the Mozambican authorities to assist visitors are merely a nuisance. They will demand money for helping you, so send them off with a firm 'No thank you'.

Komatipoort/Ressano Garcia, on the Maputo Corridor linking Witbank and Maputo, is open from 06h00 to 19h00, Ponta do Ouro from 07h30 to 17h30 and the Namaacha border post in Swaziland from 07h00 to 20h00.

IMMIGRATION

All visitors require a visa. Apply at least 10 days in advance (urgent visas are issued within two working days) to the Mozambican consulates in Pretoria, Cape Town, Durban and Nelspruit, or use a travel agency which offers visa services.

On arrival in the country you can get a visa only at Ressano Garcia or Maputo's Mavelane International Airport, but this costs far more (US$25.00) than through the embassy (there are various fees, depending on the urgency of the visa). It also takes at least 30 minutes for a visa to be issued at Ressano Garcia and at the airport (and sometimes even longer).

You have to complete an arrival form and pay a fee of R15.00 to have your passport stamped.

Extensive grasslands south of the Maputo Elephant Reserve.

MOZAMBIQUE

Customs
You are allowed to bring into Mozambique goods to the value of US$100.00 per person duty-free and 5 litres of wine, 1 litre of spirits, 400 cigarettes, 100 cigarillos and 50 cigars.

Permits for temporary export/import of goods
You need a permit to export and import your vehicle and other goods. You can get the form at the South African border post (Komatipoort) and have it completed and stamped by the South African customs officials. It is best to specify all items (such as camping equipment, cameras, etc). At Ressano Garcia hand the form to the Mozambican customs officials who will also stamp it. Keep it in a safe place as you must hand it in when you depart through Ressano Garcia/Komatipoort.

Third party insurance
Third party insurance is compulsory and you can buy it for R120.00 at the Ressano Garcia border post. There is no third party office at Pafuri so if you do the Vilankulo to Punda Maria journey in the opposite direction get insurance (known as *seguros* in Portuguese) in Vilankulo.

Vehicle documentation
Take your original vehicle registration document with you.

Driving
- You must have an international driving licence, obtainable from the Automobile Association, or the new credit card-type of licence issued in SADC countries.
- Carry two reflective warning triangles for use in the event of a breakdown.
- Wearing seat belts is compulsory.
- If you are towing a trailer, boat or caravan you must display a yellow and blue warning triangle mounted at the front of the towing vehicle and at the rear of the vehicle being towed.
- Adhere to speed limits, especially in urban areas where speed traps are not uncommon. Expect to pay a hefty fine in cash if you are caught speeding.
- Avoid driving at night as unroadworthy vehicles without lights are a constant menace on the roads.

Currency and banks
Mozambique's currency, the Metical, or plural Meticais (which is pronounced 'meticash'), is divided into 100 centavos. The exchange rate in mid-2003 was about 3 100 meticals to the Rand and 24 000 meticals to the US Dollar.

South of Inhambane, the South African Rand is generally accepted. US dollars in cash and travellers' cheques can be exchanged at banks in Maputo and all the major towns further north. Mozambican banks include Banco Comercial e De Investimentos (BCI), Banco Comercial de Moçambique (BCM) and Standard Totta.

VITAL INFO

- Consult your doctor or a travel clinic about the most effective prophylaxis as **malaria** is endemic in Mozambique, except in the high altitude areas.
- In summer **cholera** outbreaks occur from time to time so take precautions.
- **Tap water** in cities and towns is unfit for consumption and we suggest you drink bottled water. Safe drinking water is available in the Maputo Elephant Reserve and Zinave and Gorongosa national parks.
- The Mozambican government is trying to stamp out **corruption**. Despite this visitors occasionally complain about excessive fines and trumped-up charges, but we have never had any unpleasant experiences. The best way to avoid such situations is to stick to speed limits, ensure that you are in possession of all the right documentation and be courteous if stopped. If you find yourself in an awkward situation, stand your ground and ask to see a higher-ranking official. Insist on a receipt (*recibo*) if you have to pay a fine. This is not always easy as few officials speak or understand English.
- Take enough **35-mm slide film** as you are unlikely to find it anywhere in Mozambique, not even in Maputo. Colour print film is readily available.
- If your **cellphone service provider** has international roaming with the Mozambican network Mcel, you will be able to get reception along the Nelspruit/Maputo road and from Maputo at major towns northwards to Beira.

Entrance and camping fees at Maputo Elephant Reserve and Gorongosa National Park are payable in US dollars.

MAPS

The *Globetrotter Travel Map: Mozambique* is the most detailed map available. In addition to the roads it has street plans of all the major cities and towns as well as a handy place name index. The 1: 2 000 000 map (*Mozambique Carta Turística*) published by the Mozambican Directorate of Surveys is also useful. Buy it at the public information office on the corner of Avenida Francisco Orlando Magumbwe and Avenida Eduardo Mondlane.

MOZAMBIQUE

Maputo Elephant Reserve

Just across Maputo Bay (Baia de Maputo) from the capital Maputo, shimmering lakes, stretches of grassland and miles of unspoiled white beaches flanked by forested dunes all combine to create some of the most beautiful scenery of this country. Ample opportunities for bird-watching make up for the absence of large herds of game within the reserve. The offshore reefs boast a variety of colourful tropical fish, corals and other marine creatures. Take long beach walks and swim in the crystal-clear lukewarm water of the Indian Ocean.

THE PARK

The reserve was proclaimed in 1932 to protect Africa's southernmost concentration of elephant living in a natural system, and other species of game. The original boundaries stretched from Cabo de Santa Maria, the northernmost point of the Machangulo Peninsula, southwards for 85 km to the South African border. When the boundaries were redrawn in 1969, the Machangulo Peninsula was excluded, reducing the park significantly. The Maputo and Futi rivers partly form the reserve's western boundary, and to the east it is bounded by the Indian Ocean for 40 km.

The Maputo Elephant Reserve will form the core of the planned Lubombo Transfrontier Conservation Area (LTFCA) of which two-thirds will fall in Mozambique, while the other third comprises Tembe Elephant Park and Ndumo Game Reserve in South Africa's KwaZulu-Natal as well as Hlane Game Reserve and Mkhaya Nature Reserve in Swaziland. The future of the LTFCA hangs in the balance, however, as the Mozambican government plans to build a US$520 million deep-sea port and free trade development zone between Ponta Dobela in the south of the reserve and Ponta Mamoli further south.

Landscape and vegetation

Sand and dune forests, woodlands, grasslands and reed beds interspersed with numerous pristine lakes and seasonal pans create an array of habitats on the coastal plains of southern Mozambique. The reserve lies at the heart of the Maputaland Centre of Plant Diversity and over 200 of the more than 2 500 plant species recorded here are endemic or near-endemic to the centre (near-endemic usually refers to species with 40% or more of their world population in one country, and the remainder in one adjoining country or more).

Typical trees that can easily be identified by their fruit include the pod mahogany with its large (up to 17 cm long) dark brown pod. The black monkey orange, a small shrubby tree, bears round

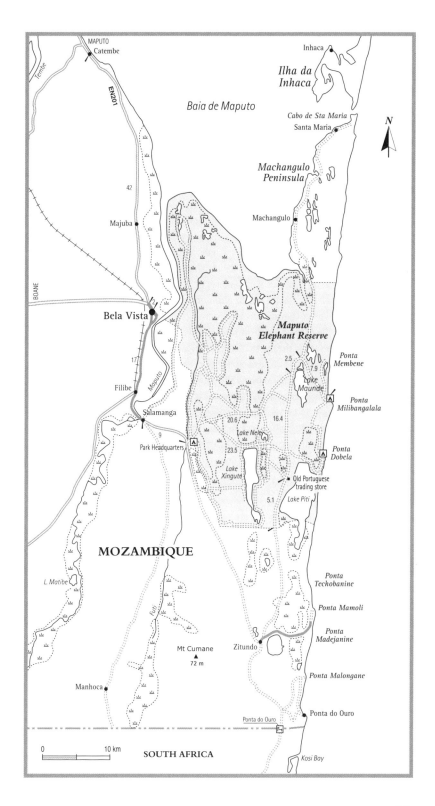

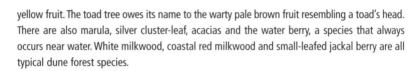

MOZAMBIQUE

yellow fruit. The toad tree owes its name to the warty pale brown fruit resembling a toad's head. There are also marula, silver cluster-leaf, acacias and the water berry, a species that always occurs near water. White milkwood, coastal red milkwood and small-leafed jackal berry are all typical dune forest species.

Fauna and game-viewing

The reserve was once home to a large population of elephant that migrated seasonally along the Futi Channel, a fossil drainage line, into the Tembe area of northern KwaZulu-Natal. The population was estimated at 350 in 1971 but, during the civil war, poaching and indiscriminate shooting took a heavy toll and numbers fell to about 120. This prompted the KwaZulu-Natal conservation authorities to create the Tembe Elephant Park in 1983. Initially the park's northern boundary was left open to enable the elephant to follow their seasonal migration route.

Fears that the population in the Maputo Elephant Reserve might be wiped out completely prompted construction of an electric fence along the northern boundary in 1989 to prevent the elephants from migrating back into Mozambique where they were likely to be poached, and a few small breeding herds, mainly bulls that were in the park at the time, were fenced in. They are the only indigenous elephant on the coastal plains of southern Mozambique and KwaZulu-Natal as all the elephant in other conservation areas in the latter were reintroduced from elsewhere.

The numbers in the Maputo Elephant Reserve have increased to over 200, and breeding herds can usually be seen in the forested areas in the vicinity of the park headquarters during the winter months. During the rainy season they migrate southwards. The population in the Tembe Elephant Park now stands at over 150. The white rhino population of 65 animals, introduced from the Umfolozi Game Reserve (now part of the Hluhluwe-Umfolozi Park in KwaZulu-Natal) in 1967, was less fortunate. These rhino were all wiped out, as were the populations of buffalo, blue wildebeest, Burchell's zebra and the large predators.

A small antelope worth keeping an eye out for is the suni which has a reddish brown coat with white underparts. It favours dense undergrowth in sand forest areas and reaches its southern limit of distribution at Lake St Lucia in KwaZulu-Natal. Common and red duiker inhabit the woodlands but for reedbuck and waterbuck you must scan the floodplains. Small numbers of kudu and nyala have managed to survive, while hippo and crocodile inhabit the lakes. Other species include vervet and samango monkeys and bushpig.

In the marine environment, pristine reefs with brightly-hued coral and shoals of tropical fish in luminous yellows, powder blues, oranges and silvers lie just offshore. Shoals of goldies and fusiliers as well as Moorish idols, anemone fish, dominoes, angelfish, the colourful but highly poisonous devil firefish, moray eels and starfish are some of the inhabitants of this underwater paradise.

Swimming with whale sharks and getting a close-up view of manta rays gliding effortlessly through the water are highlights for many divers, and schools of dolphin often frolic in the waves just off the coast. The coastline is also popular with surf-anglers, and there is a wide variety of game fish further out at sea.

Birding

With over 330 species recorded and a further 47 species awaiting confirmation, the reserve offers good sightings of birds.
Specials: Neergaard's sunbird (associated with sand forest), white-eared barbet (coastal forest), pink-throated twinspot (dense undergrowth of woodlands), African broadbill, green malkoha and Rudd's apalis.

Maputo Elephant Reserve

Water birds: greater and lesser flamingos, Goliath heron, Allen's gallinule, African jacana, yellow-billed and white-faced ducks, Cape teal, African pygmy goose and black crake.
Raptors: palm-nut vulture; African fish, African crowned and southern banded snake eagles; osprey and African marsh harrier.
Other species: crested guineafowl, orange-throated longclaw, little bee-eater, trumpeter and crowned hornbills, tambourine dove, Burchell's coucal and red-capped robin-chat.

Facilities
Basic camp sites are available at **Milibangalala** and **Ponta Dobela** in the park.
Ponta Mamoli Resort offers en-suite rooms on full-board basis and a swimming pool.
Ponta Malongane Holiday Resort has rondavels, chalets, dome tents, camp sites, restaurant, shop and swimming pool.
O Lar do Ouro Guest Lodge, Ponta do Ouro has rooms with en-suite facilities. There is dinner, bed and breakfast and a swimming pool.
Self-catering serviced cabanas are offered at the **Coco Cabanas**, in Ponta do Ouro, where you will also find the **Motel do Mar**.

Activities
Several **dive charter companies** operate in Ponta do Ouro, and the Ponta Mamoli and Ponta Malongane resorts have dive centres.
Snorkelling is a must at low tide along the reef at Milibangalala, but do keep a watch out for dangerous currents.

THE ROUTE – 330 km Maputo to Ponta do Ouro border post
The easiest route is to take the ferry from the terminal on Avenida 10 de Novembro in Maputo across the Espirito Santo River to Catembe. About 100 m south of the Catembe ferry terminal you will join the EN 201 to Ponta do Ouro; turn left here and continue for 42 km along a gravel road in fair condition before unexpectedly joining a tar road.

Ignore the road turning off to the right (to Namaacha border post on the Swaziland border) and about 500 m on you pass a turnoff to Bela Vista, a village named for its beautiful view of the Maputo River. Just over 2 km on there is a second turnoff to Bela Vista, but you continue for 14 km on tar until you reach the bridge over the Maputo River and the Temple Shree Ram.

Approximately 400 m further, you pass through the checkpoint at Salamanga where the tar gives way to a gravel road. After 9 km you reach a bridge over the Futi River and 200 m

LEATHERBACK TURTLES

The beaches of southern Mozambique are an important breeding ground of the leatherback turtle which can weigh up to 646 kg and reach a length of 2 m. Large numbers of females come ashore at night between October and February to lay their eggs in the sand above the high-water mark. They can each lay over 1 000 eggs in a season. After an incubation period of two months, the hatchlings make their way to the sea but, vulnerable as they are, they provide rich pickings for seagulls and other marine birds: only about two out of every thousand reach adulthood.

MOZAMBIQUE

beyond this is the turnoff to the park. Turn left here and continue for 2.6 km to a T-junction where you turn left again. At the park's gate, 500 m away, turn right and report to the office.

The signposted turnoff to Milibangalala splits off to the left about 300 m beyond the office. After a few kilometres you cross a grassy plain to reach a signposted split where you keep left.

The vegetation along the track varies between forested dunes, grassy depressions and marshes; 10 km from the start you reach a large reed-covered lake on your right. Beyond the lake the track winds over a dune again and 20.6 km from the gate a track joins in from your right. This is the route you will follow south to Ponta do Ouro, but for now you keep left and after less than 2 km you will have an uninterrupted view of Lake Maunde.

Milibangalala

At the split keep right, and after you have passed a small lake on your right the track heads across the shrub-covered dunes to reach Milibangalala 8 km from the last split.

Milibangalala has a small camp site under trees just off the beach; its only facilities are pit toilets and a well. It is a popular destination with anglers, and at low tide you can snorkel inside the nearby reef. You can also take a drive to Ponta Dobela, another popular camp site, further south and camp there for a day or two.

From Milibangalala backtrack for 8 km, ignoring the turnoff to Machangulo to the right and continuing for 2.5 km to a split where you keep left. After a short distance the track heads up a steep hill with loose sand where you will struggle if you don't deflate your vehicle's tyres. As you continue further south, Lake Piti comes into view, and you come to a crossroad where the ruins of an old Portuguese trading store and a house are landmarks. The track to the right leads past the northern end of Lake Xingute back to the office, but you continue south, passing through a beautiful tree-lined avenue.

You reach the southern gate about 32 km after leaving Milibangalala. From here there are so many different tracks branching off the main track that a detailed route description is not possible. During the rainy season the grasslands and depressions, which are covered in water, might be impassable.

Ponta Mamoli

Although this is easier said than done, we advise that you stick to the main track heading south until just before you reach Zitundo, a small former Portuguese settlement on a rise. Here you join a tar road that leads off to the left to Ponta Mamoli, a popular resort during the Portuguese colonial era.

The road skirts a marshy area, and after 10.8 km the road gives way to a sandy track which traverses the slopes of a high coastal dune for 1.5 km to Ponta Mamoli. Situated on the dunes high above the sea, the resort was built just before Mozambique became independent, but abandoned to the elements when most of the Portuguese fled the country soon afterwards. Ponta Mamoli is popular with divers.

> **(i) VITAL INFO**
>
> Tracks going through the seasonal wetlands in and to the south of the Maputo Elephant Reserve can be impassable during the rainy season and you could get badly bogged down.

Maputo Elephant Reserve

Ponta Malongane
Backtrack from Ponta Mamoli to the crossroad at Zitundo from where you follow the main track south (left) until you reach an airfield. Turn left at the junction 800 m further on for Ponta Malongane. Just over 7 km from the turnoff you will pass the northern edge of a small lake. A short way on you reach a junction. Ignore the turnoff to Ponta do Ouro and continue straight for 700 m to Ponta Malongane with its resort nestling under a canopy of coastal dune forest in the lee of a headland which forms a sweeping bay. Divers and deep-sea anglers frequent this place.

Ponta do Ouro
Leaving Ponta Malongane, drive straight for 600 m and then turn left to reach the outskirts of the popular seaside resort of Ponta do Ouro after 5.5 km. Less than 1 km on you will reach a tar road turning off to the left. This short stretch of tar leads to the filling station, market area, Motel do Mar and the Parque de Campismo where you can camp.

Ponta do Ouro, Portuguese for 'point of gold', lies in a sheltered bay formed by a high forested headland to the south. From the lighthouse perched on the dune there are stunning views of the ocean, grasslands and patches of forest – the perfect spot for sundowners. Several dive sites lying just offshore have given it a long-standing reputation for excellent diving. Ponta do Ouro offers deep-sea angling, spear fishing and windsurfing, but many visitors simply come here to soak up the sun and enjoy the warm water.

Heading out of Ponta do Ouro, ignore the turnoff to Ponta Malongane to the right and continue along a sandy track. In places this is difficult to follow as tracks keep on splitting off where the sand has become too soft for vehicles towing boats and trailers – an ugly reminder of how easy it is to damage sensitive coastal areas. After approximately 4 km you reach a junction where the track to Zitundo continues straight, but you must turn left here, continuing for 4 km to the Ponta do Ouro border post.

LOGISTICS AND PLANNING
Fuel: Have enough for about 300 km from Maputo to Ponta do Ouro. From the border it is just over 12 km to KwaNgwanase where fuel is available. This includes a generous allowance for exploring the tracks in the reserve.
Water: It is advisable to carry drinking water with you.
Food: You can buy food and alcoholic beverages in Maputo. A shop in Ponta Malongane Holiday Resort stocks basic groceries and toiletries, and a limited range of groceries is available in Ponta do Ouro. Resorts at both destinations have restaurants.
Best times: The cooler months from May to September are the best time to visit southern Mozambique. The summer months are hot and rainy, and humidity is high. Wetlands on the coastal plain are inundated and travelling becomes difficult if not impossible.

Booking
Maputo Elephant Reserve: No advance bookings
Ponta Mamoli Resort, tel: (+27 11) 678-0972, fax 678-0970, e-mail: scuba@saol.com
Ponta Malongane Holiday Resort, tel: (+27 12) 348-4262, fax: 348-1252
O Lar do Ouro Guest Lodge, Ponta do Ouro, tel: (+258 1) 65-0038, e-mail info@pontadoouro.com
Coco Cabanas, Ponta do Ouro, tel: (+27 11) 478-3686
Motel do Mar, Ponta do Ouro, tel: (+27 12) 362-1355, fax: 362-1321, e-mail: ponta@icon.co.za

MOZAMBIQUE

Vilankulo to Punda Maria

The unspoiled sun-drenched beaches of central Mozambique and one of Africa's great game parks, the famous Kruger National Park, are linked by this 920-km journey of discovery from Vilankulo to Punda Maria. You will explore remote and wild countryside with only the occasional small settlement set among vast woodlands and shrubveld. The little-known Zinave National Park, home to small numbers of game, but an interesting variety of trees, shrubs and birds, can be visited along the route. But hurry – there are plans to tar this route to make a direct road from South Africa to central Mozambique.

Landscape and vegetation

The route mainly traverses the *Planície Moçambicana* (Mozambican coastal plain), which lies below 200 m. There is little variation in altitude and because the bush is dense there's not much of a view.

The vegetation from the coast westwards to Lake Banamana is typically semi-deciduous miombo woodlands composed of species such as the munondo (*Julbernardia globiflora*), msasa, marula, black monkey thorn, pod mahogany and the tamarind tree.

Interspersed among the woodlands is the Lebombo ironwood, easy to recognise as it forms almost pure stands. Mopane scrub and woodlands become more dominant as you travel further west, while magnificent forests of fever trees grace the banks of the Limpopo River. Baobabs become more prevalent in the west and dense concentrations tower above the hilly landscape as you approach the Pafuri border post.

Fauna and game-viewing

Like most other parks and game reserves in Mozambique, Zinave National Park provided a supply of game meat to soldiers on both sides of the civil war and now has only small populations of impala, nyala, kudu, waterbuck and buffalo. Oribi and common duiker are among the smaller antelope. A few hippo inhabit the Save River which is also home to a large population of crocodile. Years of shooting have made the animals wary and you are likely to get just a fleeting glimpse as they dash for cover. Look out for some of the small mammals such as common duiker and mongoose that have managed to survive.

Game from the Kruger National Park has been released into the south-western corner of the Limpopo National Park (*see* Great Limpopo Transfrontier Park, page 27) but on the route to Pafuri you are unlikely to see much.

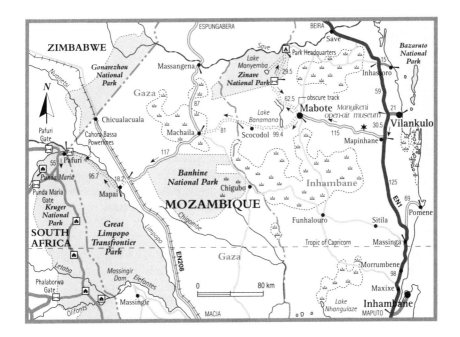

Kruger National Park is internationally known as one of Africa's top conservation areas. A sanctuary to the 'Big Five' (elephant, rhino, buffalo, lion and leopard) it is also home to over 140 other mammal species, 114 different reptiles and more than 500 bird species.

Birding

The birdlife in Zinave is poorly documented, but the park offers good birding opportunities:
Specials: Böhm's and mottled spinetails.
Raptors: white-backed vulture; Wahlberg's, long-crested, African fish and tawny eagles; African hawk-harrier.
Other species: southern ground and trumpeter hornbills, African green pigeon, purple-crested turaco, brown-headed parrot, yellow-bellied bulbul, red-necked spurfowl, black-backed puffback, southern boubou, Burchell's coucal, white-crested helmet-shrike.

Facilities

Accommodation in Vilankulo ranges from **several lodges** to the **Vilankulo camp site** where there are grassed sites shaded by trees, braai places, power points and clean ablutions with hot showers. You can camp at the park headquarters in **Zinave National Park** where water from a borehole is the only facility. There is no accommodation between Zinave and Pafuri. The area is sparsely populated so camping just off the road, away from any homesteads, is not a problem. Accommodation is planned for the **Limpopo National Park** section of the Great Limpopo Transfrontier Park. Rooms with en-suite showers, camp sites, a shop, restaurant and filling station are available in **Punda Maria rest camp**.

Activities

Take a trip on a **dhow** or **motorboat** from Vilankulo to Bangue or Benguerra, two of the islands that form part of the Bazaruto Archipelago.

MOZAMBIQUE

Margie Toens who runs Serviços Paraíso in Vilankulo will assist you with reservations for dhow trips, accommodation and information (*see* booking, page 29).

Getting there
The trail starts at Vilankulo, some 700 km north of Maputo.

THE ROUTE – 920 km Vilankulo to Punda Maria; 350 km Inchope return (no fuel at Inchope)
From Vilankulo, take road 212 for 21 km to its junction with the EN 1 where you turn left, continuing for 30.5 km to the signposted turnoff to Zinave National Park at Mapinhane. Turn right here from the tar onto a gravel road and enjoy the 115-km-long journey to Mabote. The road has been upgraded and unless it has rained you should have a smooth ride.

Manyikeni Open-air Museum
Just over 29 km after you leave the tar road a signpost points to a turnoff to the right to the Manyikeni Open-air Museum, 3 km on. A short walk from the parking area takes you to the site which was a regional centre of the Great Zimbabwe Empire. It consists of a stone enclosure of limestone blocks (originally 1.5 m high) surrounded by a settlement which could have housed up to 200 people. The site, which was inhabited between 1450 and the 1700s, has provided important information on the development of long-distance trade during this period. Archaeological finds suggest that Manyikeni was culturally and economically linked to Great Zimbabwe and the interior as well as with coastal settlements.

Continuing further west through dense miombo woodlands, you reach Mabote 86 km beyond the Manyikeni turnoff. Take the road signposted to Zinave National Park to the right at the four-way stop in the village. As you make your way to the outskirts of the village the gravel road deteriorates into a track with deep ruts and loose sand in places; you will average around 15 km an hour. About 29.5 km out of Mabote you reach a split, where you must bear sharp right.

Zinave National Park
On reaching the administrative village of the Zinave area the track improves. Continue straight to the entrance to Zinave National Park 62.5 km from Mabote; it is a further 29.5 km to the park headquarters. The track descends gradually and from the entrance gate to the park headquarters, which lies a mere 84 m above sea level, you will lose about 110 m in altitude. Sections of the track pass through clay areas where you could get bogged down after rains. You are unlikely to cover the 92 km to the park in much less than 4 hours.

INGENIOUS BEEHIVES

While travelling in this part of the country you will notice slightly roundish dark objects about 1 m long tied to forks in trees, sometimes quite high. These are beehives made by the local inhabitants by carefully stripping the bark off a tree in a sheath and enclosing the ends of the sheath with wooden nails. A small opening is left for the bees and when the trees are in flower the hive is placed in the tree. The honey is ready in about two weeks.

Bounded by the Save River in the north, Zinave was initially set aside as a hunting area in 1969 but three years later it was declared a national park. The park provided sanctuary to one of the largest concentrations of nyala in Africa and the northernmost populations of the South African subspecies of giraffe and spring-hare. In addition, it is home to the Niassa subspecies of the blue wildebeest and large numbers of roan, impala, kudu, hippo and warthog. Carnivores include leopard, cheetah, brown hyaena and black-backed jackal.

Except for the approach from the entrance gate to the park headquarters and a 24-km track to a seasonal wetland, Lake Manyemba, there were no other tracks in the park at the end of 2002. As the vegetation along the way is magnificent, the journey to the lake is worth making even if it does not have any water. The track is rather faint in places, but if you keep a sharp lookout you should have no problems.

In the absence of large numbers of game, Zinave's main attractions are its birdlife and magnificent landscape which ranges from Brachystegia woodlands, baobabs and tracts of mopane to acacia parklands and seasonal lakes.

From Zinave to Pafuri is about 580 km of hard driving and you will need to sleep somewhere en route. Backtrack to Mabote and at the four-way junction turn right (west) onto the track signposted to Pafuri. You will reach a village where the track to Mapai and Nzinani is signposted to the left after 11.6 km. Almost 15 km further along this track, a bridge takes you across an arm of Lake Banamana. This is a good birding spot and besides flocks of waterfowl you might tick African fish eagle, flamingo, pelican, black-winged stilt, avocet and African spoonbill.

Here you encounter mopaneveld, which is a sure indication of clay and hence muddy tracks after rain. You reach a village approximately 29.6 km beyond the bridge. Ignore a turnoff to the left and head straight towards a school. Facing the school, follow the track that skirts its perimeter to the right; after 20.6 km you will reach Scocodol village. About 22 km beyond Scocodol a steel bridge takes you across the Changane River where you cross from Inhambane Province to Gaza Province.

Mopaneveld becomes more dominant, and there are several clay stretches that become difficult to negotiate after rains as they are deeply rutted by logging trucks. As you travel further west, a minor track leading to Chive joins in from the left just over 46 km beyond the bridge, but your path lies to the right. After 12.5 km you reach a small settlement dating back to Portuguese colonial days, and 22.3 km on, you turn left onto a good gravel road at Machaila.

Bahine National Park

From Machaila the road heads in a south-westerly direction and later forms the north-western boundary of the little-known Bahine National Park. It joins up with route 208 immediately after crossing the railway line, 117.2 km beyond Machaila. Turn right and keep a sharp lookout for the unsignposted track to Mapai which branches off to the left after 3.5 km.

The track to Mapai initially leads through fairly thick sand and then descends to reach the village on the banks of the Limpopo River. The river, which can be crossed only when its level is low (there is no causeway or bridge), is 18.2 km beyond the last turnoff.

Great Limpopo Transfrontier Park

After crossing the Limpopo River you are in the still-to-be-developed Limpopo National Park which, with the adjoining Kruger National Park and the Gonarezhou National Park in Zimbabwe, forms the Great Limpopo Transfrontier Park. Formerly known as Coutada 16, this wild tract of land, like Zinave, was set aside as a hunting area in 1969 and became a national

MOZAMBIQUE

(i) VITAL INFO

- Since there is no bridge across the Limpopo River at Mapai, the route can be done only when the level of the Limpopo is low, usually from mid-winter to late October, depending on when the rainy season starts. Check with the South African Police Service station at Pafuri whether the river is fordable, tel: (+27 13) 735-6882.
- The Pafuri border post is open daily from 08h00 to 16h00.

park in November 2001. The Limpopo River forms its eastern boundary, while the Letaba River is another natural border in the south. In the west it borders on the Kruger National Park.

To enable conservation authorities to consult communities living in the park, a 30 000-ha wildlife sanctuary was set aside in the south-western part of the Limpopo National Park. Aspects on which the communities were consulted included the protection of their agricultural fields against damage by wild animals, the boundaries of the sanctuary and the provision of water.

As an initial step towards the introduction of game into the Limpopo National Park, a 30-km section of the Kruger's eastern fence was dismantled and in September 2001 the first 40 of a planned total of 1 000 elephant were released into the park. Among the over 5 000 other animals to be resettled in the park by the end of 2003 are giraffe, blue wildebeest, Burchell's zebra, waterbuck, impala, warthog and hippo. Roan, sable, white rhino, tsessebe and eland are on the list of game to be released in 2004.

The Great Limpopo Transfrontier Park will form the nucleus of the proposed Great Limpopo Transfrontier Conservation Area that will also include Zinave and Bahine national parks in Mozambique. Four other potential transfrontier conservation areas have been identified between Mozambique and its neighbours. They are: Liwonde/Lichinga (with Malawi), Selous/Niassa and Mnazi Bay/Quirimbas (with Tanzania) and Chimanimani (with Zimbabwe) transfrontier conservation areas.

The track winds in a north-easterly direction and 3.2 km beyond the Limpopo River crossing turns right continuing through shrubveld and patches of mopane. About 69 km beyond the Limpopo you pass under the high-tension cables that transmit electricity from the Cahora Bassa hydro-electric scheme to the South African network. Soon afterwards the road begins to wind and passes through magnificent baobab-studded veld before descending to the Limpopo floodplains lined with fever trees. The Mozambican border is 96 km beyond the Limpopo River crossing and the South African border post where you enter the Kruger National Park 500 m further.

Punda Maria

From the border post it is about 70 km to Kruger's northernmost rest camp, Punda Maria. Along the way you might encounter elephant, giraffe, impala and buffalo, and nyala is especially common in the Pafuri area. The dense riverine forest along the Pafuri River is also the only place in the park where you stand a chance of seeing the samango monkey.

The major attraction of the Pafuri area, though, is not its game but its spectacular birdlife which includes several rare species. Among these are mottled and Böhm's spinetails, Meves's starling, racket-tailed and broadbilled rollers.

Vilankulo to Punda Maria

LICHTENSTEIN'S HARTEBEEST

The northern part of the Kruger National Park, especially the area near Punda Maria, is the only place in South Africa where you may spot the rare Lichtenstein's hartebeest. You can distinguish it from the more common red hartebeest by its dull mustard-coloured coat which has a reddish tinge on the back. Its horns curve sharply inwards and backwards unlike that of the red hartebeest which curve outwards and forwards. The species became extinct in South Africa in the early 1900s. A small herd from Malawi's Kasungu National Park was reintroduced in 1985 and a second herd followed in 1987.

Visit the Thulamela archaeological site at Pafuri in the Kruger National Park on a guided tour leaving from the Pafuri picnic spot at 07h30 and 10h00. Book at the Punda Maria reception office.

LOGISTICS AND PLANNING

Fuel: Available at Vilankulo, at Vilankulo turnoff on the EN 1 and at Mapinhane, 32 km south of the Vilankulo turnoff, and at Punda Maria. You will need fuel for 920 km.
Water: Carry enough drinking water with you.
Food: Stock up in Maputo as Vilankulo has limited supplies. Between Vilankulo and Punda Maria only the bare basics are available.
Best times: The cooler months (May to September) are generally best to visit the area. Clay tracks along parts of the route become impassable in the rainy season and you might not be able to ford the Limpopo River.

Booking

Zinave National Park: No advance bookings
For **Kruger National Park or for Pafuri Rest Camp** reservations, contact South African National Parks, PO Box 787, Pretoria 0001, tel: (+27 12) 428-9111, fax: 343-0905, e-mail: reservations@parks-sa.co.za.
For **dhow trips**, **accommodation** and **information**, tel: (+258 23) 8-2228, e-mail: margie@teledate.mz

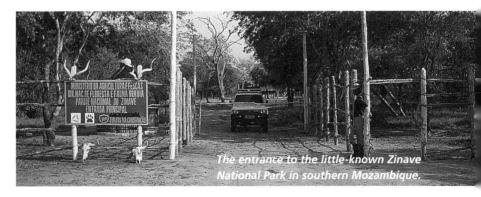
The entrance to the little-known Zinave National Park in southern Mozambique.

MOZAMBIQUE

Gorongosa National Park

Gorongosa's game numbers are slowly increasing after just over a decade of peace in Mozambique. Until the game has re-established itself, the scenery, prolific birdlife and wild atmosphere will be the main attractions of this central Mozambican reserve. Its special appeal is its magnificent vegetation which includes grasslands along Lake Urema, forests of fever trees lining seasonal pans, dense palmveld and woodlands with a rich diversity of species.

THE PARK

The nucleus of what was to become Gorongosa National Park was first set aside in 1921 as a hunting area to provide game meat to the workers of the coconut and sugar plantations being established in the region. Gorongosa was proclaimed a game reserve in 1935 to protect the prolific wildlife, and 25 years later it became a national park. A few years after this it was enlarged by the addition of the area east of the Urema River. Until the 1970s Gorongosa ranked as one of Africa's great game parks, attracting 11 000 visitors a year. The civil war in the 1980s exacted a heavy toll on the wildlife that sustained the rebels and government forces. In 1981 the park headquarters came under attack from Renamo, and the following year the park was occupied by the rebels, resulting in its closure in 1983. Over the next six years control of the park changed hands a number of times, and on several occasions rebel positions were pounded with aerial bombardments. Government forces finally overran the Renamo camps in 1989.

Landscape and vegetation

The Southern Urema Lake tourist area lies at the southern end of the Great East African Rift Valley which is about 40 km wide at this point. From the escarpment west of the park the landscape drops steadily eastwards, losing some 260 m in altitude over 17 km to Chitengo Camp which lies a mere 40 m above sea level. The scenery varies between woodlands, palmveld, floodplains, seasonal pans and Lake Urema which lies at the lowest point of the valley in the Urema River. When the Urema River floods in summer, water spills over the grassy floodplains to form a huge inland lake, and waist-deep grass fringes Lake Urema.

The woodlands consist of a rich variety of species, among them Natal mahogany, large specimens of red mahogany, marula, sausage, leadwood, black monkey orange, buffalo-thorn and red thorn trees. Especially attractive are the apple-leaf trees which reach heights of 10 m. Long cylindrical pods make it easy to identify the sjambok pod, and the striking African dog rose flowers brighten the bush between August and December. Also conspicuous are the distinctive

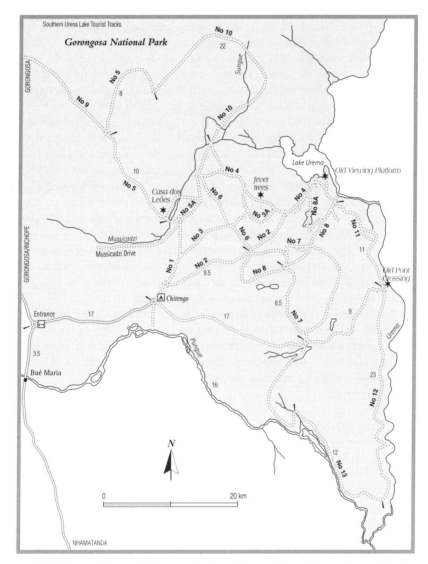

two-lobed leaves of the camel's foot tree. In the north-east of the tourist area, the woodlands give way to magnificent fever tree forests on the edges of the seasonal floodplains. On the termitaria islands in the floodplains there are groves of ana trees (or winter thorn). You cannot miss the palms – the borassus palm with a swelling halfway up its bole, the ilala palm and the wild date palm – along river banks.

Fauna and game-viewing

In the late 1970s Gorongosa boasted over 12 000 buffalo, 7 000 blue wildebeest, 3 500 hippo, 3 000 Burchell's zebra, 3 000 waterbuck and 2 500 elephant. Years of civil war changed this. The large number of snares and traps displayed near park headquarters bears silent testimony to the suffering of the animals. When the first wildlife census was conducted in 1994, two years after the war ended, a bleak picture emerged. There were only 108 elephant and the waterbuck

MOZAMBIQUE

population was down to 129. No buffalo, hippo, blue wildebeest or eland were counted. Wildlife numbers are still low, but game populations are slowly growing. By the end of 2002, the waterbuck population had increased to over 400 (they can usually be seen on the floodplains of Lake Urema); the reedbuck population stood at 250; impala, estimated around 300, inhabit the woodlands but are skittish and usually take flight on hearing a vehicle. Warthog are common and you might encounter bushpig during an early morning or late afternoon drive.

Nyala did not occur in the park before the civil war, but increased bush encroachment as a result of the decline in the elephant numbers has attracted them to the park. Bushbuck and red duiker are frequently seen, and the short grassland patches offer good opportunities for sighting oribi. This small antelope has a yellowish rufous coat, pure white underparts and a distinctive black-tipped tail. It is territorial, mostly seen in family groups of a ram, one or two females and their young. Baboon, vervet monkey, samango monkey (seen in the riverine forests) and bushbaby represent the primates. The last-named occurs on the higher ground in the west of the park.

Less frequently sighted are red hartebeest, blue wildebeest and sable. The park's sable population numbers between 40 and 50. You will sometimes see them in the vicinity of the airstrip at Chitengo Camp. The large predators are represented by small numbers of lion, leopard and cheetah, while the wetland grasslands harbour serval, a shy nocturnal species. The large grey, water and Selous' mongooses count among the smaller carnivores.

Small numbers of eland and the Sofala zebra (a subspecies of Burchell's zebra) occur east of the Urema River. Gorongosa is an important sanctuary for the Sofala zebra. As recently as 30 years ago they numbered more than 20 000. Now the population is estimated at no more than 50, with small herds in Gorongosa and the Morromeu Delta. Unlike Burchell's zebra it has no brown shadow stripes but clean black-and-white banding.

Birding

The birding at Gorongosa is phenomenal. The palm-nut vulture is just one of the 'mega ticks' worth looking out for. In South Africa it reaches its southern limit of distribution at Mtunzini and Kosi Bay where it lives and breeds in the raffia palms along the coast, but we positively identified one in Gorongosa. It is easily recognised by its white and black plumage, yellowish bill and pale blue cere. Its breeding and feeding habits are closely associated with oil palms, hence its common name. Besides ripe oil palm fruit, it eats fish, crabs, molluscs and carrion.

Specials: black-and-white flycatcher (in Chitengo Camp), collared palm-thrush, wattled and crowned cranes, racket-tailed and broadbilled rollers.

Wetland birds: Goliath, rufous-bellied and purple herons, great egret, African wattled, long-toed and crowned lapwings, African jacana, comb duck, spur-winged goose.

Raptors: African fish eagle, long-crested, crowned and martial eagles, bateleur, lizzard buzzard.

Other species: crested guineafowl, paradise flycatcher, Kurrichane thrush, purple-crested turaco, black-backed puffback, saddle-billed and marabou storks, silvery-cheeked hornbill, African green pigeon, red-necked spurfowl, bronze-winged courser and Burchell's coucal.

Facilities

Chitengo has grassed camp sites shaded by tall trees. The ablution facilities (in the bombed-out ruins and bullet-riddled walls of a building) have handbasins, cold showers and flush toilets. Firewood is available.

Casa Msika, on the Chicamba Dam 111 km west of Inchope and 5 km off the EN 6. Rooms and chalets, camp sites, restaurant, swimming pool.

Gorongosa National Park

>  **VITAL INFO**
>
> - Most maps show a road linking Chitengo and Muanza on road 213 between Dondo and Caia, but access to the park from Muanza is not possible as there is no pont or bridge at the Urema River.
> - The Southern Urema Lake tourist area is open only from May to December as the area is inaccessible during summer rains. There are plans to open the higher-lying areas in the west of the park during summer.

Biques Camping, Avenida das FPLM, Beira. Only camp site in Beira (just off the beach), restaurant.

Activities
Guided canoe trips on the Pungué River and **guided walks** around Chitengo offered by park management.

Getting there
From Inchope at the junction of the EN 1 and EN 6 go north along EN 1 for 43 km to the turnoff marked Gorongosa National Park. Turn right; drive for 12 km to park entrance. Chitengo is 5 km on.

ROUTES – 350 km Inchope return (no fuel at Inchope)
The Southern Urema Lake tourist track system covers about 120 km, most of it accessible by two-wheel drive bakkies during the dry season. After rains, only four-wheel drive vehicles can negotiate the tracks. Most tracks are numbered but some markers at intersections were not obvious in October 2002. Some were obscured by vegetation and others had been knocked over. Check the map carefully at intersections or, like us, you may get lost. A GPS can be useful to help you track your route.

Interesting features along Route 5 are magnificent baobabs and the Casa dos Leões (House of the Lions), the park's first headquarters in 1940. The site was flooded and the headquarters were moved to Chitengo, the abandoned buildings becoming the resting place of a pride of lion.

To reach Lake Urema follow routes 2, 7 (lovely palmveld along the way) and 8 to a derelict double-storey building overlooking the lake. During the Portuguese colonial era the building was a vantage point and bar. A truck laden with refreshments would set out early in the morning and by the time the tourists arrived the staff would be waiting to serve drinks. The tracks across the floodplains are not negotiable when the lake is high. In October 2002, fallen trees obstructed the 26-km track from Chitengo to the site where a pontoon crossed the Urema. The 11-km track from the old pont crossing north along the Urema was quite overgrown, but good for birding.

LOGISTICS AND PLANNING
Fuel: Not available at Inchope or Gorongosa village. Depending on your approach fill up at Save Bridge, Chimoio or Beira, respectively 320 km south, 125 km west and 135 km east of Chitengo.
Water: Available in the park.
Food: Stock up in Chimoio and Beira at a supermarket. Ensure you are self-sufficient.
Best times: The cooler months (May to September) are the best time to visit. October to December can be very hot and humid and early rains can turn the tracks into mud baths.

Booking
Biques Camping, tel: (+258 3) 31-3051, Avenida das FPLM, Beira

Main picture: *Grasslands of the Makgadikgadi Pans.*
Inset picture: *Sociable weaver nests are characteristic of the south-western Kalahari.*

Botswana

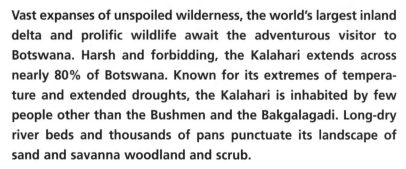

BOTSWANA

Vast expanses of unspoiled wilderness, the world's largest inland delta and prolific wildlife await the adventurous visitor to Botswana. Harsh and forbidding, the Kalahari extends across nearly 80% of Botswana. Known for its extremes of temperature and extended droughts, the Kalahari is inhabited by few people other than the Bushmen and the Bakgalagadi. Long-dry river beds and thousands of pans punctuate its landscape of sand and savanna woodland and scrub.

Seventeen percent of Botswana has been set aside for conservation, and the destinations described in this section are all in parks and reserves, except for the Makgadikgadi Pans, Tsodilo Hills and Gcwihaba Cave. Botswana has a 'high revenue–low impact' policy, and park and reserve fees are relatively expensive if you are not a Botswanan citizen or resident. Unfortunately, though, the standard and maintenance of facilities often fall far short of expectation. But the wilderness experience amply compensates for this.

Chobe National Park in the north has the world's largest concentration of elephant and the Chobe riverfront is the best place for close-up views. Puku and the Chobe sub-species of bushbuck are two 'specials' of the riverfront. Buffalo, giraffe, Burchell's zebra and impala are among the many species to be seen.

Amid the sea of sand lies the Okavango Delta with its papyrus-lined waterways, lily-covered backwaters and floodplain grasslands. Nearly a third of the Delta is protected in the Moremi Game Reserve, a sanctuary to four of the Big Five (elephant, lion, leopard, buffalo), large numbers of antelope, giraffe, zebra, as well as predators such as cheetah, wild dog and the smaller cat species. This rich diversity of habitats supports an amazing birdlife.

The Makgadikgadi Pans, the largest saline pans in the world, contrast sharply with the watery and lush green Okavango Delta. The fossil bed of a super-lake, the pans are now characterised by their desolation, dry mud-cracked floors and shimmering mirages. Only the western extremity of the pans enjoys the protection of the Makgadikgadi–Nxai Pan National Park which, in spite of its name, consists mainly of grassland.

Although the former Nxai Pan National Park and the Makgadikgadi Pans Game Reserve have been known as the Makgadikgadi–Nxai Pan National Park since their amalgamation in 1992 the scenery in the two sections is completely different and we have decided to treat them as two entities.

The landscape and wildlife of the Kgalagadi Transfrontier Park, Central Kalahari and Khutse game reserves and Nxai Pan are typical of the Kalahari. Solitude and wilderness are the main attractions. Years of drought and veterinary fences have reduced game numbers in the Kalahari significantly, but there is an array of small mammals, reptiles, birds and amphibians.

Two destinations that are not on the main tourist circuit but are fascinating all the same are Tsodilo Hills for their rock paintings and Gcwihaba (Drotsky's) Cave, an underground delight. Combining a visit to both makes an interesting tour of western Botswana.

Overview

Roads throughout Botswana have improved enormously over the last decade, and tarred roads provide easy access to gateway towns, while gravel roads have replaced most of the infamous sandy access tracks. The destinations that we describe in this book can all be explored in a four-wheel drive vehicle with reasonable ease during the dry season, although the sandy sections can be rather challenging.

Botswana has three distinct seasons. The winter months (May to August) are dry and cool during the day but it can be bitterly cold at night. Temperatures well below freezing are not uncommon. Winter is followed by a warm dry season in September and October and a hot rainy season from November to April.

The rains, accompanied by dramatic afternoon thunderstorms, and sometimes gale force winds or dust storms, may begin as early as November and last until April. Rainfall varies from 230 mm in the Kgalagadi Transfrontier Park in the south-west to 650 mm in Chobe in the north.

The rainfall is highly unpredictable, and it usually occurs as scattered thundershowers. Many years may go by without a single drop of rain on the parched earth, so extended droughts are not unusual.

Botswana has a rich diversity of cultures: in addition to the Batswana (the main group) there are many others, among them the Bayei, Hambukushu and Basubiya of the north-west, and the Bakgalagadi and Bushmen of the Kalahari.

In the Ngamiland district you might be surprised to see Herero women with their Victorian dresses and distinctive headdresses. They are the descendants of Herero who fled from Namibia to Botswana in 1904 after their defeat by the German colonial administration.

BORDER POSTS AND FORMALITIES

There are a number of border posts between South Africa and Botswana. The more popular entry points are Pioneer Gate (open from 06h00 to 22h00), Tlokweng (06h00 to 22h00), Martin's Drift (08h00 to 18h00) and Ramatlabama (07h00 to 20h00). From Namibia there are four: Mamuno Trans-Kalahari (from 07h00 to midnight), Mohembo (06h00 to 18h00), Ngoma (06h00 to 18h00) and Dobe (08h00 to 16h30).

Bleached tree skeletons create a scene of devastation on Dead Tree Island in the Moremi Game Reserve.

BOTSWANA

PASSPORTS AND VISAS
You will need a valid passport and, depending on your nationality, a visa. Citizens of SADC (except Angola, DRC and Mozambique), Commonwealth member states (except Ghana, India, Nigeria and Sri Lanka), the EU, the United States of America and a number of other countries do not need visas. An initial entry period of 30 days is granted.

CUSTOMS
Botswana is a member of the Southern African Customs Union (SACU) and the duty-free allowance includes 2 litres of wine, 1 litre of spirits and alcoholic beverages, six 340-ml cans of soft drinks/beer and 400 cigarettes, as well as new and used goods to the value of approximately R1 250, but sales tax might be levied on all goods.

ROAD SAFETY DISK
You must buy a Road Safety disk at the customs office in order to be covered by third party insurance. The disk is valid for a calendar year and costs P20.00 for a year or P10.00 from June to December.

VETERINARY REGULATIONS
To prevent the spread of foot-and-mouth and other diseases Botswana has strict veterinary regulations, but the extent to which they are enforced depends on the prevalence of diseases. There is a limit of 25 kg of meat per vehicle. Generally meat for personal consumption may be transported without a problem from south to north. If in doubt, contact the Veterinary Department in Gaborone, tel: (+267) 395-0500.

VEHICLE DOCUMENTATION
Have your vehicle registration document handy at border posts where you must provide the engine and chassis numbers. At some posts you might also be asked for the original vehicle registration document.

DRIVING
It is compulsory to wear seat belts and to carry your driver's licence. You must have two warning triangles. The speed limit on main roads is 120 km per hour and in urban areas 60 km per hour.

CURRENCY AND BANKS
Botswana's currency is the Pula, one of the strongest currencies in Africa with an exchange rate of R1.38 to P1.00. Banks and automatic teller machines are available in all major towns. Banking hours are 08h30 to 15h30 Monday to Friday and 08h00 to 10h45 Saturday.

IMPORTANT INFORMATION
Consult your doctor or travel clinic about the most effective prophylaxis if you are visiting northern Botswana where malaria is endemic.

Overview

Game is not restricted to parks and reserves and wanders freely. Don't become complacent when you leave your vehicle to collect firewood (where it is allowed), stop for lunch or answer the call of nature – even if you've seen little game all day. You could be metres away from lion and not see them, even in knee-high grass. Despite their size, elephant can suddenly appear, seemingly from nowhere. Take care wherever you are.

Don't drive on public roads after dark, as animals, game and unroadworthy vehicles are a constant menace. Sections of the Trans-Kalahari Highway are especially dangerous at night. Driving in parks after sunset is prohibited.

PARKS AND RESERVES RESERVATIONS

Reservations for the southern parks and reserves (Mabuasehube, Kgalagadi Transfrontier Park, Khutse and Central Kalahari game reserves) must be made in advance with the Parks and Reserves Reservations Office in Gaborone, PO Box 131, Gaborone, tel: (+267) 318-0774, fax: 318-0775, e-mail: dwnp@gov.bw. The office is in the Government Enclave of Gaborone, off Khama Crescent, opposite the end of Queen's Road.

Reservations for Makgadikgadi–Nxai Pan National Park, Moremi Game Reserve and Chobe National Park must be made with the Parks and Reserves Reservations Office in Maun, PO Box 20364, Boseja, Maun, tel: (+267) 686-1265, fax: 686-1264. The office, which is signposted on the main road, is close to the police station.

Payments by credit cards can be made at the Parks and Reserves Reservation offices in Gaborone, Maun and Sedudu Gate in the Chobe National Park. Payments in parks and reserves can be made in Pula, South African Rand, US Dollar, British Pound and Euro.

You must leave the park before 11h00 on the day following your final night to avoid being charged for another full day.

MAPS

The *Shell Tourist Map of Botswana* and the accompanying *Shell Tourist Guide to Botswana*, by Veronica Roodt, are very handy. They are packed with useful and interesting information as well as GPS co-ordinates.

The schematic maps and GPS co-ordinates in Mike Main's *African Adventurer's Guide to Botswana* (published by Struik) are useful.

If you intend venturing on tracks not covered by these maps, topographical maps can be obtained from the Department of Surveys and Mapping, Private Bag 0037, Gaborone, tel: (+267) 395-3251, fax: 395-2704, e-mail: botdsm@info.bw or from their offices in Francistown and Maun.

BOTSWANA

Gemsbok Wilderness Trail

Space, solitude and isolation are the attractions of this trail in the Kgalagadi Transfrontier Park, south-western Botswana. In summer a visit to the Kalahari is most likely to be characterised by unbearably high temperatures and dust storms, but you could witness the raw power of a rare Kalahari thunderstorm. Winter months can be freezing cold and on rare occasions snow has fallen in the Kalahari. Game usually occurs in small numbers, but you might encounter huge herds of migratory antelope after the rains or watch a lion proclaiming his territory over a pan at full moon. Even in the absence of large numbers of big game, there are numerous smaller creatures such as ground squirrels, suricates, agamas, barking geckos and birds to occupy your attention.

THE PARK

The first formally declared trans-border conservation initiative of its kind in Africa, the Kgalagadi Transfrontier Park came into being when the Kalahari Gemsbok National Park in South Africa's Northern Cape Province and the adjoining Gemsbok National Park in Botswana were amalgamated in 1999. Bounded by Namibia in the west and the Nossob River in the east, the Kalahari Gemsbok National Park was proclaimed in 1931, while the core of the Gemsbok National Park, a 40-km-wide strip east of the Nossob River, was proclaimed in 1938. To enable game to migrate freely, no international boundary fence was erected along the course of the Nossob River between South Africa and Botswana. (There are no foot-and-mouth disease fences in south-western Botswana which is not prime cattle farming country – the nearest fence is over 300 km away as the crow flies). In 1967 the Gemsbok National Park was enlarged nearly four-fold and, after the incorporation of the Mabuasehube Game Reserve in the 1990s, the park's size increased to 27 792 km², almost as large as Belgium.

While wildlife enthusiasts frequented the South African park, the park in Botswana was largely unknown, partly because of inadequate tourism infrastructure and roads. It was not until the opening of the Gemsbok 4x4 Trail in the late 1990s that access to the area became easier.

The Kalahari has been home to the Bushmen for thousands of years. When the Kalahari Gemsbok National Park was proclaimed in 1931, the Khomani Bushmen were allowed to remain. In 1973, Parks Board officials, decreeing that the Bushmen had acquired 'Western lifestyles and habits' (no longer pursuing a purely traditional hunter-gatherer existence), resettled

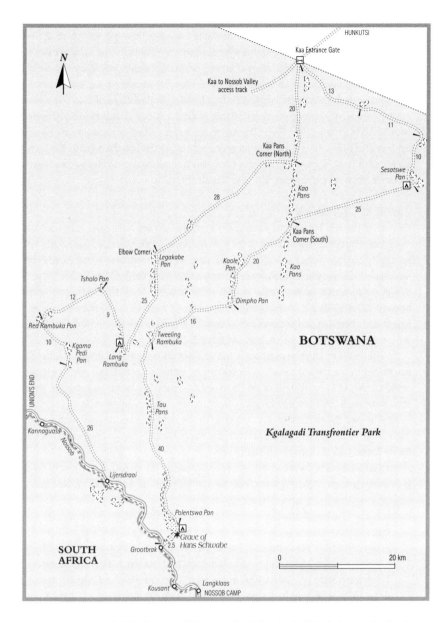

them outside the park. A land claim, which was lodged after South Africa's democratisation in 1994, resulted in an agreement to buy 25 000 ha of land adjoining the park to the south for the Khomani people. In addition, the South African National Parks Board (as it was then called) agreed in principle to make 55 000 ha of land (inside the park) available as a contractual park (see box, page 188) for the Khomani and the Mier communities living outside the park.

Landscape and vegetation
While the name Kalahari conjures up images of endless orange dunes, east of the Nossob River there are surprisingly few. The landscape is characterised by a sand mantle interspersed with

BOTSWANA

numerous pans, bounded in the east and south-east by low dunes. The vegetation is typically tree savanna with a mixture of camel and false umbrella thorns, shepherd's tree, raisin bushes, elands bean and silver cluster-leaf, and a variety of grasses. The trumpet thorn (*Catophractes alexandri*), with large white trumpet-shaped flowers after rains, is found in limestone areas around pans.

After rains the bleak Kalahari landscape is brightened by a kaleidoscope of flowering plants. Among these are the striking mauve-pink flower of the devil's claw (*Harpagophytum procumbens*), fields of yellow devil's thorn (*Tribulus zeyheri* subsp. *zeyheri*) and the similarly named but unrelated devil's thorn (*Dicerocaryum eriocarpum*) which has two sharp thorns. The tsamma (*Citrullus lanatus*), gemsbok cucumber (*Acanthosicyos naudiniana*) and the wild cucumber (*Cucumis africanus*) with its spiny fruit also flourish after rains.

Fauna and game-viewing

For most of the year the artificial water points of the Nossob and Auob River valleys are the most rewarding game-viewing areas of the park. Antelope include gemsbok, blue wildebeest, springbok, common duiker, steenbok and red hartebeest. Giraffe were reintroduced from Namibia in 1990, and you are likely to see them on a drive along the Auob River valley. The section of the park west of the Nossob River is home to about 10 prides of lion, numbering between 100 and 120 animals. Your best chances of seeing them are usually in the early mornings or late afternoons and in the vicinity of waterholes. Less frequently-seen large predators are brown and spotted hyaena, cheetah and leopard.

Since there are no boreholes east of the Nossob River the movement of the game is largely determined by the rains. If there is sufficient ground water in the trail area you should see animals. Look out for small herds of red hartebeest near pans. Spectacular migrations of eland occur sometimes. Other antelope include gemsbok, common duiker and steenbok.

An estimated 250 to 300 lions live in the area to the east of the Nossob River, with most of them favouring the game-rich areas of Mosimane Pan and Mabuasehube further east. Look out for the famed Kalahari lion with its black mane.

The Kalahari is one of the strongholds of the brown hyaena. They are nocturnal so look for them in the early mornings or late afternoons. Other large predators include leopard and spotted hyaena.

TRANSFRONTIER PARKS

Transfrontier conservation areas ensure uniform principles are applied in conservation areas on borders of neighbouring countries, promote friendly relationships between countries and enhance tourism. Over 140 transfrontier conservation areas have been established worldwide since 1932, but only in 1999 was the first such area declared in Africa. In addition to the Kgalagadi Transfrontier Park, the Maloti–Drakensberg (South Africa and Lesotho) (*see* Trans-Maloti, page 158), Lubombo (South Africa, Mozambique and Swaziland) (*see* Maputo Elephant Reserve, page 18), Great Limpopo (Kruger, Limpopo and Gonarezhou national parks in South Africa, Mozambique and Zimbabwe) (*see* page 27) and Ai-Ais/Richtersveld (South Africa and Namibia) (*see* Richtersveld National Park, page 183) transfrontier parks and conservation areas have been established. Sixteen areas in southern and eastern Africa have also been identified.

Even if you do not encounter large numbers of antelope or the large predators, there are numerous small mammals that might attract your attention. Among these are black-backed jackal, bat-eared fox, suricate, ground squirrel and the yellow mongoose. Other interesting small creatures include the leopard tortoise and the ground agama, which perches prominently at the top of shrubs in a territorial display.

Birding
The harsh climate of the Kalahari does not attract a large variety of birds, and only 78 of the 264 species recorded in the Kgalagadi Transfrontier Park are resident. Raptors are quite prominent: 43 of southern Africa's 70 species have been recorded here.
Raptors: secretary bird, bateleur, martial and black-chested snake eagles, red-necked falcon, African harrier-hawk, white-backed, lappet-faced, hooded and white-headed vultures.
Other species: ostrich, kori bustard, red-crested and northern black korhaan, Namaqua and Burchell's sandgrouse, double-banded courser, white-browed sparrowweaver, four resident lark species, Kalahari scrub-robin, ant-eating chat and the bokmakierie.

Facilities
Polentswa at the start of the trail has A-framed structures with cement slabs, but no other facilities. **Sesatswe** and **Lang Rambuka** are merely designated camp sites with no facilities. In the Botswana section of the park there are also camp sites without any facilities at **Two Rivers** (at the southern gate) and **Rooiputs**.

In the South African section of the park there are three rest camps. **Twee Rivieren**, the main camp at the southern gate, has cottages, each with one or two bedrooms, a living room, a fully equipped kitchen and bathroom; it also has bungalows with fully equipped kitchen and bathroom. In addition, Twee Rivieren offers a restaurant, shop, information centre and swimming pool. **Nossob Camp** provides accommodation in cottages, bungalows and huts, and has a small shop and a predator information centre. **Mata Mata** has cottages and huts, as well as a shop with a limited range of necessities.

There are also three wilderness camps in the South African section: at **Bitterpan** (accessible only by 4x4), **Groot Kolk** and the **Mata Mata Tent Camp**.

Activities
Be sure to view the photographic display of predator interaction in the **Predator Centre** at Nossob.

A walk through the **botanical reserve** in Nossob Camp is a useful introduction to the Kalahari flora. You can identify several well-known Kalahari plants by their nameplates as you stroll along a network of paths.

Night drives and **guided walks** are offered at Twee Rivieren and Nossob.

There are two other 4x4 trails in the Kgalagadi Transfrontier Park: the **Nossob Eco Trail** in South Africa and the **Mabuasehube Wilderness Trail** in Botswana. Bookings must be made with South African National Parks and Botswana Parks and Reserves Reservations, respectively.

Getting there
The most convenient approach is through the Twee Rivieren Gate, the southern entrance to the Kgalagadi Transfrontier Park. Only the last 60 km of the 247-km journey from Upington, the closest major town, is untarred. From Twee Rivieren it is 168 km to Nossob and another 21 km to the start of the trail.

BOTSWANA

Other options include the Kaa entrance on the north-eastern border of the park from where you can follow a track to Kannaguass in the Nossob Valley for 85 km and then continue for about 103 km to Nossob Camp. You can also follow the 170-km-long access route from Mabuasehube to Nossob Camp.

THE ROUTE – 410 km
Nossob Rest Camp return

In spite of the sandy terrain, virtually the entire trail can be done in four-wheel drive high range. The only exception is when you ascend the occasional low dune. Then low range might be necessary.

To reach the start of the trail, travel from Nossob Camp towards Union's End for about 20 km to the turnoff signposted Grootbrak. From here the trail winds past the Grootbrak windmill to reach the solitary grave of German geologist Hans Schwabe a short way on. Schwabe died here on 22 October 1958 after he set off to explore for diamonds, despite having been refused permission by the park authorities. After leaving his car at Kwang Pan, he walked north, possibly to look for water. A search party set off after his abandoned car was found at Kwang Pan, but found only Schwabe's body. He was buried here because of the legal implications of transporting a body across international borders. The camp site overlooking Polentswa Pan is just beyond the grave.

From Polentswa the first day's trail (101 km) initially strikes off in a northerly direction along the eastern edge of Polentswa Pan. After about 16 km you will traverse a few low dune ridges and further along the trail skirts the Tau Pans (*tau* is Setswana for lion) to reach Tweeling Rambuka, about four hours after setting off. Continuing through tree savanna dominated by acacias, the route now heads in a north-easterly direction to Dimpho Pan and then swings north as it makes its way to Kaole Pan. Beyond Kaole, the track winds between two of the Kaa Pans, a string of pans stretching for nearly 40 km from north to south.

For the remainder of the day you traverse slightly undulating sandveld and woodlands with little to divert you from the track ahead. At one point, the mangled remains of a burnt-out vehicle serves as a reminder that you should check regularly underneath your vehicle for grass. About 100 km after setting off from Polentswa you will arrive at the dunes on the western edge of Sesatswe Pan; these dunes offer a magnificent view over the pan which has a diameter of about 2 km. It's only a short drive from here to the camp site on the edge of the pan.

On day two (107 km) you head generally northwards for approximately 10 km. Here the trail turns north-west and traverses the dunes and inter-dune valleys. After about 11 km the track skirts a pan and further along links up with the track heading south from the Kaa entrance

ⓘ VITAL INFO

- Have your passport ready at the Twee Rivieren border post.
- Driving across pans is banned.
- Only the designated camps at Polentswa, Sesatswe and Lang Rambuka may be used.
- Sleeping outside is dangerous because of lion and hyaena.
- Keep your tent zipped up.
- Grass growing on the ridge between the tracks collects in the protection plates underneath the vehicle, and the friction can cause a fire.
- Cover your radiator with a mesh screen to stop grass seeds from clogging it up and causing the engine to overheat.

gate, completed in 2001. Heading south the trail reaches Kaa Pans Corner after 20 km and then heads in a south-westerly direction to Legakabe Pan through scenery similar to that seen on the first day. Finally, it winds along the dunes on the eastern side of Lang Rambuka Pan from where there is a magnificent view over the pan. The camp site, situated on the western edge of the pan, is not far.

The final day's trail (57 km) could be called the 'day of the pans' as it leads up and along several low dunes and a number of pans. Head north into the dunes and after 4 km the track ascends steeply to the crest of a dune from where you look down over some saline and vegetated pans. Further on you reach Tsholo Pan and then continue to Red Rambuka Pan about 12 km on. Through typical tree savanna, the trail skirts Kgama Pedi Pan (*kgama* is the Setswana name for red hartebeest) and then Munugo Pan. In mid-summer these pans are covered in carpets of pinkish-mauve nerines (*Nerine laticoma*). Just beyond Munugo Pan you gaze over the plains and on approaching Lijersdraai waterhole where the trail ends, you pass through magnificent open tree savanna. You reach Nossob Camp 77 km beyond the end of the trail, while Twee Rivieren is another 168 km (about 4 hours) on.

Linking routes
You can link up with Mabuasehube (*see* page 46) by following the 170-km track from Nossob Camp. One night is spent camping in the wilds.

LOGISTICS AND PLANNING
Fuel: Available at Twee Rivieren, Mata Mata and Nossob rest camps in the park. You will need enough fuel to cover a round trip of 355 km from Nossob.
Water: Take enough for at least three days (and spare water for emergencies) as there is no water at the overnight stops along the trail.
Food: The shop at Twee Rivieren has a wide range of groceries, frozen meat, firewood, soft drinks and liquor. The selection at Nossob Camp is less extensive.
Firewood: Take enough with you as you are not allowed to collect wood.
Best times: April/May and September/October are popular months as temperatures are generally pleasant. Game-viewing is best between August and the start of the rains, when the game is concentrated along the Auob and Nossob rivers. If you can bear the heat of summer, you might see a variety of flowering plants, large herds of migratory antelope or a thunderstorm.

Maps
A sketch map of the trail can be obtained at the Two Rivers office. The map does not contain GPS references, but the track is clearly defined so you shouldn't get lost.

Booking
Wilderness trail: Advance bookings, Parks and Reserves Reservations Office, Gaborone, tel: (+267) 318-0774, fax: 318-0775, e-mail dwnp@gov.bw. The trail is booked for the exclusive use of one group (two to five four-wheel drive vehicles). Report to the Two Rivers office (at the Twee Rivieren gate) to check in and collect a trail baton. On completion, check out at Two Rivers and hand in the baton. Vehicles may not deviate from the trail route.
Accommodation: For reservations at Twee Rivieren, Nossob, Mata Mata and the three wilderness camps, contact South African National Parks, PO Box 787, Pretoria 0001, tel: (+27 12) 428-9111, fax: 343-0905, e-mail: reservations@parks-sa.co.za.

BOTSWANA

Mabuasehube

Mabuasehube in the east of the Kgalagadi Transfrontier Park is a patchwork of tree and scrub acacia, and pans that seasonally attract large numbers of springbok, eland, red hartebeest, gemsbok and the predators following them. Set in the south-western corner of Botswana it is well off the usual tourist routes, and although access and facilities have been improved in recent years it remains an unspoiled tract of Kalahari. Here you can still feel the atmosphere of wild Africa and during a visit to Mabuasehube you will experience solitude and silence interrupted only by the roar of a lion or the call of a jackal.

THE PARK
Small groups of hunter-gatherer Bushmen and Bangologa (one of the five Bakgalagadi groups) once lived in the area. Mabuasehube was proclaimed as an extension to the Gemsbok National Park in 1974 in order to protect the complex of pans that are important in the migration of antelope from the sandveld in the west. Unlike Gemsbok National Park which remained largely closed to visitors until the late 1990s, Mabuasehube has been open since its establishment. The main track linking Tsabong in the south and Hunkutsi in the north used to run through the reserve. The reserve was amalgamated with the adjoining Gemsbok National Park to the west in the mid 1990s and forms part of the Kgalagadi Transfrontier Park which came into being in 1999 (see Gemsbok Wilderness Trail, page 40).

Landscape and vegetation
Three large pans and a number of outlying pans set amid a landscape of sandveld form the focal point of Mabuasehube. Adding to the scenic beauty are the spectacular dunes, some rising 30 m above the pan floor, along the south-western edges of the pans. They were formed when winds from the north-east deposited sand and silt from the pan floors on the leeward side of the pans and in time the dunes became stabilised by vegetation.

Mabuashehube, which is a Kgalagadi name that means 'place of red earth', is a large barren pan. The early pastoral Bangologa people managed to prolong their stay at Mabuasehube by deepening the pan along its western edge. In this way water was retained well into the dry season. In 1948 when the pan eventually dried up they were forced to leave. These days large numbers of antelope, especially gemsbok and eland, visit the pan to lick the salt from its floor to supplement the mineral deficiencies in the vegetation.

Lesholoago Pan to the north-east and Mpaathutlwa and Bosobogolo pans south of Mabuasehube are covered in short grass. In the east lies the complex known as the four Monamodi Pans.

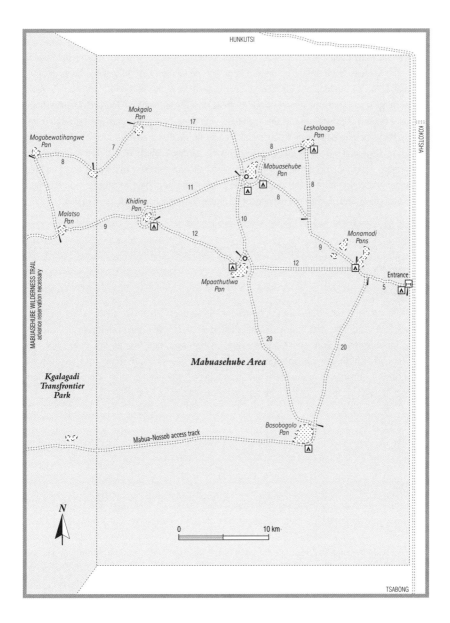

The vegetation of the sandveld in Mabuasehube is similar to that occurring elsewhere in the Kgalagadi Transfrontier Park (*see* page 40).

Fauna and game-viewing

After good rains the pans at Mabuasehube can hold water for several months, and antelope are attracted in large numbers by the nutritious grazing on the grass-covered pans. Not all the antelope converge on Mabuasehube as there is enough water in the seasonal pans and grazing in the sandveld west of Mabuasehube to sustain them. But as the pans dry up the animals migrate from the sandveld eastwards to the pumped waterholes at Mabuasehube and Mpaathutlwa pans.

BOTSWANA

These pans are the only permanent water sources east of the Nossob River (which has numerous artificial water points). Game-viewing depends on whether, where and how much it has rained.

The Mabuasehube area is home to a large lion population that follows the herds of antelope, so be on the look-out for them. Brown hyaena are active in the late afternoon or early morning. If you study the densely-wooded areas closely you might see leopard (Mabuasehube has a healthy population) while the open pans with their short grasses are ideal cheetah country. Packs of wild dog range through the area as do smaller predators such as black-backed jackal, Cape and bat-eared foxes, caracal and the aardwolf which lives almost exclusively on termites. Springbok occur throughout the year while large numbers of migrant eland and red hartebeest concentrate in the area at times. Small numbers of blue wildebeest crop the short grassy plains and, as they are dependent on water, they stay here until it has rained.

Birding
The birdlife of the Mabuasehube section of the Kgalagadi Transfrontier Park is similar to that occurring elsewhere in the park (see page 40).

Facilities
At the entrance gate there are camp sites and an ablution block with showers and flush toilets. Four camp sites with thatched shade shelters, rustic showers and bush toilets are available at **Mabuasehube Pan**, and **Mpaathutlwa**, **Lesholoago**, and **Monamodi pans** have two sites each. **Khiding** and **Bosobogolo** pans have two sites each with shade structures, shower enclosures (bring your own water!) and bush toilets. For accommodation options in the more popular western section of the park see Gemsbok Wilderness Trail, page 40.

Activities
From Mabuasehube a two-day wilderness 4x4 trail leads westwards to the Nossob Rest Camp. You spend the night in total wilderness. Groups must consist of at least two vehicles.

Getting there
Sand on the road from Tsabong in the south used to be axle deep years ago but the road is now partly surfaced. The road no longer runs through the reserve, but follows the eastern boundary to a new entrance gate 112 km from Tsabong. Approach from the east along the Trans-Kalahari Highway, turn left onto the tarred road to Werda/Tsabong at Sekoma and follow it for 50 km to the settlement of Khakhea. After another 40 km you will reach Khokhotsa Pan on your left where a microwave communication tower to the right serves as a useful landmark. Turn right and follow the road (which soon turns into a track) past the tower. Following a cutline, the track heads almost dead straight in a westerly direction through scrub and bush, and after 100 km you join the Tsabong/Tsane road. Turn left (south) and continue for roughly 16 km to the entrance gate.

Mabuasehube can also be reached by following the 170-km-long access track from Nossob Camp to Bosobogolo Pan. One night is spent camping in the wilds.

ROUTES – 530 km Tshabong return; 900 km Jwaneng return
The network of tracks around the pans covers just over 80 km; this is the only part of the area that has been made accessible, since there is little likelihood of seeing game away from the pans. In this way you can watch birds and view game at leisure, without having to cover long distances.

From Mpaathutlwa Pan you can also travel south for about 20 km to Bosobogolo Pan which lies alongside the old unused access route from the south. It is a seasonal pan and the game comes and goes, but there are large herds of springbok on the open pan after the rains.

Another option is the 52-km circuit from Mabuasehube Pan to Mokgalo Pan and then on to Mogobewatihangwe and Malatso pans before heading back via Khiding Pan.

Linking routes

You can link the Mabuasehube section of the Kgalagadi Transfrontier Park to Nossob Rest Camp in the more popular western section of the park by setting off on a two-day/one-night self-guided Mabuasehube Wilderness Trail. For safety reasons you may not do this trip with fewer than two vehicles. Travelling is only allowed from east to west. Reservations must be made through Botswana's Department of Wildlife and National Parks office in Gaborone (e-mail: dwnp@gov.bw). Alternatively, you can use the 170-km-long access track from Bosobogolo Pan and Nossob Camp. One night is spent camping in the wilds.

LOGISTICS AND PLANNING

Fuel: Available at Tsabong (112 km south of the entrance gate), Hunkutsi (175 km north of the gate) and Jwaneng on the Trans-Kalahari Highway (290 km from the gate). Plan your fuel requirements according to your approach and return routes and make allowance for game drives.

Water: Can be obtained at the entrance gate but should be boiled for drinking purposes.

Food: Only basic groceries can be bought in Tsabong and Hunkutsi so stock enough food for the duration of your visit.

Best times: The rainy season (December to March/April) is generally the best time to visit Mabuasehube. Game-viewing and birding are likely to be most rewarding as game is attracted to the new growth on the pans, and summer migrants add to the numbers of resident bird species.

Booking

Reservations must be made with the Parks and Reserves Reservations Office, Gaborone, tel: (+267) 318-0774, fax: 318-0775, e-mail dwnp@gov.bw.

Red hartebeest and gemsbok grazing on Khiding Pan, one of several large pans in Mabuasehube.

BOTSWANA

Khutse Game Reserve

Seasonal pans set among the sands of the central Kalahari form the focal point of Khutse Game Reserve. While large herds of antelope sometimes gather around the pans and are followed by predators such as lion, cheetah and hyaena, game-viewing is not Khutse's main attraction. It's the wild and unspoiled atmosphere of this area that makes a visit worthwhile, and any large concentrations of game should be considered a bonus. The ultimate allure of all the Kalahari parks is the wild, open spaces, clear atmosphere, the pleasure of sitting round the campfire at night listening to the night sounds and sleeping in a camp site which is unfenced. There is also always the possibility of seeing something unexpected (a honey badger, African wild cat or three southern pale chanting goshawks co-operating to catch a mongoose). What makes Khutse particularly attractive is the open pans for easier game-viewing.

THE RESERVE

Located in the Kalahari thirstland, Khutse was established in 1971 to protect the complex of seasonal pans and wildlife of the area. Before that, small groups of nomadic Bushmen and Kgalagadi people wandered through the region, while the Bakwena settled here later. The Kgalagadi name Khutse, which means 'to kneel down and drink', is a reference to the pans' importance as a water source. Khutse shares its northern border with the Central Kalahari Game Reserve, but as there is no fence, game is free to migrate between the two reserves.

Landscape and vegetation

Khutse's complex of grassy and saline pans lies amid a mosaic of gently undulating dunes, sandy plains, grasslands and tree savanna, dominated by acacia trees and scrub. The pans lie in a fossil river system which once flowed into a super-lake that dried up when the climate became arid and shrank to form the Makgadikgadi Pans (*see* pages 36 and 61). It has been suggested that the pans in Khutse were formed during an earlier, wetter period, some 15 000 to 10 000 years ago.

Fauna and game-viewing

Although Khutse does not support large concentrations of game, throughout the year animals can usually be found near the open pans. A spurt of nutritious new growth after the rains generally attracts antelope to the grassy pans, while the salinity of the pans supplements the

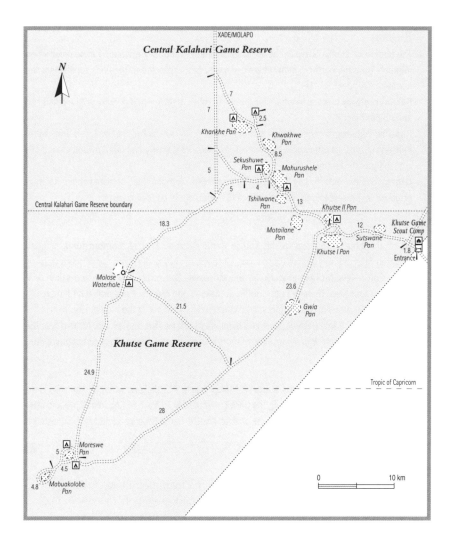

mineral deficiencies in the vegetation. Antelope eat the highly concentrated minerals on the pans during the dry months and during the rainy season drink the mineral-rich water.

Once the seasonal pans have dried up many animals migrate out of the reserve. Others move to the Molose and Moreswe waterholes where boreholes provide water during the dry season.

You are likely to see springbok and giraffe throughout the year, and you may possibly see gemsbok, red hartebeest and blue wildebeest. In the more densely wooded areas you might come across kudu. Although eland are found in the reserve they migrate over vast distances and are not often seen. Common duiker and steenbok favour grassland with scrub and shrubs.

Lion, leopard, cheetah and spotted and brown hyaenas represent the large predators, but your chances of seeing them depend on the whereabouts of their herbivorous prey. Smaller predators you might see during an early morning or late afternoon drive are the bat-eared fox, black-backed jackal, African wild cat and caracal.

Other smaller animals that might catch your attention are warthog, yellow mongoose and ground squirrel.

BOTSWANA

Birding
The birdlife of Khutse is typical of the Kalahari and is especially rewarding in summer when migrants from the northern hemisphere and water birds attracted to the pans supplement the number of resident species.
Summer migrants: capped wheatear, European roller, great spotted cuckoo, yellow-billed kite and Abdim's stork.
Raptors: bateleur, southern pale chanting goshawk, white-backed, lappet-faced and white-headed vultures, secretary bird, black-chested snake eagle, tawny and martial eagles, amur falcon and greater kestrel.
Other species: ostrich, kori bustard, northern black korhaan, lilac-breasted roller, Kalahari scrub-robin, fawn-coloured lark, magpie shrike and double-banded courser.

Facilities
There are three camp sites in the Khutse Game Reserve. **Khutse Campground**, situated between Khutse I and Khutse II pans, has 10 spacious sites under large camel thorn trees as well as pit toilets. **Molose waterhole** and **Moreswe Pan**, which are close to a saline pan, both have four sites. There are no facilities at Molose, and Moreswe has only a pit latrine.

Three camp sites with no facilities are administered from Khutse in the southern extreme of the Central Kalahari Game Reserve. Four sites overlook **Khankhe Pan**, and two are located near the edge of **Mahurushele Pan**. A large camel thorn tree shades the single site at **Sekushuwe Pan**.

Getting there
The easiest approach is from the south via Molepolole and Letlhakeng where the tar road ends. From the traffic circle in Letlhakeng the track continues for 25.5 km to Khudumelapye and after 35.9 km you reach Salajwe where the split to Khutse Game Reserve should be signposted if

GAME MIGRATIONS

Drought, rains and instinct influence the migration of species such as blue wildebeest, red hartebeest, eland and springbok. Rainfall in the Kalahari is extremely unpredictable and erratic so it is difficult to anticipate migration patterns.

In times of drought, blue wildebeest and red hartebeest migrate from the southern Kalahari through Khutse and the Central Kalahari game reserves to the Boteti River and Lake Xau in search of water and grazing. The erection of foot-and-mouth disease fences across Botswana since the 1950s has disrupted these migration patterns and caused the death of tens of thousands of animals. The herds are trapped behind the fences as they lie across the animals' traditional migration routes to the seasonally flooded pans, the waterholes and new grazing, resulting in death from thirst and starvation.

To discourage the animals from migrating during the dry season, water pumps have been installed at two pans in Khutse (Molose and Moreswe) and at a number of pans in the Central Kalahari Game Reserve.

Khutse Game Reserve

the sign has not, as sometimes happens, been knocked down by cars, or removed. Continuing further, you reach Kaudwane and from here the track deteriorates into thick loose sand all the way to the reserve boundary. The Game Scout Camp is 1.8 km beyond this.

Khutse can also be approached from either Xade in the west of the Central Kalahari Game Reserve or along the Trans-Kalahari route, a 330-km journey that takes two days of hard driving.

ROUTES – 600 km Molepolole return

You can explore the pan area and the sandveld along a network of tracks covering about 200 km. A rewarding early morning or late afternoon drive from the Khutse Campground is the Pans Track which follows a fossil valley containing a series of pans, all worth investigating. There is a chance you may see a herd of giraffe gathered on one of the grass-covered pans, large numbers of vultures socialising around a waterhole or a pride of lion. You may even be privileged to see something totally unexpected like a tawny eagle stealing a snake from a secretary bird and then having a mid-air battle with two other tawnies trying to wrest the snake away, or you may have a really close-up view of an African wild cat – a shy species that is not easily seen.

From the Khutse Campground the track heads in a north-westerly direction and about 7.1 km after the first junction to Moreswe Pan (which you must ignore) crosses into the Central Kalahari Game Reserve. For administrative purposes the network of tracks and three camp sites in the very south of the reserve fall under the control of Khutse.

Beyond Motailane Pan, (the first pan you reach after setting off from Khutse Campground) you reach Tshilwane Pan and then Mahurushele Pan where you keep right, ignoring the turnoff to Molose waterhole and Moreswe. The track continues along the fossil valley and after passing Sekushuwe Pan you reach Khwakhwe and Khankhe. It will take you about an hour to reach Khankhe from Khutse Campground, and from here it is best to retrace your tracks and to check the pans for animals again – just in case.

It is a short drive from Khutse Campground to the viewpoint overlooking Khutse I Pan, which is the best spot to enjoy sundowners. Here a sand dune provides a natural vantage point over the pan and the endless Kalahari savanna to the south. The viewpoint is a mere 5.4 km from the campground, along a short loop road, which gives you enough time to enjoy sundowners on the sand dune and get back to the camp before dark.

From Khutse Campground you can also do a full-day circuit of about 130 km to Moreswe Pan in the south-west of the reserve via Molose waterhole. Beyond Motailane and Tshilwane pans the track traverses gently undulating duneveld where you might spot kudu and giraffe, the latter especially where there are acacias. Molose, which is about 40 km from Khutse Campground, has an artificial waterhole.

On leaving Molose, you are less likely to see game as you head once again through sandveld scrub and shrubs. About 18 km beyond the pan, a signboard provides a welcome respite from driving. It marks the Tropic of Capricorn and is a popular photographic stop. From here the track continues for another 7 km to Moreswe Pan where a figure-of-eight track circles Moreswe and Mabuakolobe (*kolobe* is Setswana for warthog) pans. There is a good chance of seeing game in this area during the dry season if water has been pumped into the artificial waterhole at Moreswe, a small saline pan, and at Molose.

From Moreswe, the track heads in a north-easterly direction, and there is little to distract your attention from the track ahead until you reach Gwia Pan, where game congregates during the rainy season. The remaining 12 km, which goes through shrubs and scrub, can be rather tiring at the end of a long day's drive.

BOTSWANA

KGALAGADI

The first black people, a number of related groups who speak a language related to, but separate from, Setswana, migrated into what is today referred to as the Kalahari about 2 000 years ago. These people became known as the Bakgalagadi, or 'people of the Kgalagadi', a name said to be derived from Makgadikgadi and which is translated as 'area of many pans' or 'salt pans'. The name Kalahari itself is a corruption of Kgalagadi.

Linking routes
A visit to Khutse can be extended into the Central Kalahari Game Reserve, but you would need to carry enough fuel to cover at least 1 100 km if you plan to exit at Mananga Gate close to the north-eastern corner of the reserve. Xade is 290 km from Khutse, and Deception Pan a further 160 km. The Trans-Kalahari Traverse from Khutse office to Mananga Gate is 330 km long and takes two days of hard driving to complete. As this track is used only infrequently, you should not attempt it alone.

LOGISTICS AND PLANNING
Fuel: You should have sufficient fuel to cover at least 600 km, from Molepolole back to Molepolole and game drives in Khutse. The nearest filling station is at Letlhakeng, about 104 km from the Game Scout Camp, but it is advisable to fill up at Molepolole 57 km further south, as the filling station at Letlhakeng might occasionally be out of fuel.
Water: Water is available only from the Game Scout Camp near the park entrance, but, as it is slightly brackish, it is best to take your own.
Food: You can shop at supermarkets and liquor outlets in Gaborone (about 220 km from Khutse). A more limited range of supplies can be bought at Molepolole and Letlhakeng, as well as small shops en route to the reserve.
Best times: In spite of the summer heat, and depending on the rains, December to April is generally the best time for game-viewing. Large concentrations of game graze the nutritious new grass on the pans. Birding is also more rewarding during these months when the summer migrants can be ticked.

Booking
Reservations must be made with the Parks and Reserves Reservations Office, Gaborone, tel: (+267) 318-0774, fax: 318-0775, e-mail dwnp@gov.bw.

Unfenced camp sites in Botswana's parks and reserves add to their wilderness atmosphere.

Central Kalahari Game Reserve

Grass-covered valleys stretching to the horizon, interrupted occasionally by clumps of acacias and shimmering pans, create the essence of this reserve in central Botswana. For many months of the year the game seems to hide, but it is the stark scenery and remoteness, rather than herds of game, that attract visitors. You need to be prepared to rough it in this unspoiled part of southern Africa that covers almost 10% of the whole country. In the solitude and infinite space you will witness how animals eke out an existence in this forbidding land.

THE RESERVE

The largest conservation area in Africa after the Selous National Park in Tanzania, the Central Kalahari Game Reserve stretches for just over 260 km from north to south and is 280 km at its widest point from east to west. It was set aside in 1961 to enable the G/wi and Gana Bushmen (or Basarwa as they are known in Botswana) to continue their hunting and gathering way of life and to protect the wildlife and habitats of the Kalahari. Traditionally the Bushmen were nomadic peoples, moving between dry-season and wet-season camps in the southern half of the reserve and the Khutse Game Reserve. Their numbers fluctuated from as many as 3 000, during times when conditions were favourable, to as few as 800 during times of drought.

A borehole pump installed at Xade in 1969 changed the lives of the Kalahari Bushmen forever. Within 15 years Xade's population increased from one extended family to more than 1 000 people who turned to subsistence crop and stock farming to supplement their hunter-gatherer lifestyle. The provision of water elsewhere in the reserve also enticed the Bushmen to settle in smaller semi-permanent villages at Molapo, Metsimanong, Gope, Mothomelo, Kikao and Kumana.

In 1986 the Botswana government announced that it would resettle people outside the reserve to provide them with facilities such as schools and clinics. They were encouraged to move voluntarily, but many refused to leave their ancestral lands. In 1997 over 1 000 people were resettled at New Xade, 45 km west of the reserve. Each family was given goats, cattle and 15 000 Pula in compensation, but some decided to remain in the reserve. Another settlement, Kaudwane, was established south of Khutse Game Reserve. The defiant inhabitants were eventually forced to move when government officials removed the water pumps in 2002.

The reserve was closed to visitors until the early 1990s when Deception Valley was opened. Access was later extended to other areas of the park, such as Passarge Valley, which became accessible only in 1998.

BOTSWANA

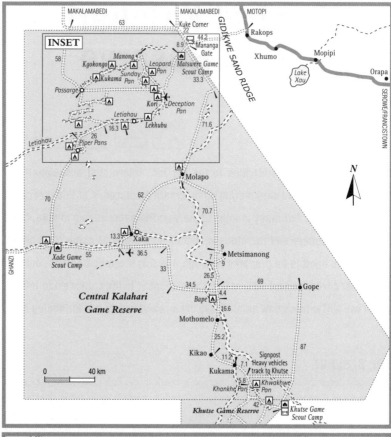
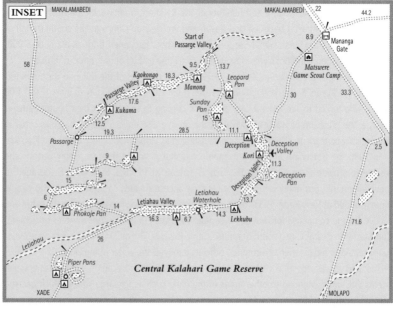

Central Kalahari Game Reserve

Landscape and vegetation
An immense sea of low dunes dominates the landscape. The Kalahari began taking shape some 65 million years ago when rivers dumped vast quantities of gravel, clay and sand into the Kalahari Basin, which was formed when the Great Escarpment of southern Africa was uplifted. These deposits were subsequently eroded and over millions of years the sand was redistributed by strong winds over an area of 2.5 million km^2, the largest unbroken expanse of sand in the world. It stretches from just north of the Gariep River in South Africa's Northern Cape Province across two thirds of Botswana, eastern and northern Namibia, western Zimbabwe, Zambia and Angola and into the Democratic Republic of the Congo.

Numerous seasonal pans punctuate the dunescape in the north, while four fossil rivers snake their way through the dunes. The best known of these fossil rivers, the Letiahau, carved Deception Valley. It has been suggested that these rivers flowed as recently (in geological terms) as 16 000 years ago into a vast super-lake which shrank to what is today the Makgadikgadi Pans (*see* page 61) when a drier period set in.

The grass-covered dunes are interspersed with camel thorns, Kalahari sand acacia, shepherd's tree and raisin bushes. The trumpet thorn (*Catophractes alexandri*) is characteristic of calcrete areas and the perimeter of pans, while the silver cluster-leaf is common in the sandveld in the south of the reserve. There is also a mosaic of grasslands, shrub savanna and scrub, grass-covered pans and patches of acacia woodland.

After rains the valley floors are covered in nutritious, golden, waving grasslands that attract large numbers of antelope. Conspicuous, especially in Deception Valley, are the acacia and buffalo-thorn 'tree islands' that provide a shady retreat for the game during the heat of the day. The 'islands' consist of dense clumps of umbrella thorn and buffalo-thorn trees and are widely scattered along the floors of fossil valleys. They often form around shallow depressions.

Fauna and game-viewing
Springbok and gemsbok can be seen throughout the year, but don't count on seeing large numbers of animals unless you visit the park after good rains when the game concentrates on the grasslands in the valleys. Red hartebeest and eland, two migratory species, are present in small numbers, while vast herds of blue wildebeest migrate through the reserve from time to time. The most publicised of these migrations took place in August 1979 when thousands of blue wildebeest died of thirst when their migration to Lake Xau, east of the park, was halted by the Kuke veterinary fence.

Tracking the herds of antelope are the predators. Lion are fairly common. Brown hyaena can be seen in the early mornings or late afternoons. Cheetah, wild dog and leopard also inhabit the park but don't expect to see them easily.

Other large species to keep a watch for are giraffe and kudu, while steenbok and common duiker also occur. Deception is a good place to see the Cape fox with its silvery coat and a distinctive dark, bushy tail. It favours semi-arid open grassland and scrub and can often be found resting during the day in the shade of acacia trees fringing shallow depressions. Also do not neglect the other smaller species such as bat-eared fox, African wild cat, ground squirrel and suricate that can be as interesting to observe as the larger animals.

Birding
The birdlife of the reserve is typical of the Central Kalahari and is characterised by species that are adapted to survive in arid conditions and nomadic species.

BOTSWANA

Raptors: tawny and martial eagles, black-chested snake eagle, lanner falcon, secretary bird, lappet-faced, white-backed and white-headed vultures, greater kestrel and bateleur.
Other species: ostrich, kori bustard, red-crested korhaan, Burchell's sandgrouse, Kalahari scrub-robin, double-banded courser, crimson-breasted and southern white-crowned shrikes, lilac-breasted roller, Marico flycatcher, grey-backed sparrowlark and fawn-coloured lark.

Facilities
There are several camp sites with no facilities in the popular northern section of the reserve. For an ideal wilderness experience, **Deception**, **Kori** and **Sunday Pan** camp sites have six, four and three sites respectively, while the others have only a single site. **Piper Pans**, the southernmost camp site in the northern section, and **Xade** in the south-west, both have two sites. There are sites with no facilities at **Molapo**, **Metsimanong**, **Bape** and **Kukama** on the Trans-Kalahari route.

Getting there
As you approach from the north there are two access routes. The most direct route is to take the signposted turnoff, 82 km east of Maun, to Motopi, and continue to the post office tower 3.3 km north of Rakops. You turn right and travel for 44.2 km to Mananga Gate along a hard surface track for most of the way, except where you cross the Gidikiwe Sand Ridge. This ridge marks the shores of the ancient Makgadikgadi super-lake. From Mananga Gate it is 8.9 km to the Matswere Game Scout Camp. The alternative is to turn south onto the road to Makalamabedi. The turnoff is 56 km east of Maun on the Maun/Nata road. Makalamabedi is reached about 19 km on and the track, with rather sandy stretches, follows the veterinary fence for 77 km to Kuke Corner. Continue for another 22 km to Mananga Gate, 174 km from Maun.

The park can also be approached from the west. Take the signposted turnoff onto a gravel road, 9.5 km west of the T-junction opposite the airfield in Ghanzi. The track to Xade splits off to the left after about 26.3 km and 116 km on you enter the park. Xade is 23 km away and 175 km from Ghanzi.

From the south, the park can be accessed via Khutse Game Reserve from Molepolole and Letlhakeng where the tar road ends. Most of the track to the Khutse gate is sandy. The gate is about 104 km beyond Letlhakeng and 161 km from Molepolole. From Khutse there are two options: the 330-km Trans-Kalahari to Mananga Gate or, via Xade to Deception Valley, a 450-km journey.

ROUTES – 660 km Rakops return, including Deception and Passarge valleys and Piper Pans
There are several camp sites in the Deception Valley vicinity which give a rewarding sense of the wilderness and isolation of the Central Kalahari.

Deception to Piper Pans
A visit to Deception Pan is not to be missed. The hard clay track in the Deception and Letiahau valleys is easy to negotiate in the dry season, but it can be challenging in the rain.

> ### (i) VITAL INFO
> - After the rainy season cover your radiator with a mesh screen to prevent grass from clogging it up.
> - Stop often to remove grass from the protection plates and under the driving shaft, as it can ignite.

Central Kalahari Game Reserve

From Deception Camp Site, follow the scenic wide valley southwards for nearly 9 km to the Deception Pan turnoff. Notice the acacia tree 'islands'. As you crest a low dune, the pan comes into view and, unless it has rained recently, Deception will live up to its name: from a distance the pan appears full of water, but when you get to its edge there is only the dry cracked surface of the pan floor and you realise that you've been deceived by a mirage.

About 15 km beyond the Deception Pan turnoff you reach Lekhubu Camp Site, a beautifully shaded spot with one site. The valley now swings west; 15 km beyond Lekhubu you reach Letiahau waterhole. Surrounded by a dense clump of buffalo-thorn trees, Letiahau is the only pumped waterhole along the length of the valley. You should see game here: expect the unexpected. We were startled to find a python on the edge of the waterhole. When it saw us, it slithered into the water where it remained submerged for quite some time before coming up to breathe. Eventually it eased itself out of the water and disappeared into the bush. Letiahau Camp Site is 6.7 km further west and Deception Valley assumes its rightful (indigenous) name, Letiahau Valley.

About 16 km beyond Letiahau Camp you can link up with the track to Phokoje (black-backed jackal), San and Tau (lion) pans or continue to Piper Pans. If you are headed for Piper Pans, the track leaves the Letiahau Valley a short way on, and continues for 26 km through easily negotiable sandveld covered with Kalahari shrub and scrub savanna to a split. Either of these tracks will take you to Piper Pans, where there is a pumped waterhole (good game-viewing potential). One camp site is among a clump of trees on the edge of the pan and the other is shaded by camel thorn trees on the dunes south of the pan. There is no view of the pan from the latter.

South of Piper Pans the terrain is sandier and vegetation denser but as there are no pumped waterholes, there is little incentive to go to Xade, unless you are leaving the park in the west or going to Khutse Game Reserve.

Deception to Passarge Valley

A worthwhile full-day trip from Deception Camp Site is the 156-km-long circuit through Passarge Valley which can be difficult to negotiate after rains, because of clay. The rest of the circuit is on sand that is easily negotiated, especially when wet after rains.

There is not much game during the dry season as there are no pumped waterholes, except at Sunday Pan. The scenery along the 48-km-long valley, which winds through the dunes, makes this a rewarding trip. About 15 km north-west of Deception, Sunday Pan has three sites and is an excellent alternative to the Deception Camp Site, which can sometimes be a little busy.

You pass Leopard Pan Camp Site (one site) and after 13.7 km you reach the start of Passarge Valley, a fossil valley that flowed in a north-westerly direction to the Makgadikgadi super-lake. It was named after a German scientist, Siegfried Passarge, who undertook an expedition through the Kalahari from 1896 to 1898. In addition to his detailed study on the physical geography of the area, Passarge published a book on the Bushmen in 1905.

If you want absolute solitude there are three camps, Manong, Kgokongo, and Kukama, each with only one site, along the valley. After travelling along Passarge Valley for 48 km the track climbs out of the valley into the dunes and links up with the cutline. Take a short detour to the pumped waterhole at Passarge Pan before you tackle the long, straight track back to Deception: you might spot something unexpected. Known as the Trans-Kalahari Traverse, the track was made in 1973 when a geological survey of the Kalahari was undertaken.

Just before the turnoff to Tau Pan you reach the crest of a dune, with far-reaching views over the flat expanse. Further on the dunes provide the only distraction from the dead-straight track, and after about 47 km on the Traverse you finally reach Deception Camp Site.

BOTSWANA

TAMPANS (TICKS)

Beware of sand tampans when camping or stopping for lunch under trees. These reddish-brown soft ticks live up to 8 cm under the sand and are activated by the carbon dioxide exhaled by humans and animals. Minutes after the arrival of animals and humans they emerge from the sand and puncture the exposed skin of their hosts to feed on the blood. Although treatment of the bites is normally not necessary, you could become very ill, in which case you should consult a doctor.

Trans-Kalahari route

The Trans-Kalahari route in the eastern section of the park links Mananga Gate and Khutse Game Reserve. Since there are no artificial waterholes in this section of the park, this 330-km drive can be tedious. Due to the remoteness of this area, two vehicles are advisable.

Do not underestimate the time it will take to reach Khutse: two days of hard driving and some deep sand in the dunes 40 km south of Mananga Gate. If you start early you can reach Bape Camp Site; if not you will have to break your journey at Molapo.

LOGISTICS AND PLANNING

Fuel: Ghanzi and Maun have reliable supplies. Fuel is usually also available at Rakops. The nearest filling station south of the reserve is at Letlhakeng (104 km from Khutse), but Molepolole (161 km from Khutse) has a more regular supply. If you plan to travel extensively and visit Khutse, take enough fuel for 1 250 km.

Water: Available only from the game scout camps at Matswere in the north-east and Xade in the south-west and Khutse Game Reserve. It is a good idea to boil the water for drinking.

Food: Supermarkets and liquor outlets in Gaborone, Francistown and Maun stock a wide range of fresh produce, frozen and canned foods, meat, groceries, cool drinks and liquor. If you approach via Khutse, you can do last-minute shopping at Molepolole; villages en route sell basic groceries and canned goods.

Best times: The best time to see game is between December and April, despite the heat. You may experience a typical Kalahari thunderstorm or get caught up in a dust storm. Summer migrants make birding most rewarding during these months.

Maps

Obtain a copy of the Department of Wildlife and National Parks map of the northern section of the park on arrival. It indicates the Phokoje, San and Tau pans, as well as the Passarge Valley tracks. The tracks are indicated on the latest *Shell Map*.

Booking

Reservations must be made with the Parks and Reserves Reservations Office, Gaborone, tel: (+267) 318-0774, fax: 318-0775, e-mail dwnp@gov.bw.

Makgadikgadi Pans

Expanses of cracked salt and silt melting into dancing heat waves to the distant horizon typify the Makgadikgadi Pans in central Botswana, the largest salt pans in the world. Driving across these flat featureless pans is a journey into a surrealistic world of boundless space and timelessness. In the middle of nowhere lies Lekhubu (Kubu) Island, a mysterious place where people lived at a time when Makgadikgadi must have been a more hospitable environment. During the rainy season the harsh saline desert of Makgadikgadi is transformed into vast sheets of water that attract hundreds of thousands of water birds. (*Also see* page 66.)

THE PANS

It is difficult to imagine that the vast expanses of sun-bleached salt and clay of the Makgadikgadi Pans once formed an enormous inland lake of the same proportions as Lake Victoria in East Africa. Sowa Pan in the east lies at the lowest end of the Makgadikgadi Basin and is seasonally fed by the Nata and four other rivers.

Mystical Lekhubu Island in the south-west of Sowa Pan is the main attraction of a visit to the Makgadikgadi Pans. Granite boulders and grotesquely shaped baobab trees rise unexpectedly from the nothingness surrounding them. In the late afternoon the silhouettes of the ancient baobabs with their unusual reddish sheen enhance Lekhubu's unique setting and its spirituality.

Tools found here provide clear evidence that Lekhubu was inhabited thousands of years ago by Stone Age people and later by the Bushmen. Other people lived here too, but their origins are unclear. Archaeological sites include piles of stone and the ruins of a village that was inhabited in some period, possibly about 1 500 years ago. A semi-circular, 1-m-high stone wall at Lekhubu's south-eastern corner shows similarities to the Zimbabwean building tradition in the 16th century and the Lekhubu settlement might have been an outpost of Khame or Great Zimbabwe.

Ntwetwe Pan is separated from Sowa by a ribbon of land. Its irregular outline has many inlets, bays and grass-covered 'fingers'. At its longest extremity it stretches over 150 km in a northeast/south-west direction and it is up to 80 km wide. The monotony of its shimmering white pan is interrupted in places by grassy horseshoe-shaped 'islands', formed when Kalahari sands were blown onto the dry pan floor and were eventually stabilised by grass. In ancient times the waters carried by the Boteti River flooded the pan, but it is now inundated only by rain and run-off.

Indications are the early Okavango, Kwando/Chobe and Upper Zambezi rivers once flowed via the Makgadikgadi Basin to the Limpopo River. Around 2 million years ago the flow was blocked by upheavals of the earth's crust (the Kalahari–Zimbabwe Axis) to the east of the basin. Water, unable to find an outlet to the sea, formed a huge inland lake. Over aeons the courses of the Upper Zambezi and Kwando/Chobe rivers changed, reducing the flow of water into the lake.

BOTSWANA

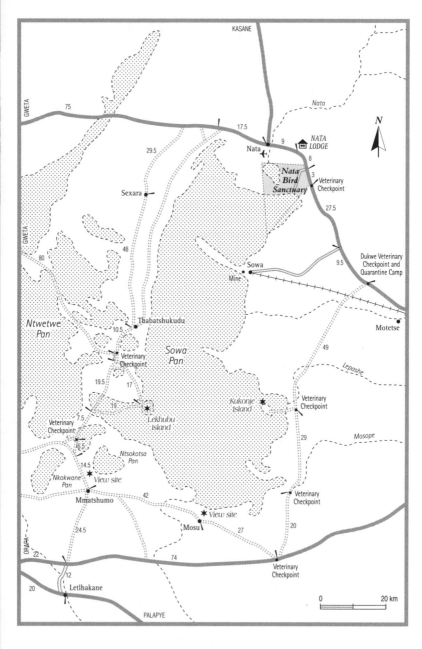

Crustal movements and climate changes have caused considerable fluctuations in the level of the lake over the last million years. Research suggests that Lake Makgadikgadi was linked to the Mababe and Ngami basins via the Boteti River Valley, some 40 000 to 35 000 years ago. Covering the same size as Lake Victoria, this super-lake was 55 m deep in places. Its shores are marked by the Gidikwe Sand Ridge west and north of the Makgadikgadi Pans and the Magikhwe Sand Ridge west of the Mababe Basin. A drop in the level of Lake Makgadikgadi separated it from the Mababe and Ngami basins which formed a single lake, Thamalakane, between 17 000 and 13 000 years ago. The overflow of this lake spilled into a much-reduced Lake Makgadikgadi via the Boteti River. In time, Mababe and Ngami dried up and Lake Makgadikgadi's main source of water was the overflow from the Okavango Delta along the Boteti Valley. During wet cycles, rivers from the southern Kalahari also flowed into the lake from the west.

Lake Makgadikgadi dried up completely less than 10 000 years ago when the Okavango Delta and the Kalahari rivers stopped flowing into it. All that remained was a series of saline pans which are now fed by rain and five rivers from the east.

The pans are a saline desert without any vegetation except on the fringes where species such as the salt bush (*Salsola*) grow. Grass, scrub and shrub veld grow on the edges of the pan and the 'fingers' of land jutting from the pans.

Fauna and game-viewing
Other than the occasional gemsbok that might wander onto the pan to lick the salt, the pans are devoid of animal life. The only exception is in the north-western corner of Ntwetwe Pan which falls in the Makgadikgadi–Nxai Pan National Park. Here the grasslands and the complex of seasonal pans attract vast numbers of Burchell's zebra and antelope, usually from April onwards (*see* Makgadikgadi, page 66).

Birding
In years of good rains, tens of thousands of lesser and greater flamingos arrive at the pans virtually overnight, and if conditions are favourable they breed on Makgadikgadi, one of only three major flamingo breeding sites in Africa. They fly in from the distant coastal lagoons in Namibia, wetlands in South Africa and even the lakes as far away as East Africa. Single colonies of up to 60 000 flamingo have been counted.

The feeding ground of both flamingo species is the highly nutritious brine at the delta of the Nata River. The lesser flamingo feed on microscopic algae and the greater flamingo on small crustaceans such as fairy shrimps.

Once the pans have dried up and the flamingo and other water birds have departed, only the chestnut-banded and Kittlitz's plovers remain on the cracked surface.
Specials: wattled crane (numbering up to 1 000 at times) and crowned crane on the grasslands.
Commonly seen (in good rainy years): white and pink-backed pelicans, Caspian plover, black-winged stilt, pied avocet, African spoonbill, marsh sandpiper, black-necked grebe, Cape and red-billed teals, white-backed duck, grey-headed gull, several species of herons and plovers.

Facilities
Lekhubu Island and the camp site are managed by the people of Mmatshumo as a community-based tourism project, and entry and camping fees are payable at the island. You should be totally self-sufficient as there are no facilities.
Nata Sanctuary, 17.5 km south of Nata on the road to Francistown. Entrance and camping fees payable. Camp sites, ablutions.
Nata Lodge, 9.2 km south of Nata on road to Francistown. Chalets, camp sites with clean ablutions, restaurant, swimming pool.

Getting there
Approach from Nata, the most popular access point to the Makgadikgadi area situated 300 km east of Maun and 190 km north-west of Francistown.

BOTSWANA

> ### ⓘ VITAL INFO
>
> - Driving across the pans can be dangerous. What appears as a hard surface can turn out to be only a thin crust disguising a bottomless pit of mud and brine that can swallow a vehicle.
> - Parties should have at least two vehicles. Follow fresh tracks, a sign that someone has negotiated the pan successfully.
> - Deflating tyres, especially 'bakkie tyres', will increase their 'footprint' and give better flotation. Put your free-wheel hubs in the 'lock' position in case you need to engage four-wheel drive.
> - Keep your speed above 60 km. This will give the vehicle momentum which gives it a better chance of crossing soft patches.
> - If you get bogged down, let the vehicle come to a standstill without braking and do not attempt to drive further. Jack up the vehicle (use your spare wheel as a base) and place available material, eg stones or wood, under the wheels until you can drive it out gently. This is easier said than done when you are in the middle of nowhere but this might be your only option; if you have a winch you can use the spare wheel as an anchor.

ROUTES – 650 km Nata return, including Nata Sanctuary

Makgadikgadi can be traversed from north to south along two routes: from Gweta across Ntwetwe Pan to Mopipi, and from the Maun/Nata road to Lekhubu Island and Mmatshumo village; the latter route is described below.

Lekhubu Island

From Nata follow the tar road towards Maun for 17.5 km until you reach the signposted turnoff (marked Lekhubu 72 km). Turn left (south) and ignore tracks turning off to the right. When you link up with a clearly defined track, you again turn left. You are now heading generally south along the crest of an old shoreline of Lake Makgadikgadi with views of Sowa Pan to the left.

A soda ash and salt mine is situated on the Sowa Spit, the peninsula extending into Sowa Pan. During its life as a lake the Basin had a vast quantity of sediment washed into it which accumulated to a depth of over 600 m in places. As the water evaporated, huge deposits of soda ash, or sodium (used in the glass and chemical industries and for the production of steel and paper), sodium bicarbonate, sodium chloride and potassium chloride stayed behind. The mine was opened in the early 1990s to exploit the vast reserves of soda ash and salt in the pan.

Just over 55 km after you turn off the tar road, a track splits off to the right. Go straight for 18.5 km to Thabatshukudu, a settlement overlooking Sowa Pan. Here another approach, a track from Zoroga on the Nata/Maun road, joins in from the north. South of the village the track skirts the eastern fringes of a pan and after about 10 km you will reach the Tswagong veterinary gate.

Continue south for 2 km beyond the gate and then go left for 3.2 km to Kebetseng's cattle post (the cement reservoir is a landmark). Ignore the track joining from the right and continue straight in a south-easterly direction to Lekhubu just over 14 km on, and 120 km from Nata. Lekhubu, a 'Desert Island' and a 'Lost City', is best appreciated in the late afternoon or early morning.

Retrace your tracks to Kebetseng's cattle post if the pan is wet. Turn left, and after 2.5 km, left again. The 'dry' option is to follow the track from Lekhubu Island across a stretch of pan in a south-westerly direction for just over 19 km before joining the main north/south track. Turn left here and after 7.5 km you will reach a veterinary gate on Tsitane Pan.

About 6 km beyond the gate you reach the end of the pan and the track soon begins to ascend a series of terraces that mark the fluctuating levels of Lake Makgadikgadi. It is hard to imagine that waves once lapped these shores but the rounded pebbles offer evidence that they did. From the summit of the highest ridge you are treated to awe-inspiring views of the vast pans below.

Five kilometres beyond the summit you reach Mmatshumo village, where you can buy cold drinks before tackling the last 24 km to the tar road to Francistown, just over 200 km to the east.

Nata Bird Sanctuary

Nata, Botswana's first community tourism project, was established in the early 1990s when four communities made available 23 000 ha of land adjoining Nata Delta in the north of Sowa Pan. Some 3 000 head of cattle were moved out of the area and in 1993 the sanctuary was fenced.

If you're a birding enthusiast, make a point of visiting the viewing platform on the edge of Sowa Pan. The Nata Delta is a feeding ground for thousands of flamingos, waterfowl and migrant waders. When conditions are favourable up to 6 000 white pelicans breed here.

The turnoff to the sanctuary is signposted 17 km south of Nata on the road to Francistown. Find out at the camp site if the pan has water and the track is negotiable. Don't attempt this route in the wet season. We once did against our better judgment and got through with difficulty. There are no rocks or dead branches to use for traction, so you will be in serious trouble if you get stuck.

From the camp site follow a well-defined track through grasslands and across several small pans for 6.9 km to a junction. The track to the right continues to the Nata River (a good spot to tick waterfowl) but to get to the viewing platform continue straight for another 1.9 km. The platform provides magnificent views over the pan and thousands of water birds feed here if there is water. To return retrace your tracks to the camp site.

Linking routes

You can combine Makgadikgadi Pans and Lekhubu Island with the Makgadikgadi–Nxai Pan National Park to the west of Ntwetwe Pan. Read Mike Main's *African Adventurer's Guide to Botswana* for his detailed descriptions of other routes in the Makgadikgadi Pans area.

LOGISTICS AND PLANNING

Fuel: Available at Francistown, Nata, Gweta and Maun.
Water: Take your own water.
Food: You can shop at supermarkets and buy alcoholic beverages in Maun and Francistown, while Nata provides a limited range of supplies.
Firewood: Take your own firewood and charcoal.
Best times: You should go to Lekhubu Island and across the pans only when they are dry, usually May to September, depending on how much water the pans held during the rainy season.

Booking

Lekhubu Island: No advance booking.
Nata Sanctuary: No advance booking.
Nata Lodge, tel: (+267) 621-1260, fax: 621-1265, e-mail: natalodge@inet.co.bw

Makgadikgadi

After the dry season, the grasslands of the former Makgadikgadi Pans Game Reserve in north-eastern Botswana are host to the second largest migration of ungulates in Africa, a spectacle rivalled only by the annual wildebeest migration in Maasai Mara and Serengeti in East Africa. Perhaps fortunately, few people witness this event and you can visit Makgadikgadi without being swamped by large crowds. Rain dictates the movement of the game but, if you don't see large numbers, the golden grasslands, wide-open spaces and solitude provide compensation of a different kind. Although the former Makgadikgadi Pans Game Reserve and Nxai Pan National Parks have been called the Makgadikgadi–Nxai Pan National Park since their amalgamation in 1992, the scenery in the two sections is quite different and we have decided to treat them separately. The accessibility of the park which is bisected by the Nata/Maun road makes it an ideal stopover en route to destinations such as the Moremi Game Reserve.

THE PARK

The area was declared a game reserve in the early 1970s at the same time as Nxai Pan to protect the wildlife moving seasonally between the two areas. Its northern boundary followed the old main road between Francistown and Maun, and the Boteti River and the shimmering Makgadikgadi Pans form its western and eastern boundaries respectively. The reserve was amalgamated with the Nxai Pan National Park when the latter was extended southwards to Kanyu Flats and Baines' Baobabs in 1992 and the combined park became known as the Makgadikgadi–Nxai Pan National Park.

Landscape and vegetation

The area once formed the floor of a super-lake that has long since dried up and shrunk to what is today the Makgadikgadi Pans (see page 61). Vast flat open grassy plains interspersed with occasional clumps of acacia trees dominate the landscape which also features clusters of stately makalani palms in the north and east. Further west the vegetation changes to tree and bush acacia savanna with camel and black thorns and silver cluster-leaf trees conspicuous in sandy areas, while riverine woodlands fringe the dry channel of the Boteti River.

The north-western corner of Ntwetwe Pan, one of the two major pans forming the Makgadikgadi Pans complex, extends into the park in the south and south-east. Coves, inlets and

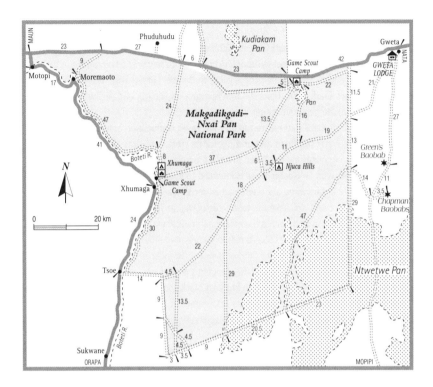

grass-covered peninsulas characterise its irregular shoreline, fringed by many small seasonal pans. During the dry season the cracked salt crust on the surface of the pans forms abstract patterns, and mirages on the stark white surface of Ntwetwe Pan can deceive you into believing that it holds water. But it is only after rain that the pans are covered by a thin sheet of water, providing a lifeline to the game and a habitat for wetland birds. In total the combined area of the pans accounts for less than 20% of the surface of the Makgadikgadi section of the park.

Fauna and game-viewing

The nutritious short grasslands of Makgadikgadi support between 25 000 and 35 000 Burchell's zebra and provide the setting for one of Africa's great game migrations. Towards the end of the dry season (November and December), the game concentrates along the Boteti River which winds from the Thamalakane River, the Okavango Delta's major outlet, to Lake Xau and Ntwetwe Pan. Since the river stopped flowing two decades ago the game has relied on pools from underground seepage and local rainfall.

Unlike springbok, gemsbok and red hartebeest, Burchell's zebra and blue wildebeest are dependent on water and soon after the first rains thousands of zebra and wildebeest migrate north to Nxai Pan. Here they remain until April when they return to the panveld in the south-eastern corner of the park, moving gradually westwards as the field water diminishes until they reach the Boteti River once again and begin their next migration.

Springbok can be seen throughout the year while other antelope on the grassy plains and bush savanna are gemsbok, blue wildebeest and red hartebeest. Bushbuck inhabit the Boteti riverine fringe but the population has declined as a result of snaring. Common duiker can also be found here, while steenbok favours tall grass with bushes and scrub.

BOTSWANA

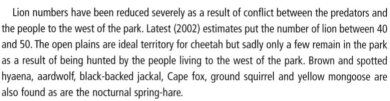

Lion numbers have been reduced severely as a result of conflict between the predators and the people to the west of the park. Latest (2002) estimates put the number of lion between 40 and 50. The open plains are ideal territory for cheetah but sadly only a few remain in the park as a result of being hunted by the people living to the west of the park. Brown and spotted hyaena, aardwolf, black-backed jackal, Cape fox, ground squirrel and yellow mongoose are also found as are the nocturnal spring-hare.

The drying up of the Boteti has resulted in increased competition between the game and cattle for scarce water resources and grazing. Cattle cross freely into the unfenced park and deplete the grazing alongside the Boteti River. A proposal to enclose the Makgadikgadi–Nxai Pan National Park with an electric fence is intended to keep predators and game in and cattle out. While fences in Botswana are often blamed for the large-scale death of migratory antelope, such a fence could well save the vast herds of Makgadikgadi.

The Makgadikgadi spiny agama is a special inhabitant of the area, but is usually overlooked. This small (excluding the tail it is 55–70 mm long) grey and brown agama, with dark blotches on the back and yellow ones on the sides of the neck, is endemic to the area. It lives in small tunnels at the base of salt bushes (*Salsola*) fringing the pans.

The leopard tortoise (named after the irregular black spots or streaks on its carapace) and flap-necked chameleon might show themselves. A series of click-click calls will betray the presence of barking geckos but, since at the slightest vibration they retreat into their burrows, they are extremely difficult to locate. After rains, African bullfrogs and marsh terrapins emerge in large numbers from the soil where they spend the dry season.

Birding

The open short grasslands of Makgadikgadi are the favoured habitat of the northern black korhaan, one of the most common birds in the Makgadikgadi area. The male is easily recognised by its raucous 'kraaak, kraaak' call when it is disturbed and when it proclaims its presence with short display flights during the breeding season. The head and belly of the male are black, while the back is barred black-and-buff. Its diet consists mainly of insects but it does also eat seeds and other plant material. As conspicuous and vocal as the male is, so is the female secretive and quiet. Birding is most rewarding during the summer months when summer migrants and water birds attracted by the seasonal pans supplement the numbers of resident species.

Typical grassland birds: ostrich, Burchell's sandgrouse, red-capped and rufous-naped larks, double-banded courser, scaly-feathered finch, spotted thick-knee and capped wheatears.
Boteti riverine forest birds: Meyer's parrot, African green pigeon, grey lourie, African mourning dove, Burchell's starling and Hartlaub's babbler.
Raptors: secretary bird, bateleur, white-backed and lappet-faced vultures, tawny eagle, black-chested snake eagle, lanner and red-necked falcons and greater kestrel.
Summer visitors: European bee-eater, Caspian plover, lesser kestrel, red-footed falcon, black-winged pratincole and lesser grey shrike.

Facilities

Large camel thorn trees on the sandy banks of the Boteti River provide welcome shade at **Xhumaga Campground**. There are five camp sites, a water standpipe and an ablution block with showers, hand basins and flush toilets.

Njuca Hills, an ancient dune and one of the few elevated points in the park, has two camp sites shaded by acacia trees. Two pit toilets are the only facilities.

Makgadikgadi

> **UNGULATES**
>
> Ungulates are herbivores (plant-eating animals) that are divided into two orders: odd-toed ungulates (for instance zebra and rhinoceros) and even-toed ungulates (among them hippopotamus, pigs, giraffe, antelope and buffalo).

LODGES WITH CAMPING FACILITIES NORTH OF MAUN:
Island Safari Lodge, signposted 10 km north of Maun, just before crossing the Matlapaneng bridge. Chalets, restaurant, swimming pool, camp sites.
Audi Camp, signposted 1.7 km north of the circle near Matlapaneng bridge, north of Maun en route to Shorobe. Tents, camp sites, restaurant, swimming pool.
Crocodile Camp Safaris, signposted 2.2 km north of the circle near Matlapaneng bridge, north of Maun en route to Shorobe. Chalets, camp sites, restaurant, swimming pool.
Okavango River Lodge, signposted 2.5 km north of the circle near Matlapaneng bridge, north of Maun en route to Shorobe. Chalets, tents, camp sites, restaurant, swimming pool.
ACCOMMODATION OPTIONS WHEN APPROACHING FROM NATA:
Nata Lodge, 9.2 km south of Nata on the Francistown road. Chalets, camp sites with good clean ablutions, restaurant and swimming pool.
Gweta Rest Camp, in Gweta village, 42.5 km east of the turnoff to the Makgadikgadi office. Rondavels, camp sites, restaurant.
Planet Baobab, 5 km east of Gweta. Bushman grass huts, traditional mud homesteads, camp sites, restaurant, swimming pool and several guided activities.

Getting there

The turnoff to the Game Scout Camp (where you should report on arrival) is signposted 140 km west of Nata and 162 km east of the junction of the Nata/Maun and Toteng roads. From here it is 8 km to the office.

ROUTES – 350 km park turnoff return; 140 km Nata–park t/off; 165 km Maun–park t/off
You can explore the grasslands, pans and environs of the Boteti River along a network of tracks covering the park. Some of the tracks can be combined into circular drives, but others could involve travelling long distances along the boundary cutlines, or retracing your tracks.

Another option is to visit Green's and Chapman's baobabs, two well-known landmarks a few kilometres beyond the park's eastern boundary. Green's Baobab is named after the intrepid hunter, trader and explorer Frederick Joseph Green who hunted along the Boteti River in the early 1850s. He carved his initials into the baobab in 1858/59 while passing through the Makgadikgadi area en route to western Zimbabwe. Other early hunters and explorers who carved their name in the bark of the tree include P Viljoen and H van Zyl.

Chapman's Baobabs lie to the south-east and owe their name to the renowned explorer and trader James Chapman who also hunted in the area in the 1850s. Towering nearly 25 m above its surroundings, the group consists of a cluster of six baobabs. The British artist and explorer Thomas Baines accompanied Chapman on his 1861 to 1863 expedition from Namibia to Victoria Falls. Their journey took them across Kanyu Flats and Kudiakam Pan where Baines painted the now-famous Baines' Baobabs (*see* Nxai Pan, page 75).

BOTSWANA

BOTETI RIVER

In the early 1970s a weir was built on the Boteti River and water diverted into a natural pan, Mopipi, to supply water to the Orapa diamond mine. To improve the flow of water to the reservoir a stretch of one of the Okavango Delta's main rivers, the Boro, was dredged and for several years the waters of the Boteti filled the dam. During the drought of the 1980s the river stopped flowing just short of the Mopipi reservoir and dried up in 1982. Crustal movements along the Thamalakane Fault, where the waters of the Delta are channelled into the Thamalakane River, could have caused the drying up of the Boteti River.

In December 1990 plans were announced to dredge a 45-km section of the Boro River and to raise its banks to rejuvenate the flow of the Boteti; this would provide water for subsistence farmers living along its course and feed into a new dam and the Mopipi reservoir further downstream. Local and international opposition by conservationists and local inhabitants put a stop to the scheme.

LOGISTICS AND PLANNING

Fuel: Available at Nata, Gweta and Maun.
Water: Available at the main entrance and at Xhumaga, but Xhumaga's water has a sulphurous taste.
Food: You can shop for groceries at supermarkets and buy alcoholic beverages in Maun and Francistown. Being smaller, Nata and Gweta offer only a limited choice.
Firewood: Bring your own supply of firewood, or charcoal, as it is not available in the park.
Best times: May to December are generally the best months as the herds of herbivores have migrated back from Nxai Pan. Game usually congregates along the Boteti River in November and December before migrating to Nxai Pan and remaining there until about April.

Booking

Reservations for **Xhumaga** and **Njuca Hills** must be made with the Parks and Reserves Reservations Office, Maun, tel: (+267) 686-1265, fax: 686-1264.
Island Safari Lodge, tel: (+267) 686-0300, fax: 686-2932, e-mail: island@info.bw
Audi Camp, tel: (+267) 686-0599, fax: 686-0581, e-mail: audicamp@info.bw
Crocodile Camp Safaris, tel: (+267) 686-0265, fax: 686-0793
Okavango River Lodge, tel and fax: (+267) 686-3707
Nata Lodge, tel: (+267) 621-1260, fax: 621-1265, e-mail: natalodge@inet.co.bw
Gweta Rest Camp, tel and fax: (+267) 621-2220
Planet Baobab, tel: (+267) 241-2277, e-mail: unchart.res@info.bw

Nxai Pan

Baines' Baobabs, which have been a famous landmark of the Kalahari for well over a century, together with a network of fossil pans are the focal points of this section of the Makgadikgadi–Nxai Pan National Park (*see also* Madgadikgadi, page 66) in north-eastern Botswana. Large herds of antelope and zebra concentrate on the pans which provide them with nutritious grazing after the annual rains. The full spectrum of predators follows closely. Once the herds have returned to their winter grazing areas the game-viewing can be disappointing, but the wilderness atmosphere of Nxai Pan is reward enough in itself. For the purposes of this book, we have described Nxai Pan separately from the former Makgadikgadi Pans Game Reserve because of the enormous difference in scenery and vegetation of the two areas.

THE PARK
The Nxai Pan National Park was proclaimed in the 1970s to protect the wildlife that is attracted seasonally to the complex of pans north of the Kanyu Flats. In 1992 the Kanyu Flats and Baines' Baobabs were incorporated into the park, increasing its size by almost 50% and linking it to the Makgadikgadi Pans Game Reserve to the south: only the main road between Francistown and Maun separates these two sections of the park.

Landscape and flora
The park lies amid a complex of pans, which once formed the floor of the Makgadikgadi super-lake (*see* Makgadikgadi Pans, page. 61). As the shores of the super-lake began to shrink, a series of smaller lakes was left behind to the west of Makgadikgadi. The largest of these, Nxai Pan, is about 14 km long and has an average width of 5 km. It is shaped like a kidney and is bounded to the south and the west by sand ridges. To its east lies an unnamed pan and further north-east is Kgama-Kgama Pan.

Nxai and Kgama-Kgama pans are covered in short grassland dotted with acacia scrub, shrubs and 'islands' of umbrella thorn trees. Mopane veld and corkwood trees (*Commiphora*) are conspicuous just south of North Camp, while a mosaic of baobabs, mopane, trumpet thorn (*Catophractes alexandri*), black thorn and croton bushes occurs along the Baobab Loop. You will also see swathes of acacias and buffalo-thorn. Bushwillow, trumpet thorn and poison bush grow along the southern edge of Nxai Pan. Silver cluster-leaf, bushwillow and coffee neat's foot, a scrambling shrub with large white summer flowers, are conspicuous in sandy areas.

BOTSWANA

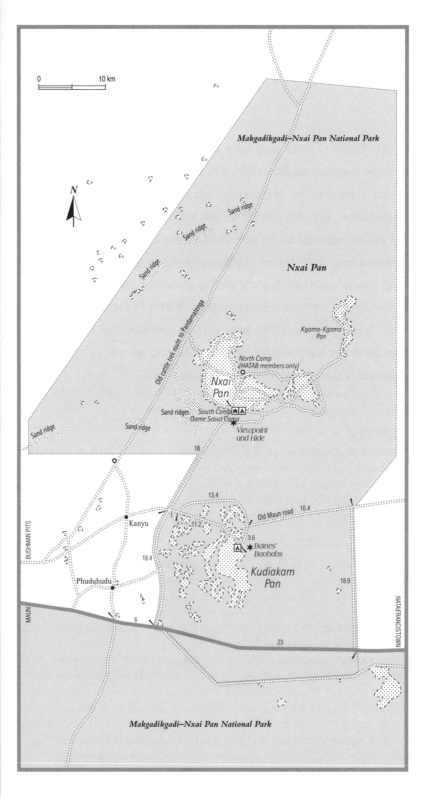

Kudiakam Pan and a network of some 20 smaller pans, which dominate the Kanyu Flats in the south of the park, lie amid extensive grasslands interspersed with acacia scrub and raisin bushes. Unlike Nxai Pan, these are typical salt pans with no vegetation.

Fauna and game-viewing

As is the case elsewhere in the Kalahari, a combination of drought, rains and instinct dictate the movement of migratory antelope. After good rains – which usually occur in November or December, but it could be later – large herds of blue wildebeest, Burchell's zebra and gemsbok migrate from the Boteti River northwards to Nxai Pan. They remain here until March or April when they move south to their winter grazing areas in the Makgadikgadi section of the Makgadikgadi–Nxai Pan National Park (*see also* page 66).

During years of good rain, herds of buffalo and elephant migrate from the north into the Nxai Pan section of the park.

With its mixture of open grass plains and wooded stretches, Nxai Pan is the only place in Botswana where you can see springbok and impala in the same area. Springbok, blue wildebeest and Burchell's zebra graze on the grassy pans, while impala and kudu favour wooded places. Herds of giraffe often browse the acacia trees on the pans, and gemsbok, red hartebeest and eland can be spotted too.

Of the large predators, you are most likely to see lion, but leopard and brown hyaena also occur here. Nxai Pan was formerly a stronghold of cheetah, but now they are rarely seen. Their decline has been attributed to conflict with cattle farmers neighbouring the park and the drought of the 1980s, which resulted in a decline in the prey species.

Wild dogs move through the park occasionally. Chancing upon a pack of these much-maligned predators is a rare treat.

In the absence of the more prominent large game, small mammals such as steenbok, common duiker, Cape hare, suricate, bat-eared fox and yellow mongoose take centre stage. With some luck and perseverance you could track down African wild cat.

Birding

With over 210 bird species recorded to date, Nxai Pan offers good birding opportunities, especially during the rainy season.
Raptors: white-backed, lappet-faced and white-headed vultures; southern pale chanting goshawk; tawny, black-chested snake and steppe eagles; greater kestrel; secretary bird; and yellow-billed kite.
Other species: kori bustard, red-billed buffalo-weaver, yellow-billed oxpecker, northern black korhaan, Burchell's and double-banded sandgrouse, lilac-breasted roller, African grey, red-billed and southern yellow-billed hornbills, arrow-marked babbler, white-browed and Kalahari scrub-robins, several lark, cisticola and shrike species.

Facilities

You have a choice of two camp sites within Nxai Pan section of the park. **South Camp** with its shady grove of purple-pod cluster-leaf trees has four sites and an ablution block with showers and flush toilets. A viewpoint and hide are situated close by. Three informal camp sites without facilities are available at **Baines' Baobabs**.

North Camp is no longer open to visitors, except for members of HATAB (the Hospitality and Tourism Association of Botswana).

BOTSWANA

THE SMALL TREASURES OF NATURE

During midsummer while we were returning from Baines' Baobabs we found ourselves caught in a heavy downpour. The two tracks were transformed into rushing streams and during a temporary break in the rain we hopped out of our vehicle to photograph the running water in this usually parched environment.

We were amazed to hear a chorus of frogs. It started raining again and we sat in the car listening to the chorus intensify. We didn't see the frogs but we imagined that there must have been thousands. Once again we were reminded that smaller inhabitants can be quite as thrilling as the 'Big Five'.

Getting there

Take the signposted turnoff to Nxai Pan 66 km west of Gweta or 136 km east of Maun to reach South Camp. The first 18.4 km of the track to the Baines' Baobabs turnoff is sandy and the going is slow in the dry season. On the rain-compacted sand it's an easy drive. From here you continue north for another 18 km. The track traverses broken calcrete with deep depressions that fill with water during the rains.

ROUTES – 300 km park turnoff return; 165 km Nata–park t/off; 140 km Maun–park t/off

The Nxai Pan area has a network consisting of 120 km of tracks. You can explore these tracks during a three-day trip from South Camp. During the rainy season you might find the clay tracks rather challenging.

Lookout

The flat terrain of Nxai Pan has few landmarks, but a lookout point 5.5 km (one way) from South Camp has an expansive view of the surrounding landscape. The lookout is on a sand ridge and the drive there takes you through the only deep sand in the Nxai Pan area. The vegetation of the sand ridge differs noticeably from that of the pans, with silver cluster-leaf, coffee neat's foot and bushwillow much in evidence.

The platform near South Camp provides the only elevated view of the Nxai Pan area.

Nxai Pan

Baobab Loop

From South Gate head north for 1.7 km to a turnoff to a waterhole set on the open grassy pan. In the dry season game-viewing can be rewarding here since water is pumped into the waterhole. Watch the nearby clump of acacias closely as lion often wait here for the animals to come and quench their thirst. Backtrack to the main track north and ignore two tracks leading off to the right (they lead to the eastern edge of Nxai Pan) and one to the left.

As you continue north the grassy plains and acacias give way to mopaneveld interspersed with corkwood (*Commiphora*) trees. A short way after you pass a green watertank, a track branches right to a waterhole. Take a break and see what shows up before backtracking to the main track where you turn right.

A short drive brings you to a junction and North Camp which is open to HATAB members only. The track to the right leads to Kgama-Kgama Pan but to get to the Baobab Loop you turn left. Just short of 2 km along the track after you have turned left, you will reach the first of the baobabs after which the road is named. A short way on the loop track splits off to the right. Unlike the open grasslands and scrub that dominate the pan, this area is fairly well wooded and you might see impala. About 9.3 km beyond the last turnoff you will reach another baobab which is small by comparison with some of the giants found elsewhere in southern Africa. A few kilometres on a four-way junction offers three options. The track to the east (left) is the direct route back to the camp.

The track to the west (right) continues for 5 km to the old Cattle Trek Route, which was used from the 1950s to 1963 as a short-cut from Maun via Pandamatenga to Kazungula on the border between Botswana, Zambia and Zimbabwe. There is little game in this area and, as the route is indistinct in places, we do not recommend that you explore here.

The track heading south (straight) meanders near the outer edge of Nxai Pan, then passes three small pans that attract game if there is water. About 9 km beyond the crossroads you reach the Game Scout Camp and South Camp.

Kgama-Kgama Pan

Another option from South Camp is a trip to Kgama-Kgama Pan. If rain has fallen large numbers of game will concentrate on the pan to graze the nutritious grass. The lack of permanent surface water in the area means there is not much game in the dry season.

From South Camp head north to the junction at North Camp where you turn right onto a track which alternates between woodland, scrub and grassland to an unnamed saline pan and a four-way junction. For just over 8 km the track to Kgama-Kgama Pan passes through scrub veld to a 13.5-km loop around the northern part of the pan. Khama III, who ruled as Chief from 1875 to 1923, once had a cattle post in this grass-covered area.

Once you have completed the loop, backtrack to the four-way junction where you have the option of two tracks that will take you back to South Camp. The two tracks eventually join and once again you have a choice of either continuing directly to South Camp or travelling west across Nxai Pan until you join the main north/south track.

Baines' Baobabs

You reach the turnoff to Baines' Baobabs at the Old Francistown/Maun Road, 18.4 km north of the A3 (18 km south of South Gate). After 1 km the track splits but your choice will be dictated by the season. The right-hand track is slightly shorter (11.2 km) but, since it leads through a narrow tongue of Kudiakam Pan, it should be avoided during the rainy season. The left-hand

BOTSWANA

track continues along the Old Maun Road, and 13.4 km beyond the last junction you turn right, continuing for 3.6 km to Baines' Baobabs which are perched on the edge of the pan.

The seven baobabs are named after the British artist Thomas Baines who passed by in 1862 when he and explorer James Chapman were undertaking a two-year expedition from Namibia to Victoria Falls. Baines did a water-colour painting of the baobabs on 22 May 1862. A comparison of his painting and a photograph taken just over 100 years later showed that they had hardly changed in that time.

The clump of baobabs is sometimes also referred to as the 'Seven Sisters' or the 'Sleeping Sisters'.

Linking routes

A visit to Nxai Pan can easily be combined with the adjoining Makgadikgadi section of the Makgadikgadi–Nxai Pan National Park (*see* page 66).

LOGISTICS AND PLANNING

Fuel: The nearest available fuel is at Gweta and Maun.

Water: You can obtain water at South Gate office.

Food: You can buy a wide range of produce, incuding fresh meat, frozen and canned foods and other groceries, and both soft drinks and liquor from supermarkets and liquor outlets in Francistown and Maun.

Firewood: Bring your own supply of firewood or charcoal with you, as firewood is not available in the park.

Best times: The best time to visit Nxai Pan is between December and April, in spite of the heat. This is when the animals congregate around the pan, especially after rain. Summer lures avian migrants so keep a look out for them.

Booking

Reservations for **South Camp** must be made with the Parks and Reserves Reservations Office, Maun, tel: (+267) 686-1265, fax: 686-1264.

Book the **Baines' Baobabs Camp Site** for the last night of your stay, as you must first check in at the South Gate office before going there.

Visiting Nxai Pan during the rainy season is a rare treat.

Moremi Game Reserve

Moremi in north-western Botswana consists of mopane woodlands, riverine forests, grassy floodplains, papyrus-lined waterways carpeted with water lilies and seasonal pans. The reserve, on the eastern fringe of the largest inland delta in the world, the Okavango, offers superb game-viewing – large herds of elephant, lion, buffalo, giraffe, impala, red lechwe, waterbuck, blue wildebeest and Burchell's zebra. Be prepared for the unexpected: a buffalo calf killed by lion in the camp site, a stand-off between a leopard and a baboon in the tree above your tent, or an elephant ambling past your camp.

THE PARK
The nucleus of Moremi was set aside by the Batswana as a wildlife reserve in 1963 and named after the late Chief Moremi III. In the 1970s the reserve was extended to include Chief's Island, his traditional hunting ground, and it was proclaimed a game reserve. In 1991 Moremi was further increased when a large triangle of permanent swamp to the north-west of the reserve was incorporated, providing protection for nearly a third of the Okavango Delta.

Landscape and vegetation
The Mopane Tongue or dryland area of the Moremi Game Reserve is a delicate combination of woodlands interspersed with tall grasslands, sandveld, lush riverine forests and pans. When the water level in the Delta is high, vast areas of seasonal wetlands are flooded.

The vegetation of the Moremi dryland area consists mostly of mopaneveld (about 80%). Prominent along the edge of the floodplains are tall jackal-berry and sausage trees, while silver cluster-leaf and camel thorn trees are sure indicators of deep sand. Other prominent trees include knob and umbrella thorns, apple-leaf, mokolwane palm and leadwood.

Seasonally flooded areas of grassland, termitaria (see box, page 144) and channels adjoin the dry land to the south. An intricate network of rivers, narrow channels, quiet backwaters, lagoons and palm-studded islands characterises the permanent swamp to the west of the dry land.

Fauna and game-viewing
A wildlife paradise and sanctuary to large breeding herds of elephant and other game, Moremi offers a superb experience in the wild. You could encounter elephant throughout the reserve and see the destruction they have caused to the mopaneveld in the woodlands south of Xakanaxa.

Large herds of red lechwe graze or rest on the floodplains, also favoured by waterbuck – identified by the white ring around the tail. If you are looking for common reedbuck, watch the tall grassland, usually close to water. On an early morning or late afternoon drive it is not

BOTSWANA

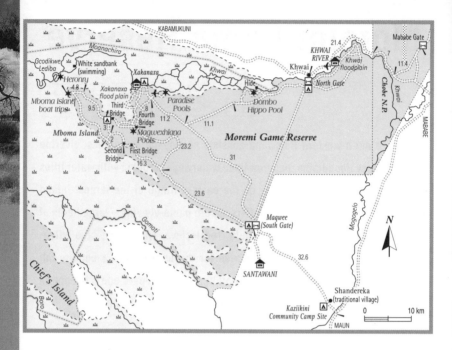

uncommon to see herds of buffalo numbering several hundred, especially in the vicinity of Fourth Bridge. Impala is the most commonly seen of all the antelope in this reserve, but you may also see blue wildebeest, tsessebe and Burchell's zebra, especially on the Khwai floodplains. Giraffe frequent the acacia and mopane woodlands, while the woodlands are favoured by sable and roan but sightings are not common.

If you want to see lion, an early morning or late afternoon drive to a waterhole will usually be rewarding. Leopard, cheetah and wild dog also occur, but are less frequently seen. Spotted hyaena are common visitors to the camp sites, sneaking right up to your camp at night.

Well-known spots to see hippo in the dry season include Magwexhlana Pools near Fourth Bridge, Dombo Pool and Saguni Pool in the Khwai River.

Other species you could see – warthog, baboon, vervet monkey and black-backed jackal – are not restricted to particular areas and may be spotted anywhere in the reserve. Also make a point of looking for the smaller species such as a family of banded mongoose or a spotted genet that might be tempted to visit your camp at night.

Birding

Moremi's rich diversity of habitats attracts an array of birds. Some 450 species recorded in the Okavango Delta to date make the reserve a birder's paradise. Species such as arrow-marked babbler, pied barbet and greater blue-eared starling have become very tame in the camp sites.
Raptors: bateleur; African fish, black-chested snake and Wahlberg's eagles; osprey; and African marsh-harrier.
Water birds: white-faced duck, long-toed and African wattled lapwings, pied and giant kingfishers, squacco heron, slaty egret and African jacana.
Summer migrants: broadbilled roller and carmine bee-eater (there is a good chance of seeing them hawking the plains just south of North Gate Camp Site after rains) and African openbill.

Other species: Meyer's parrot, woodland kingfisher, African grey, southern yellow-billed and red-billed hornbills, grey lourie, black-collared barbet, Arnot's chat (in mopane woodlands), water thick-knee, Swainson's spurfowl, Senegal and coppery-tailed coucals, fan-tailed widowbird, African stonechat and African paradise flycatcher.

Facilities

LODGES IN MAUN:

Island Safari Lodge, signposted 10 km north of Maun, just before the Matlapaneng bridge on the western bank of the Thamalakane River. Chalets, restaurant, swimming pool, camp sites.

Audi Camp, signposted 1.7 km north of the circle near the Matlapaneng bridge, north of Maun en route to Shorobe. Tents, camp sites, restaurant, swimming pool.

Crocodile Camp Safaris, signposted 2.2 km north of the circle near the Matlapaneng bridge, north of Maun en route to Shorobe. Chalets, camp sites, restaurant, swimming pool.

Okavango River Lodge, signposted 2.5 km north of the circle near the Matlapaneng bridge, north of Maun en route to Shorobe. Chalets, tents, camp sites, restaurant, swimming pool.

Kaziikini Community Camp Site, 62.5 km north of Maun, is good for a night in the bush. Five spacious camp sites under acacia trees, four rondavels with cold showers, a bar and restaurant.

The 16-bed **Santawani Lodge** is in a small concession area in a prime game-viewing region just south of the Moremi Game Reserve. It is suitable for self-drive, self-catering tourists. Santawani offers eight two-bed chalets, a communal kitchen and hot showers, and individual travellers can be accommodated if a group hasn't booked the whole camp. The camp site must be booked en bloc for 16 people. Chalet residents have to pay a compulsory game drive fee of P50.00 per person per day.

In the Moremi Game Reserve there are four camp sites. **Maqwee** at South Gate is convenient if you leave Maun too late in the day to continue to Third Bridge or if you are travelling from the reserve to Maun and need to get there early the following morning. Nestling among mopane woodland are seven camp sites, ablutions with cold showers, handbasins and flush toilets, as well as two water standpipes.

The camp site at **Third Bridge,** named after the mopane polebridge spanning a channel, is characterised by tall sausage trees, and elephants frequently drink close by. It has seven camp sites, ablution block with showers, handbasins and flush toilets, and a water standpipe.

Xakanaxa Camp Site is shaded by tall jackal-berry, acacia and apple-leaf trees on a low sandy ridge on the edge of the Delta. It has seven sites, an ablution block with showers, handbasins and flush toilets, fireplaces and water standpipes. In December 2002 it was by far the best maintained of the four camp sites.

North Gate Camp Site is situated on the banks of the Khwai River under a swathe of acacia and apple-leaf trees. Located close to Khwai village, it lacks the remoteness of Xakanaxa. There are seven camp sites, ablution blocks with showers, handbasins and flush toilets, as well as water standpipes.

Activities

Take a **boat** or **_mokoro_ (dugout canoe) trip** along the winding channels of the Delta from Mboma Island or Xakanaxa to get a different view of the Okavango.

Visit **Shandereka traditional village** (north of Maun en route to South Gate) for a glimpse of the culture and way of life of the Bayei people who settled on the islands and along the margins of the Okavango Delta some 250 years ago.

BOTSWANA

Getting there
Moremi Game Reserve can be accessed through two gates: South Gate, 95 km north of Maun, and North Gate, 40 km from Chobe National Park's Mababe Gate.

ROUTES – 460 km Maun via Xakanaxa to North Gate; 125 km Maun–North Gate (direct)
There is an extensive network of mainly hard tracks that are easily negotiated during the dry months. During the rainy season, however, these tracks become waterlogged with muddy pools and stretches of thick black mud which often traps vehicles.

Check your route and distances carefully at every crossroads, especially when exploring the Xakanaxa and Khwai floodplains, to avoid getting lost. Veronica Roodt's *Shell Map of the Moremi Game Reserve* is essential unless you are familiar with the area and have a good sense of direction.

From Maun take the tarred road north for 27 km to Shorobe (measured from the last traffic circle north of Maun near Audi Camp) where you might want to look at the basketry. At Shorobe the tar gives way to a gravel road which continues for 19 km to the veterinary checkpoint at the Buffalo Fence.

The track now alternates between sandy patches and a hard clay surface and less than 2 km beyond the Buffalo Fence the track to Moremi splits off to the left, while the right-hand path continues to Khwai. About 3 km beyond the split you reach the Kaziikini Community Camp Site and the Shandereka traditional village.

About 1.6 km beyond Shandereka, take the split to the left and continue for just over 22 km past the turnoff to Santawani Lodge. After another 5 km a track from Santawani joins in from the left and South Gate is reached 300 m on.

From South Gate you can head to Xakanaxa (42 km), Khwai (30 km) or turn left and continue to Third Bridge via Mboma Island, a sandveld tongue extending into the seasonally flooded areas of the Okavango Delta. After passing First and Second bridges (they are used only in very wet seasons and are easily overlooked), either continue directly to Third Bridge or take the southern loop on Mboma Island.

Third Bridge is conveniently close to Mboma Island which is traversed by two loops, one of which covers the south and the other the north of the island. The track on the western side of the northern loop is a delightful drive for those keen on trees. Conspicuous among them are enormous sausage, leadwood, apple-leaf and knob thorn trees. This route is perfect for a late afternoon sundowner trip and, although there is usually not much game, here you might come across elephant and buffalo.

Follow the blue Mboma signs, which depict a *mokoro* (dugout canoe) and poler, to the northwestern corner of Mboma Island for a most rewarding and different perspective of the Delta.

GCODIKWE HERONRY

Gcodikwe is famous for its mixed roosts of storks, herons and egrets which can number up to 1 000 birds. The peak season is from August to November when up to 24 species breed in the water fig 'islands' of the Gcodikwe Lagoon. In addition to large numbers of marabou stork you can see yellow-billed and open-billed storks, purple heron and sacred ibis. The lagoon can be reached only by boat.

Guides offer *mokoro* trips of the Delta's waterways from here during the dry season. During the wet season the last few kilometres of the track become waterlogged. A motorboat trip takes you to the Gcodikwe Lediba (Lagoon), which is famous for its heronry (*see* box, opposite page). Although this trip can be done in two hours, you can extend the outing by another hour and go to a quiet backwater with a white sandbank for a refreshing dip if you dare (the waterways of the Delta are home to a large population of crocodiles, but the combination of shallow water and white sand makes this a safe place to swim). This is about as close as you will get to swimming in the Delta, but your guide will assure you that it is quite safe.

A rewarding game-viewing drive from Third Bridge is the track to Fourth Bridge, stopping at Magwexhlana Pools to see hippo and the large crocodile population. Lion are usually never far off when game gathers in the vicinity of the pools during the dry months. In addition to red lechwe, impala and giraffe, you might see significant herds of buffalo. Fourth Bridge lies within the home range of a pack of wild dogs. The best time to see them is either early morning or late afternoon.

North of Fourth Bridge the vegetation changes dramatically as you get closer to Xakanaxa, at the northern end of the Mopane Tongue. Exceptional stands of mopane woodland occur here and in some places they almost form a forest. This is elephant country. Few other large mammals favour this habitat type although giraffe do eat the mopane leaves during the dry season.

A network of tracks allows you to explore the floodplains south of Xakanaxa in the dry season. Few tracks are signposted but they are interlinked, making it easy to wander about. Game is plentiful in this mix of riverine woodlands fringing the floodplains, pans and seasonally flooded areas. You are likely to see elephant, giraffe, waterbuck, impala, red lechwe and Burchell's zebra.

Not to be missed is a visit to Dead Tree Island, with the bleached skeletons of a large number of dead trees that drowned when the area was flooded, possibly as a result of seismic movements. You reach the island after crossing a pole bridge. The island is about 1.5 km wide in the vicinity of the dead trees which point skyward creating a picture of devastation.

Permanent flooding of the first section of the road from Xakanaxa to North Bridge has necessitated its being re-routed. The old route can now be followed only as far as Paradise (Kai-oro and Goma-oro) Pools, a good bird-watching spot.

The new route follows the South Gate road from the Xakanaxa office for 11 km through tall mopane forest and shrubveld before branching off in a north-easterly direction to reach the original road after another 11 km. An extensive network of tracks criss-crosses the Khwai floodplain. A detour to Dombo Hippo Pool, which is overlooked by a hide, is especially worthwhile.

> **VITAL INFO**
>
> - Collecting firewood is permitted in the reserve, but you may meet lion, elephant or buffalo.
> - Moremi's lodges are for their own guests – out of bounds to casual visitors.
> - Moremi lies in a malaria-endemic area so consult your doctor about the most effective prophylaxis.
> - Do not leave your camp unattended while game-viewing as baboons sometimes rip tents open. If the camp cannot be guarded, collapse your tent and pack everything in your vehicle.

BOTSWANA

BUFFALO FENCE

Buffalo are potential carriers of foot-and-mouth, a highly contagious viral disease that is fatal to cattle and other domesticated cloven-hoofed animals. To prevent the spread of the disease to cattle in the areas adjoining the Okavango Delta, the 240-km-long Buffalo Fence was erected along the Delta's south-eastern edge in 1982. The 140-km Northern Buffalo Fence stretching north to the Namibian border along the western side of the Delta was completed in 1997.

Take an early morning or late afternoon game-viewing drive along the Khwai Loop with its network of tracks traversing the floodplains. Some of the loops meander along the Khwai River, allowing you to see water birds and hippo at Saguni Pool. On the adjoining floodplains, look out for red lechwe, waterbuck, tsessebe, blue wildebeest, Burchell's zebra and impala. In the open woodlands you might come across roan and sable, which are sighted infrequently.

Linking routes
A visit to Moremi Game Reserve can easily be combined with a visit to the Chobe National Park.

LOGISTICS AND PLANNING
Fuel: Available only in Maun and Kasane. If you are visiting Moremi and returning to Maun, take fuel for at least 550 km, including game-viewing drives. If you are going to Savute and Kasane, you will be covering about 850 km with game drives. In sandy areas fuel consumption is higher.
Food: You can buy meat, fresh fruit and vegetables, frozen foods, cold drinks and alcohol in Maun and Kasane. Basic supplies are available at Khwai village just outside North Gate.
Best times: The dry winter months are generally the best time to visit as game concentrates around the shrinking water supplies. If you are a birder the summer months will be more rewarding as there is an influx of migrant species. This is also the time when many of the antelope foal. Unfortunately tracks can be totally impassable or very muddy after sustained rains.

Map
The *Shell Map of the Moremi Game Reserve* by Veronica Roodt is extremely useful, especially when you are exploring the network of tracks on the Xakanaxa and Khwai floodplains.

Booking
Reservations for the **four camp sites** in Moremi Game Reserve must be made with the Parks and Reserves Reservations Office, Maun, tel: (+267) 686-1265, fax: 686-1264.
Island Safari Lodge, tel: (+267) 686-0300, fax: 686-2932, e-mail: island@info.bw
Audi Camp, tel: (+267) 686-0599, fax: 686-0581, e-mail: audicamp@info.bw
Crocodile Camp Safaris, tel: (+267) 686-0265, fax: 686-0793
Okavango River Lodge, tel and fax: (+267) 686-3707
Kaziikini Community Camp Site: No booking.
Santawani Lodge, Sankuyu Tshwarango Trust, tel: (+267) 686-1165, fax: 686-2992, e-mail: starlings@info.bw

Chobe National Park

During the dry season, thousands of elephants emerge from the woodlands in the late afternoon, making their way to the Chobe riverfront. As they smell the water, the need to slake their thirst becomes increasingly urgent and, as their pace quickens, so clouds of dust rise from under their heavy feet. Also crowding the riverfront are herds of sable, giraffe, impala and buffalo, often by the hundreds. On the nearby floodplain grasslands, herds of red lechwe graze peacefully, while an African fish eagle throws its head back to sound its hauntingly beautiful cry. Savute in the south-west of the park is famous for its prides of lion and large herds of bull elephant. Although the Savute Channel last had water more than two decades ago, vast numbers of antelope and zebra are still attracted to the grasslands on the open plains of the Savute Marsh after good rains. These spectacular scenes make the Chobe National Park one of the most famous wildlife destinations in Africa.

THE PARK
The park is named after the Chobe River which bounds it in the north for nearly 60 km. This vast conservation area stretches southwards for more than 150 km and is 120 km at its widest point. It was proclaimed in 1961 and is the second largest park in Botswana, after the Central Kalahari Game Reserve (*see* page 55).

Landscape and vegetation
Each of the park's four distinct ecosystems – the Mababe Depression (including the Savute Marsh and Savute Channel), Linyanti, the Nogatsaa/Tchinga area and the Chobe riverfront – has its unique atmosphere and attractions.

    The Mababe Depression in the south-west of the park formed part of a super-lake as recently (in geological terms) as 10 000 years ago and is bounded in the west by the Magwikhwe Sand Ridge. The ridge marks the 'shores' of this vast lake which covered an area that was, at times, as large as Lake Victoria.

    The Savute Marsh, which stretches south-eastwards for about 20 km and is up to 10 km wide, dominates the scenery in the north-west of the Mababe Depression. Scattered tree 'islands' punctuate its floor and, when there is no grass, the skeletons of dead trees along the margins of the Marsh create a desolate scene. Camel thorn and other acacias, leadwood and

BOTSWANA

× 195.2

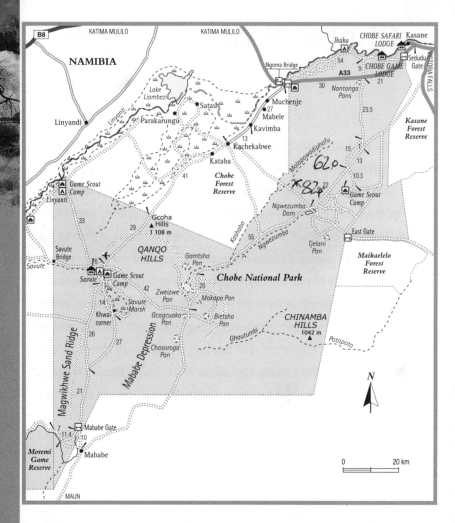

Kalahari apple-leaf trees are found in areas beyond the edge of the Marsh, which can in turn be a dust bowl, a vast field of waving grassland or a depression filled with knee-deep water.

Water from the Kwando/Linyanti/Chobe system flows intermittently from the Linyanti Swamps along the 100-km-long Savute Channel. After cutting through the Magwikhwe Sand Ridge the water spills onto the floor of the Marsh, the deepest point of the Mababe Depression. When this happens, the marsh is transformed into a spectacular wetland that attracts vast numbers of animals and water birds.

Since 1981, when the Channel last flowed, the Marsh has been watered only by local rainfall and a number of artificial water points have been provided for the dry winter months.

The flow of the Savute is highly unpredictable. The erratic moods of the Savute Channel have been attributed to seismic movements that appear to have altered the flow of water from the Linyanti Swamps, making it unpredictable. The channel last flowed from 1967 to 1979. Prior to that it flowed from 1957 to 1966 after it had stopped flowing in the late 1880s. It was probably during this period that the camel thorn trees in the channel and on the edge of the marsh drowned, leaving only bleached skeletons.

Chobe National Park

The Gubatsa Hills, or the Seven Hills of Savute, at the northern end of the Marsh, are a surprise after you have travelled through featureless countryside for hundreds of kilometres. Volcanic activity forced magma (molten matter) up from deep inside the bowels of the earth and, not surprisingly, the vegetation of the hills differs markedly from that of the surrounding landscape. Conspicuous among the rocks are the carrot tree, white syringa and paperbark false-thorn.

Linyanti in the north-western corner of the park is characterised by lush riverine forest along its namesake river. Floodplains, reed beds and marshes adjoin the river and attract herds of red lechwe, waterbuck, the elusive sitatunga with its elongated hooves, allowing it to walk on marshy ground, and a rich diversity of water birds.

The Nogatsaa/Tchinga area in the east of the park is dominated by mopane woodland and scrub interspersed with mixed bushwillow veld, patches of grassland and teak forests. A complex of large and small seasonal pans punctuates the area, while solar-powered pumps at a few pans ensure that there is water for the game when the seasonal pans dry up.

A strip of riverine forest comprising jackal-berry, apple-leaf, leadwood and camel thorn trees and floodplain grasslands lines the Chobe riverfront, in the north of the park. The destruction of the vegetation, especially by the large concentrations of elephant, is obvious and has become a serious environmental concern. Away from the river, open bushwillow scrub, mopane and teak woodlands dominate the vegetation of the deep Kalahari sands.

Fauna and game-viewing

Chobe's huge elephant population (the park has an estimated 25 000, the largest concentration in Africa) and the diversity of game have earned it a place among Africa's great game parks. Savute is famous for its numbers of bull elephants, especially during the dry season, and during the heat of the day you are likely to encounter small groups of elephant sheltering under the shade of acacias fringing the Marsh. Breeding herds also occur, sometimes numbering over 200.

Soon after the first good rains, the Marsh is transformed into waving grassland that attracts vast herds of migratory blue wildebeest, Burchell's zebra and buffalo. Towards the end of summer, tsessebe congregate on the Marsh. Among the other game to be seen are giraffe, kudu, impala and warthog.

The herbivores attract the full spectrum of predators, including Savute's famous large prides of lion. If you want to spot cheetah, keep your eyes on the open plains. Look for leopard in the vicinity of rocky outcrops, tree 'islands' and the more densely wooded areas fringing the Marsh. Packs of wild dog also occur, and other predators include spotted hyaena and black-backed jackal.

On the journey between Savute and the Nogatsaa/Tchinga area (if the pans hold water) look out for elephant, kudu, eland, impala, roan and Burchell's zebra. At Nogatsaa you should see large populations of elephant and buffalo or chance upon eland and maybe gemsbok. Giraffe are often sighted at Tchinga. Sable, kudu and Burchell's zebra also roam the area.

The Chobe riverfront is by far the most popular area of the park and access to the eastern section is through Sedudu Gate. It offers possibly the best elephant-viewing in Africa and is also renowned for its vast numbers of buffalo. Exploring the network of tracks along the river banks is especially rewarding in the late afternoon during the dry months.

Two animals of special interest here are the puku with its golden-yellow coat and the Chobe subspecies of the bushbuck. Chobe is the only place in southern Africa where the puku occurs, and it is easily mistaken for red lechwe. A drive on Puku Flats will usually reward you with a sighting. The Chobe bushbuck can be distinguished from the more common southern subspecies by its characteristic white transverse lines and white spots on

BOTSWANA

> ### ⓘ VITAL INFO
>
> - Advance reservations are necessary for entry and camping within Chobe National Park.
> - Don't leave food in your tent as it could attract animals, including predators.
> - Don't attempt to take the Marsh Route after heavy rains.
> - Exercise caution when driving through densely wooded areas as you could have an unexpected encounter with an elephant.
> - Elephant frequently pass through the Savute Camp Site and, as they can move amazingly silently, you should be cautious especially at night when you should also beware of spotted hyaena and lion.
> - The collection of firewood is permitted inside the park, but be aware of the possibility of encountering potentially dangerous animals, for instance elephant, lion and buffalo.
> - The lodges in Savute and Chobe cater exclusively for their own guests and are out of bounds to non-guests.
> - Leaving your camp unattended while you are game-viewing in Savute is not a good idea as baboons may rip tents open. If the camp cannot be guarded, collapse your tent and pack everything in your vehicle.
> - Chobe is in a malaria endemic area, so consult your doctor about the most effective prophylaxis.

the shoulders and hindquarters. Other mammal species that may be spotted in the Puku Flats section of the park include red lechwe, reedbuck, waterbuck, kudu, impala and giraffe. Sable are more common in the east, but roan and Burchell's zebra are more frequently sighted in the western section of the Chobe riverfront.

Lion are plentiful and can usually be seen along the riverfront, and the best place for tracking down leopard and wild dog is in the Serondela area.

Birding

For birding enthusiasts, Chobe National Park offers an opportunity to tick approximately 400 species. It owes this rich diversity of species to its four different ecological zones and variety of habitat types.

Savute area: ostrich, kori bustard, southern yellow-billed, red-billed and Bradfield's hornbills, lilac-breasted roller, red-billed francolin, double-banded sandgrouse, Burchell's starling, yellow-billed oxpecker and marabou stork.

Summer migrants: European and blue-cheeked bee-eaters, woodland kingfisher, African openbill and Abdim's stork. Along the Chobe riverfront look out for African skimmer, broad-billed roller and carmine bee-eaters.

Chobe riverfront: martial and African fish eagles, African marsh-harrier, bateleur, red-winged and collared pratincoles, slaty egret, long-toed lapwing, black coucal and rosy-throated longclaw (on floodplains). In summer hundreds of marabou storks roost in the dead trees in Sedudu Valley.

Facilities

Set on the banks of the Savute Channel, the public camp site at **Savute** was re-opened in 2000 after the original site was closed down because elephants had damaged the ablution block.

Elephants are sometimes curious, especially when they encounter artificial structures and often damage them when they inspect them. When they smell water they usually pull things like taps, water pipes and windmills apart to get to the source of the water. The spacious ablution block is now surrounded by an elephant-proof wall, and it has solar-powered hot showers, handbasins and toilets. There are 10 camp sites, with braai places, shaded by tall camel thorn trees. The taps in the camp site have, however, been damaged by the elephants and the best place to refill your water containers is at the entrance gate.

A new camp site was opened at **Ihaha** in 1999 after repeated damage by elephants forced the closure of the well-known Serondela Camp Site. It consists of 10 camp sites on a high bank overlooking the Chobe River, an ablution block with solar-powered hot showers, handbasins and flush toilets. Ihaha is about 33 km west of the Sedudu Gate and 22 km east of the Ngoma Gate.

Linyanti has three camp sites with an ablution block with cold showers, handbasins and flush toilets.

The camp sites at Nogatsaa and Tchinga were closed a number of years ago after they too were destroyed by elephants.

Activities

Arrange an afternoon **boat trip** on the Chobe River with one of the tour operators in Kasane. You are almost guaranteed excellent views of elephant, bushbuck and a variety of other game. A boat trip on the Chobe is a must for birders as there are so many species to see here including riverine forest, floodplain and open water species, many with a restricted distribution elsewhere in southern Africa.

Getting there

Approaching from Maun, it is a 130-km journey to Mababe Gate, Chobe's southern entrance. Alternatively, if you are travelling from Moremi, you enter the park 21 km north-east of North Gate, with the Mababe Gate 18 km on. From Kasane the most direct route to Savute is to take the A33 tar road from Kasane westwards for 51 km. Just after passing through the checkpoint near Ngoma, turn left onto the B334. The first 40 km of sometimes badly corrugated gravel road to Kachekabwe

ARTIFICIAL WATERHOLES

Once the seasonal pans in the Nogatsaa/Tchinga area have dried up, the game is forced to migrate to the Chobe River, the only perennial water source in the area. To relieve the Chobe River frontage from the pressure of large concentrations of game, artificial or pumped waterholes have been created to encourage animals, especially elephants, to remain in the area during the dry season.

BOTSWANA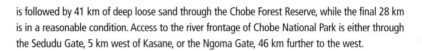

is followed by 41 km of deep loose sand through the Chobe Forest Reserve, while the final 28 km is in a reasonable condition. Access to the river frontage of Chobe National Park is either through the Sedudu Gate, 5 km west of Kasane, or the Ngoma Gate, 46 km further to the west.

ROUTES – 465 km North Gate (Moremi Game Reserve) to Kasane via Ngoma Gate and Chobe riverfront; 550 km North Gate (Moremi Game Reserve) to Kasane via Nogatsaa/Tchinga and Chobe riverfront

You can explore Chobe's four different ecological zones along a network of tracks covering over 800 km. Our route descriptions start from Moremi's North Gate, as a visit to Chobe National Park is often combined with Moremi Game Reserve (see page 77).

A short distance from North Gate, the track reaches Khwai village where people who lived on the Khwai floodplain were resettled when the Moremi Wildlife Reserve was proclaimed. The Babukakhwae (Bushmen) were among these groups and they still live at Khwai village, a small settlement of about 400 people. Babukakhwae, which means 'people of the river', alludes to their mobility on the waterways of the Delta in *mekoro*, or dugout canoes (see box below). You can stock up on basic necessities, soft drinks and beer at a few small shops in Khwai village.

Approximately 14 km beyond North Gate the track meanders along the northern bank of the Khwai River where you can see water birds and raptors. After following the river for nearly 7 km, the track splits at a signpost (broken in December 2002) where you must keep left. About 800 m on, a noticeboard indicates the boundary of Chobe National Park and here you keep straight. The track briefly returns to the river's edge (an area much favoured by elephant) and 7 km beyond the park boundary you will reach a concrete signpost indicating the turnoff to Mababe Gate to the left. About 2.6 km on you will reach the Magwikhwe Sand Ridge and, after going through deep loose sand for just over 2 km, the track leads through mopaneveld. Here, numerous short detours around deep clay potholes are sufficient evidence that travelling along this section after heavy rains can be a nightmare. About 11.4 km beyond the last turnoff you reach Mababe Gate.

North of Mababe Gate the vegetation opens out to grassland interspersed with shepherd's trees, acacias, woolly caper-bush and scrub. After heavy rains the first 10 km of the track can be challenging as you have to try to avoid deep potholes and ruts. About 21.6 km from Mababe Gate turn left onto the Sand Ridge track, which winds through dense woodland along the base of the Magwikhwe Sand Ridge and offers little opportunity for game-viewing, or take the Marsh track.

THE MOKORO

The *mokoro*, the African equivalent of the gondola of Venice, has been used for centuries by the Bayei and Hambukushu people as a means of transport in the Okavango Delta. Traditionally the *mokoro* (plural *mekoro*) was made by hollowing out the trunk of a tree that was specially felled for this purpose. The end of the trunk closest to the roots was shaped into the prow, and it took at least a month to hollow out the trunk and to ensure it was balanced and waterproof. Like a gondolier, a man stands in the stern of the *mokoro* using a three- to four-metre-long pole to punt the boat along the waterways.

The scenery along the Marsh track is more diverse as it alternates between mopaneveld, patches of coarse grass, open scrubveld and the fringe of the Savute Marsh. This route is recommended during the dry season, but it should not be attempted after rains and during the wet season. After travelling for 27 km the track winds along the edge of the Savute Marsh with its scattered tree 'islands'.

To view the rock paintings at Tsonxhwaa Hill take the signposted turnoff about 3.2 km before reaching Savute Camp. Follow the track to the car park on the eastern side of the hill and look for a fault where the rocks have been displaced, to the right of a small overhang. After a short scramble up the rocks you will see the paintings to your left. The eland, an elephant superimposed on a giraffe and a sable were painted in red ochre and are stylistically similar to the paintings at Tsodilo Hills, some 220 km to the east (*see* page 91). The rocks are smooth so make sure that your footwear has a good grip.

Savute is the gateway to Linyanti and, although the distance between them is only 39 km, you are unlikely to average more than 10 km an hour in the soft loose sand. Since most of the Linyanti area falls within private concessions there is only about 7 km of track along the river. However, the diversity of game that is attracted to the river, especially during the dry season, makes the journey worth the effort.

From Savute most travellers follow the recommended route via the Chobe Forest Reserve and Kachekabwe to the A33 tar road linking Ngoma Bridge and Kasane. The 41-km-long stretch through the forest reserve is through deep soft sand that requires low range, is dead straight and offers little possibility of seeing game.

On reaching the A33, turn right and after passing through the control point go left to pass through the Ngoma Gate. From here it is about 22 km to Ihaha Camp or if you're heading for Kasane it is a 51-km journey. Bear in mind that the speed limit on the tar road is 80 km an hour and keep a look out for game crossing the road, especially in the late afternoon.

A more interesting alternative is to follow the track to the Nogatsaa/Tchinga area. Not only is the scenery more diverse along this route, but there's a better chance to see game. Since the closure of the Nogatsaa and Tchinga camping sites due to elephant damage a number of years ago, few travellers follow this route and for safety a minimum of two vehicles is highly recommended. This route should be avoided during the peak rainy season when the tracks in the Zweizwe area become a vehicle trap of slippery black mud. If you plan to stop at one or two of the game-viewing platforms, start really early as the 220-km trip (including detours for game-viewing) will take at least 8 hours.

From the camp site cross the dry Savute Channel; after 300 m turn right and follow the track to Qumxhwaa Hill. From here the track heads south-east through mopane scrub for 36 km before taking a more northerly course, past a series of pans. Soon after crossing the Sand Ridge, the track follows the ephemeral Ngwezumba River, but for most of the way you won't notice it. Once over the sand ridge you will be struck by the marked change in vegetation which alternates between patches of teak forest, apple-leaf, acacias, silver cluster-leaf and leadwood scrub. As you approach the Nogatsaa/Tchinga area mopane dominates again and about 120 km after setting off you will reach the first signpost since leaving Savute ('Kasane 86 km'). The turnoff to Nogatsaa is 500 m on.

An extensive network of tracks leading past numerous seasonal pans traverses the area east of the main track to Kasane, usually negotiable after rains. However, in the pan area, the tracks are often flooded, rendering them impassable. During the dry season the game concentrates around the pans with solar water pumps, and game-viewing from the hides at Sarigho, Tchinga, Nogatsaa and Tambiko can be superb.

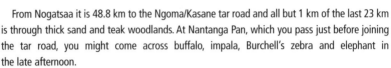
BOTSWANA

From Nogatsaa it is 48.8 km to the Ngoma/Kasane tar road and all but 1 km of the last 23 km is through thick sand and teak woodlands. At Nantanga Pan, which you pass just before joining the tar road, you might come across buffalo, impala, Burchell's zebra and elephant in the late afternoon.

From the junction with the tar road it is about 25 km to Kasane. Alternatively, if you are headed for Ihaha, cross the A33 and drive for 9 km through teak woodlands to the main Chobe riverfront track. You will join this track just before the old Serondela Camp. Turn left and continue for about 15 km to Ihaha where lion and other species may be seen.

Linking routes
Chobe is often combined with a visit to the Moremi Game Reserve (*see* page 77).

LOGISTICS AND PLANNING
Fuel: Available only in Kasane and Maun. If you are visiting Chobe only and plan to return to Kasane, have enough fuel for a distance of at least 450 km including game-viewing drives. Should you continue to Moremi and Maun, work on covering about 850 km. Remember that fuel consumption is higher in sandy areas.
Food: There are supermarkets in Maun and Kasane where you can stock up on meat, fresh fruit and vegetables, frozen foods, cold drinks and alcoholic beverages. A limited range of basic food items, cold drinks and beer can be bought in Khwai village just outside North Gate.
Best times: The dry winter months are generally the best time to visit the Chobe riverfront and the Nogatsaa/Tchinga area as the game is forced to congregate around the shrinking water supplies. Temperatures are also more tolerable. At Savute large herds of herbivores converge on the grass-covered plains during the rainy season. In spite of the heat, the summer months are rewarding for birders and those interested in flora.

Maps
The only section of the park for which a map is provided at the entrance is the Chobe riverfront. This makes a copy of the *Shell Map of the Chobe National Park* indispensable.

Booking
Reservations must be made with the Parks and Reserves Reservations Office, Maun, tel: (+267) 686-1265, fax: 686-1264.

WESTERN BOTSWANA'S HILLS

Tsodilo Hills (*see* page 91) are the best-known group of the hills of north-western Botswana but several dolomite hills punctuate the landscape to the south-west. The most prominent of these are the Aha Hills which rise almost 120 m above the Kalahari sands and straddle, for nearly 40 km, the border with Namibia where most of the range is situated. South-east of the Bushman settlement of Caecae lies a cluster of six low hills in a fossil valley, the well-known Gcwihaba Hills (*see* page 91). The Koanaka Hills lie 19 km to the south-west.

Tsodilo Hills & Gcwihaba Cave

Tsodilo Hills, also known as the 'Mountains of the Gods', have held symbolic and religious importance for the inhabitants of the remote north-western corner of Botswana for thousands of years. The early inhabitants used the rock faces as open-air canvases, creating what has justifiably been called the 'Louvre of the Desert'. A visit to Tsodilo Hills, which are steeped in myth, mystique and a sense of spirituality, is likely to make a deep impression on you. Bushman folklore has it that the three hills represent the male, female and child, while the fourth hill, unnamed and slightly apart, is the male's first wife. Further south, Gcwihaba, an inconspicuous range of hills, hides a largely unexplored series of caves and narrow passages. There is no artificial lighting and you will see the magnificent stalactites, stalagmites and flowstones only if you brave the pitch-black depths with a strong torch.

Landscape and vegetation

Other than the occasional fossil valley in the seemingly endless expanse of sandveld there are few prominent landmarks in this part of Botswana. The exception is in the north-western corner of Botswana where several outcrops contrast strikingly with the flat and featureless countryside surrounding them.

The vegetation of the area is typical Kalahari tree and scrub savanna composed of acacias, raisin bushes, western rhigozum (*Rhigozum brevispinosum*), bushwillows, coffee neat's foot and lavender fever-berry trees. Teak woodlands, the sand corkwood with its flaky chestnut-brown bark, silver cluster-leaf, the manketti tree with its grey to light-golden bark and marula trees are conspicuous in deep sand. The outcrops have their own distinctive vegetation of which the mopane aloe (*Aloe littoralis*) and the Namaqua fig are noteworthy at Gcwihaba Hills.

Fauna and game-viewing

Since the antelope migrate widely in this vast thirstland in search of food and water, you are not likely to see many. Bull elephants cover an extensive range through the sandveld during the rainy season, and you might find spoor at Tsodilo Hills or Gcwihaba Cave. Large herds of eland and gemsbok also trek through the area. You might chance upon kudu, steenbok and common duiker.

BOTSWANA

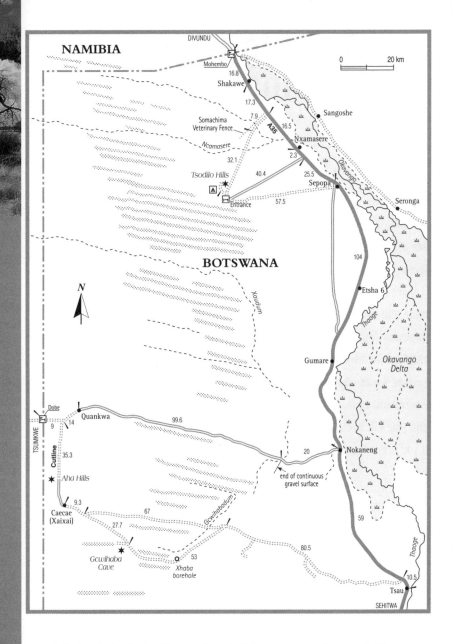

Following the herds of antelope are lion, cheetah and hyaena, and packs of wild dog roam the area in search of prey. Leopard inhabit the Tsodilo Hills, but you may count yourself fortunate if you see one of these highly secretive cats.

The Tsodilo thick-toed gecko (*Pachydactylus tsodiloensis*) is endemic to these outcrops and does not venture away from the rocks. It is small (about 50 mm long) and light greyish-brown with uneven white bars edged with brown across its back. It has a pale dark-edged 'headband' running from behind each nostril through the eye to the back of the head. The larger Turner's thick-toed gecko, without the 'headband' and with less distinct crossbands, is more widely distributed.

Dark caves are usually associated with bats and Gcwihaba is no exception. Among the bats found in Gcwihaba is Commerson's leaf-nosed bat, southern Africa's largest insectivorous bat.

Birding
The early mornings are the most rewarding time for birding.
Common species: crimson-breasted and red-backed shrikes, northern black korhaan, southern yellow-billed hornbill, Cape and glossy starlings, pied babbler, bee-eater, bronze-winged courser, southern pale chanting goshawk and bateleur. The rocks at Tsodilo Hills are home to pearl-spotted owl. You may hear their call if you spend a night at Makoba Woods Camp Site.

Facilities
Tsodilo Hills has several camp sites without any facilities. An exception is **Makoba Woods Camp Site**, close to the office, where there are solar-powered hot showers, handbasins and flush toilets. If Makoba is busy, **Malatso Camp Site** 4.7 km north of the office is a quiet alternative and ideal to walk the Cliff Trail. There are also a number of informal sites along the northern base of the Male Hill.

Two informal camping areas are available at **Gcwihaba Cave**, one just below the main entrance and the other near the western entrance. The latter site is an excellent vantage point to watch the sunset and the large numbers of bats that leave the cave at dusk.

Between Etsha 6 and Shakawe/Mohembo border post there are several accommodation options that include the following:

Drotsky's Cabins, signposted 8 km south of Shakawe. Chalets, camp sites, restaurant, boat hire, fishing, excellent birding.

Shakawe Fishing Lodge, signposted 12 km south of Shakawe. Chalets, camping, restaurant, swimming pool, fishing.

Swamp Stop, signposted at Sepopa turnoff, 58 km south of Shakawe. Serviced tents, camp sites, restaurant, boat hire, fishing, *mokoro* trips.

Nxamaseri Lodge, turn off at Nxamasere, 30 km south of Shakawe. Chalets, restaurant, fishing, boating, *mokoro* trips, horseback safaris, guided walks.

Guma Lagoon Camp, turn off at Etsha, 13, 86 km south of Shakawe. Fully catered and self-catering tents, restaurant, boat hire, fishing, *mokoro* trips, birding.

Activities
Visit the **display centre** (allow about 30 minutes) at the Tsodilo Hills office where fascinating information about the people, history and paintings of Tsodilo Hills and the area is displayed on boards. There is a small selection of curios on sale. **Four trails** have been laid out: Rhino, Lion, Cliff and Male Hill.

- The **Rhino Trail,** which should not be missed, leads along and over the Female Hill (which has the highest concentration of paintings) and takes about 2 to 2.5 hours to do. The best-known site, the Van der Post Panel, is named after Sir Laurens van der Post who visited the hills in 1958. Two eland (one measuring 60 cm), a giraffe, two unidentifiable antelope and handprints are visible high up on a rock face on the western side of the Hill. Other highlights include the Rhino Frieze, the White Painting Shelter (the crude paintings are all in white) and paintings of geometric shapes.

- You can start the **Lion Trail** at the parking area near the White Painting Shelter, but it is not very exciting as there are only three marked sites and a few unmarked sites, including the feline

which gives the trail its name. The Dancing Penis Panel is the most interesting site. Several male figures with erect or semi-erect penises with a short line across the penis-ends are depicted in this panel. It is situated a short walk from the White Painting Shelter, and an easy detour from the Rhino Trail.

- The **Cliff Trail** follows the northern end of the Female Hill and the **Male Hill Trail** entails a steep climb to the summit of the Male Hill which towers nearly 400 m above its surroundings.

Getting to Tsodilo Hills

Tsodilo Hills can be approached along three routes. The new main access is signposted 2.3 km south of the turnoff to Nxamasere (30 km from Shakawe, 250 km from Sehitwa). From here follow a gravel road for 36 km to the entrance. The office is 4.4 km on.

The northern approach starts immediately to the south of the Somachima veterinary fence (17 km from Shakawe, 263 km from Sehitwa) and follows the fence along a sandy track for 7.9 km before the Tsodilo track branches off to the left. This track soon makes its way into the dunes but, since it is infrequently used, it is overgrown and might damage the paintwork of your vehicle. The sandy nature of the terrain makes the going slow and you are unlikely to complete the 40-km journey in under four hours.

The southern approach 600 m south of the Sepopa turnoff (56 km from Shakawe, 223 km from Sehitwa) is seldom used nowadays. The journey takes much longer – branches encroach into the track and the second half traverses thick sand. Most travellers now use the 'centre' route and the track is thus seldom used.

ROUTES – 800 km Maun to Shakawe via Gcwihaba Cave and Tsodilo Hills

Although Tsodilo Hills and Gcwihaba Cave are some distance apart, it makes sense to visit both over a few days as they are in the remote west of the country and accessible from the same access road (the A35).

Tsodilo Hills

Tsodilo Hills were once considered one of the most remote places in Botswana and only a year or two ago the 40-km journey from the tar road along the 'centre' route through deep soft sand could easily take you up to four hours. The declaration of Tsodilo Hills as a World Heritage Site in 2001 has made the Hills more accessible, and all but 6 km of the road approaching the entrance gate had been gravelled by December 2002.

Rising to 390 m above the surrounding Kalahari dunes, the Tsodilo Hills are among the few prominent landmarks in the north-western corner of Botswana. The name Tsodilo, derived from the Setswana word *sorile* which means 'sheer', refers to the towering light yellow rock faces and sheer cliffs of the hills. Other local names are translated as Hill of Great Stones and Copper Hills.

With over 4 500 individual paintings in less than 10 km^2, Tsodilo Hills have one of the highest concentrations of rock paintings in the world. The paintings were recorded as early as 1907 in a book by the German geologist Siegfried Passarge but Sir Laurens van der Post's book *The Lost World of the Kalahari* drew the world's attention to them when it was first published in 1958.

If you look closely at the Tsodilo paintings you will see more similarity to rock engravings than to other paintings in southern Africa. Many of the animals are depicted in heavy outlines shaded with one colour and there are hardly any human figures or human scenes. Another interesting feature is that many of the animals have only one foreleg and one hindleg. The earliest visible paintings are estimated to be about 3 000 years old but most date back 1 300 to 900 years.

Tsodilo Hills & Gcwihaba Cave

> **ⓘ VITAL INFO**
>
> - At the time of writing (December 2002) permits were not required for Tsodilo Hills, but it is likely that an entrance fee will be charged in future
> - Gcwihaba Cave falls within a community-controlled hunting area. An entrance fee of P50.00 and and a camping fee of P10.00 per person are charged. Visitors travelling via Caecae (also spelt Xaixai) are usually stopped and asked to pay, but there is no system to collect the fees if you are approaching from Tsao. The onus is on the visitor to pay, but this may be impractical if you are using the track from and back to Tsao.
> - Do not enter Gcwihaba Cave without a reliable torch with a strong beam and at least one other source of light (pocket torch or matches) in case you lose your torch in the dark or the bulb fuses.

Getting to Gcwihaba Cave

There are two routes to Gcwihaba Cave making an interesting circular journey. Approaching from Maun and Sehitwa, turn left (west) 10.5 km beyond the microwave comunication tower at the turnoff to Tsau and continue for 81 km along a narrow sandy track to a turnoff sign-posted Xhaba Borehole. Turn left here and continue for 53 km to the cave.

The other approach is to turn right if you are approaching from Shakawe, left if approaching from Sehitwa at Nokaneng (171 km from Shakawe and 110 km from Sehitwa) and to travel via Quankwa (also spelt Qangwa) and Caecae to the cave. This track used to be sandy but these stretches have been resurfaced with gravel.

After you leave the tar road at Nokaneng, the first 20 km is a good gravel road and then there are alternate stretches of gravel and hard clay. After crossing a flat landscape the track leads across rolling dunes and follows the course of the Quankwa, a fossil river. Looking at the harsh, arid landscape we found it inconceivable that there was a lake in this valley between 23 000 and 22 000 years ago. About 120 km after leaving the tar road you reach Quankwa, a settlement inhabited by Mbanderu/Herero people.

From Quankwa the track heads south-west to the settlement of Mahopa 12.4 km on. Bear left (if you miss the turnoff and continue west you will end up at the Dobe border post); the track joins a cutline which heads almost due south through dense bush. Further along a notice informs you that you are entering a community-controlled hunting area. The track climbs through deep sand to the Aha Hills. A short way after cresting the last hill you follow a gravel road for 8.5 km to Caecae.

A number of tracks turn off into the village, but you should stick to the edge of the pan on the outskirts of the village and follow the track that ascends a small dune. Just over 9 km beyond Caecae the track to Gcwihaba Cave splits off to the right. The hills first come into view only when you crest a dune about 3.7 km before reaching the main entrance, 27.7 km beyond the last turnoff.

BOTSWANA

THE PEOPLE

Archaeological research has shown that the earliest inhabitants of Tsodilo Hills, the Middle Stone Age people, lived here from 100 000 to 35 000 years ago and were succeeded by Later Stone Age people and then by Iron Age people. These Later Stone Age inhabitants were the ancestors of the Ju/'hoan Bushmen who live near Tsodilo Hills and in settlements such as Caecae (Xaixai). They were followed by the Hambukushu, Mbanderu/Herero who fled from Namibia to Botswana in 1904 and live at Quankwa.

Gcwihaba Cave

Exploring the passages and chambers of Gcwihaba Cave with only a thin string on the dusty floor and a torch to guide you is an exciting adventure that will remain fresh in your memory for a long time.

Gcwihaba is a Bushman word that translates as 'hyaena's lair'. This is the official name and preferred to Drotsky's Caves, a name given to it by Marthinus Drotsky, a farmer from Ghanzi who drew attention to the cave after a Bushman guided him there in 1932. It was declared a National Monument in 1934 and has been earmarked as a possible World Heritage Site. Other caves in the area that are closed to the public will also form part of this Site.

Gcwihaba Cave was formed at least two million years ago when the climate was wetter. Rainwater seeping along fractures dissolved the dolomite rock, creating large cavities and passages. Subterranean rivers ran through the cave during wet cycles and sand blew in during alternating dry cycles (45 000 to 4 000 years ago). The stalactites, stalagmites and flowstones were formed over thousands of years when water rich in calcium carbonate seeped through the roof into the dry cavities and caverns. Seismic movements probably caused many of the stalactites to break off about 50 cm above the cave floor. The two entrances were formed when the roof collapsed. A plaque marks the main entrance while the other entrance is about 250 m to the west.

From the main entrance, clamber down some rocks and look for a bright yellow string along the right-hand side of the main chamber. Now make your way into a large chamber with its spectacular collection of stalactites. Further on, you have to duck to get underneath some low rocks and as you get deeper into the cave don't forget to look at the fascinating stalactites, stalagmites and flowstones around you.

Still further on you reach a fairly deep hole where the route seems to come to an end. Here you have to climb down, and once you're out on the other side look for the string. The surface underfoot gets softer because you're walking over a deep accumulation of bat droppings. Sensing your presence the bats start flying around but fortunately the chamber is large enough for everyone.

Your route continues along a passage which becomes quite narrow in places, and at one point you are forced to crawl through a tight gap. After about 45 minutes in the dark (and, no doubt, much to your relief) the dim light filtering through the western entrance signals the end of your subterranean journey.

You are likely to be hot and dusty after your underground exploration, so take enough water for a well-deserved clean-up.

Tsodilo Hills & Gcwihaba Cave

Linking routes
Visits to Tsodilo Hills and Gcwihaba Cave can easily be combined with various routes in Namibia, specifically Nyae-Nyae, formerly known as Eastern Bushmanland (*see* page 129) and Khaudum Game Park (*see* page 134) in eastern Namibia, via the Dobe border post. The border is open from 08h00 to 16h30 daily.

You can also link up with Namibia's North-Eastern Parks (*see* page 139) via the Mohembo border post (06h00 to 18h00).

LOGISTICS AND PLANNING
Fuel: Available at Shakawe, Etsha 6, the turnoff to Gumare along the A35, Maun and Ghanzi.
Water: Obtainable at the Tsodilo Hills office, but at Gcwihaba Cave there is no water nor any other facilities.
Food: A wide range of fresh, frozen and canned foods, as well as cold drinks and liquor, is available at supermarkets and liquor outlets in Maun. Ghanzi, Shakawe and Sepopa have a less extensive selection of foodstuffs.
Best times: Autumn and spring, when the weather is cooler, are the best times to visit Tsodilo Hills and Gcwihaba Cave. Winter days are generally cool, but minimum temperatures can be very low in mid-winter.

Maps
Familiarise yourself with the map in the office as no maps of the trails at Tsodilo Hills were available in December 2002, in spite of the World Heritage Site status of the Hills. Alternatively, arrange a guide who can point out the paintings. The fee is P50.00 per trail.

Booking
Drotsky's Cabins, tel: (+267) 687-5035, fax: 687-5043
Shakawe Fishing Lodge, tel: (+267) 686-0822/3, fax: 686-7509, e-mail: t.wild@info.bw
Swamp Stop, tel: (+267) (radio phone) 687-7073, e-mail: philkay.island@info.bw
Nxamaseri Lodge, tel: (+267) 687-8016, fax: 687-8015, e-mail: nxa.lodge@info.bw
Guma Lagoon Camp, tel: (+267) 686-0351, fax: 686-0571

Tsodilo Hills in north-western Botswana is a World Heritage Site.

Main picture: Damaraland is a wilderness of mountains, hills and boulder-strewn slopes.
Inset picture: The former Sperrgebiet, north of Lüderitz.

Namibia

NAMIBIA

Namibia, named after the harsh and inhospitable desert which lies along its west coast, is also bounded in the east by the Kalahari Desert. By association with the Namib Desert, the country's very name conjures up visions of sand dunes, gravel plains and endless space. But in sharp contrast with the desert is the well-watered north-east, with its wide rivers fringed by green ribbons of riverine vegetation, water-lily carpeted side channels and floodplain grasslands. Kaokoveld, on the other hand, is a lonely wilderness of towering mountain peaks, boulder-strewn slopes and wide valleys where desert-dwelling elephants and black rhinos have managed to survive against all odds.

Fourteen per cent of Namibia has been set aside as conservation areas and the country's large game species are to be found mainly in the north and north-east of the country. But there are still vast tracts of wild land in communal areas where people like the Himba and the Ju/'hoan continue to pursue their traditional way of life. Communal conservancies have been established in many of these areas to enable local communities to benefit from tourism through the establishment of community-run camp sites. They also exercise control over natural resources, concerning themselves for instance with wildlife, including such aspects as game counts, trophy hunting and the reintroduction of game. All income derived is used for projects that will create socio-economic upliftment for people living in the community.

We have selected a mixture of routes that we believe represent the real spirit of Namibia – land of contrasts.

Two of the routes through the dune sea of the Namib (Saddle Hill and Conception) can be done only as an organised trail because of the sensitivity of the desert, as well as the risks of travelling through uncharted territory. Nyae Nyae and the Kaokoveld offer spectacular scenery and the chance to experience the culture of two of Africa's most renowned indigenous peoples – the Himba and the Ju/'hoan Bushmen.

A journey through Khaudum and the North-Eastern Parks takes you to some of the remotest corners of Namibia. Although game is not as abundant here as in the Etosha National Park, Namibia's flagship conservation area, you will experience wildest Africa and camp in the bush with no facilities. Game-viewing is not the essence of a visit to Namibia, though. It is rather the country's raw, magnificent scenery, its ever-changing landscapes, wide expanses melting with the horizon, solitude and absolute wilderness. The absence of large numbers of game is amply compensated for by the superb birdlife.

An excellent road system links the country's main centres, and, as many of the top tourist attractions are accessible either by tar or well-maintained gravel roads, they are not described in this section. Among these are the Etosha National Park, the Hoba Meteorite near Grootfontein (the world's largest meteorite) and Otjikoto Lake outside Tsumeb. Twyfelfontein and the Brandberg have

Overview

the largest concentrations of rock engravings and rock paintings respectively in the world, and in the south the awe-inspiring Fish River Canyon is up to half a kilometre deep. Most of these attractions can be explored en route to the destinations described here.

Namibia is the driest country south of the Sahara, with an average rainfall of only 270 mm. Along the coast the rainfall averages a mere 10 mm a year but fog occurs on average once every three days. In the late afternoon dense banks of fog blanket the coast but they usually lift around mid-morning. Rainfall increases from south to north and west to east, and averages 700 mm in the far north-east, which receives the highest rainfall. The rainy season stretches from November to March/April and the rains are usually accompanied by violent thunderstorms. The only exception is the area south of Lüderitz which receives most of its rain in winter – but rain also occasionally falls in summer.

The north-east has three distinct seasons. Late April to August is the cool dry season, but be prepared for cold nights in mid-winter when frost can occur. The hot dry season from September to November is followed by a hot wet season from December to March/early April when maximum temperatures exceed 35°C. The humidity is high, and the only relief from the oppressive heat comes with the rains.

Oshiwambo, Bushmen, Himba, Herero, Nama and Damara are among the cultures that make up the Namibian nation. German is still widely spoken in many small towns, especially the coastal towns of Lüderitz and Swakopmund with their Continental atmosphere. The country became independent on 21 March 1990 after a bitter liberation struggle against South African rule that claimed thousands of lives on both sides. Since independence peace has prevailed and you will find Namibians friendly and good hosts.

BORDER POSTS AND FORMALITIES

The main ports of entry from South Africa are Noordoewer in the south and Ariamsvlei in the south-east, both of which are open 24 hours.

From Botswana you can enter Namibia via Buitepos on the Trans-Kalahari Highway (07h00 to midnight), Mohembo near Shakawe, and Ngoma close

Driving skills are tested to the limit in the dune sea of Namibia's Namib Desert.

NAMIBIA

to the western side of Chobe National Park (both open 06h00 to 18h00) and Dobe (08h00 to 16h30) where you can link up with the road to Tsumkwe.

IMMIGRATION
You will need a valid passport and entry is usually granted for 30 days but can be extended to 90 days. Exempt from visa requirements are: nationals of the European Union (as at 2003), SADC countries (except DRC, Seychelles and Mauritius), the following Commonwealth members: Australia, Canada, Malaysia, New Zealand, Singapore and the following countries: Cuba, Iceland, Ireland, Japan, Liechtenstein, Malaysia, Norway, Russian Federation, Switzerland and the United States of America. As entry regulations can change, check with the Ministry of Home Affairs in Windhoek, tel: (+264 61) 292-2102 or the relevant government department in your home country.

CUSTOMS
Duty-free allowances include personal effects, sporting and recreational equipment, and the following consumables: 2 litres wine, 1 litre spirits, 400 cigarettes, 50 cigars and 250 grams cigarette or pipe tobacco, and goods with a total value not exceeding N$500 per person.

ROAD-USER FEE
All vehicles not registered in Namibia must pay a N$70.00 road-user charge on entering the country. Ensure that you keep proof that you have bought your road-user disk.

VEHICLE DOCUMENTATION
It is advisable to travel with your original vehicle registration papers as you might be required to show them at border posts.

DRIVING
The speed limit is 120 km an hour on major roads, 100 km an hour on gravel roads and 60 km an hour in urban areas.

Kudu, warthog and in some areas domestic stock make travelling in the late afternoon and at night hazardous.

When travelling on gravel roads check the condition of tyres regularly and take an occasional break on long journeys. On long lonely trips it is easy to forget that there might be other vehicles on the road, so keep a watch in your rear-view mirror for vehicles approaching from behind. Headlights should be switched on when you are driving in the dust of a vehicle ahead or when a vehicle approaches.

Loose gravel and sand ridges that accumulate alongside defined tracks on gravel roads can cause your vehicle to lose traction if you overtake or switch from one set of tracks to the other. Do not brake suddenly if this happens but decelerate and steer gently.

Slow down when you approach riverbeds or when the road surface deteriorates as this could cause you to lose control of your vehicle.

Overview

> ## ⓘ VITAL INFO
>
> - Khaudum, the North-Eastern Parks and Kaokoveld fall within malaria areas (Kaokoveld falls in an epidemic area, and malaria can be contracted along the Kunene River even during the winter months). Consult your doctor or travel clinic about the most effective prophylaxis.
> - The Caprivi Strip between Kongola and Bagani is safe for travellers and the military convoy was discontinued in the second half of 2002. Travelling after dark is still not advisable.

CURRENCY AND BANKS

The Namibian Dollar, the country's currency, is on a par with the South African Rand (which is also legal tender). Make sure that you convert your Namibian Dollars into South African Rand before leaving the country as they cannot be exchanged at banks outside of Namibia.

Banks and automatic teller machines are available in all major towns but ensure that you have enough cash when visiting the Kaokoveld. The last banks en route to Nyae Nyae are at Grootfontein. In the north-east there are banks at Rundu and Katima Mulilo. Credit and debit cards are not accepted at garages – only petrol/garage cards – and in remote towns and villages cash is usually the only acceptable form of payment.

DAYLIGHT SAVING

From the first Sunday in April to the first Sunday in September, Namibian time is one hour behind South African standard time. Border posts remain open in accordance with South African time. For the remainder of the year Namibian time is the same as South African standard time.

MAPS

The Automobile Association *Map of Namibia*, or any other good road map, will suffice when travelling on the major roads, and maps of Kaokoland and Caprivi are available at booksellers in Windhoek and Swakopmund. Topographical maps can be bought from the Office of the Surveyor-General, Ministry of Lands, Resettlement and Rehabilitation, Private Bag 13182, Windhoek, Namibia, tel: (+264 61) 24-5056. The office is situated on the corner of Robert Mugabe Avenue and Lazarette Street.

NAMIBIA

Saddle Hill Guided 4x4 Trail

On this exclusive guided trail through the sand sea of the former *Sperrgebiet* along the Namibian coast you will experience the exhilaration of driving up fearful dunes and 'sliding' down slip faces. You will feel the adrenaline rushing through your veins as you roar up the dunes and take split-second decisions to overcome the challenges facing you. Long-abandoned diamond mines that have been reclaimed by the desert, shipwrecks, untouched beaches, solitude and endless expanses of rolling dunes add to the allure of this amazing journey.

Landscape and vegetation
Pale yellow dunes stretching as far as the eye can see dominate the southern Namib landscape. Sharp dune crests and sweeping 'arms' extending to the surrounding dunes create intriguing patterns and shapes along the coast. This belt of crescentic dunes is about 20 km wide and owes its haphazard arrangement to the strong south-south-westerly winds. The linear dunes further inland are influenced by medium-strong south-south-westerly and easterly winds and are oriented in a north-east/south-west direction. Wide dune streets separate them.

After good rains the gravel plains are transformed into waving grasslands but, except for the hardy Namib dune bushman grass (*Stipagrostis sabulicola*) and the spiky ostrich grass (*Cladoraphis spinosa*), the shifting dunes are devoid of vegetation. The rocky outcrops provide a foothold for arid-adapted species such as the bushman's candle (*Sarcocaulon*), dollar bush (*Zygophyllum*) and corkwood (*Commiphora*). The bunch-of-grapes mesemb (*Jensenobotrya lossowiana*) is endemic to coastal cliffs in the area, its common name referring to the appearance of its fleshy leaves. It bears small pink flowers in autumn and winter. Brakbos (*Salsola*) plays an important role in trapping wind-blown sand along the coast.

Fauna and game-viewing
You might encounter herds of gemsbok and springbok on the plains south of the dune fields if there is grazing. Black-backed jackal and brown hyaena patrol the coastline to scavenge whatever has washed ashore and also catch seal pups at the Mercury Island seal colony.

The larger animals aside, the desert is home to a fascinating variety of smaller creatures specially adapted to life in this inhospitable environment. There are numerous tenebrionid beetle species, commonly called tok-tokkie beetles, spiders, dune ants and fish moths. The Namaqua chameleon and the many-horned and Peringuey's adders are among reptiles you might chance

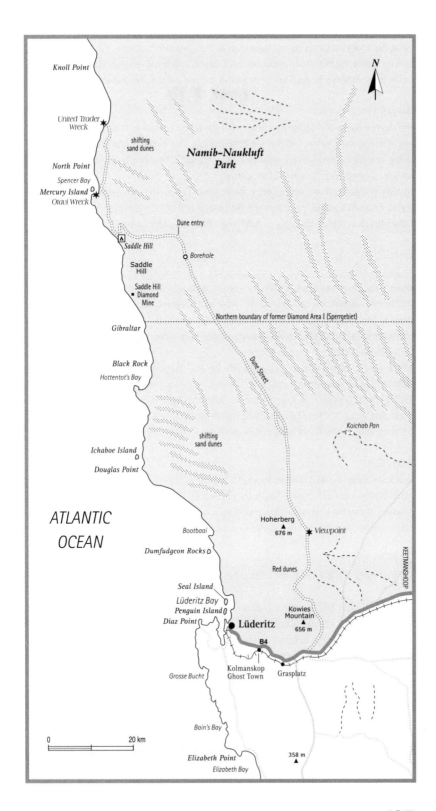

NAMIBIA

upon. Peringuey's adder is commonly known as the sidewinder because of its unusual way of moving across the hot desert sand. By continuously contorting its body it moves sideways rather than slithering forward like other snakes, leaving a distinctive pattern on the dunes.

Birding
The coastal dunes and sandy flats from northern Namaqualand to Walvis Bay are the only places in the world where you can see the dune lark. This medium-sized lark is usually seen singly, in pairs or groups of between four and eight birds. Its diet consists of insects such as ants, grass seeds and the leaves of succulents.
Marine species: white-breasted and Cape cormorants, African black oystercatcher (in rocky areas), kelp and Hartlaub's gulls, various tern, plover and other wading species.
Other species: ostrich, Ludwig's bustard (only after rains), rock and greater kestrels.

Facilities
At Saddle Hill North an old mine workshop has been converted into a living room with a kitchen, fireplace, gas stove, paraffin lamps, chairs, benches and tables. You will find basics (mattresses and pillows) in some of the other old buildings, but you must bring your own sleeping bag. Flush toilets and cold showers are also provided.

Accommodation in and around Lüderitz ranges from camp sites to *pensions* and hotels.
OPTIONS INCLUDE:
Shark Island camp site, Namibia Wildlife Resorts' magnificent site on Shark Island in Lüderitz. Can be very windy.
Kratzplatz, in Lüderitz. Self-catering rooms, communal kitchen, braaiplace.
Klein-Aus Vista, 220 km east of Lüderitz. Rooms with en-suite facilities, kitchen/lounge area, camping sites, guided horse trails, nature drives.

Activities
Visit **Kolmanskop ghost mining town**, 10 km east of Lüderitz, or book a guided trip to the ghost-mining town of Elizabeth Bay, south of Lüderitz.
Head out aboard the schooner *Sedina* to view the rocky coastal town of **Lüderitz** from out at sea.
Take a **guided 4x4 trip** to Koichab Pan. See the famous **Namib horses** from Klein-Aus Vista.

Getting there
The trail starts in Lüderitz 340 km west of the southern Namibian town of Keetmanshoop.

THE ROUTE – 500 km Lüderitz return
From Lüderitz the convoy heads east for about 25 km along the tar road towards Aus/Keetmanshoop and then turns north into what was formerly known as the *Sperrgebiet*. Here you deflate your tyres to 1 Kpa and you will be briefed on how to drive in the sand. A gradual climb along a sandy track brings you to a saddle on Kowies Mountain. Expansive views of dunes sweeping down to a vast plain greet you and, as you traverse the plains, the dunes loom ever larger until you are at their base.

This is where you will get your first taste of dune driving as you now head east along the base of the dunes. Travelling at an angle can be unnerving and the technique is to maintain enough momentum (at least 40 km an hour) to prevent the tail end from sliding. After a few kilometres you head up and into the dunes which you traverse for the next 10 km. There

Saddle Hill Guided 4x4 Trail

are several slip faces that are pretty daunting when you negotiate them for the first time. This section is a good training ground for what's to come, as these dunes are relatively small.

After about 10 km you emerge onto a plain and then return to the dunes before traversing easy terrain. After a further 50 km you reach the site where an old borehole was sunk in the 1940s to provide water for the Saddle Hill diamond mine.

About 7 km from here you arrive at the belt of coastal dunes, and for the next 20 km you weave your way up, over and through the dunes. There are several challenging dunes, some of which require a sharp turn just as you crest the dune. To overcome these obstacles you have to have enough momentum and be in the right gear.

Once you're through the dunes it's an easy drive to Saddle Hill base camp, which you reach 150 km after turning off the tar road – seven or eight hours of hard driving. The remainder of the day is spent at leisure.

On the second day you explore some of the attractions in the area. The sightseeing trip north leads past an old diamond camp where weather-beaten jigs, screens and water barrels are reminders of the mining days of the 1920s. The low diamond price of 11 shillings a carat forced the closure of the mine in 1932 until it was recommissioned in the mid-1940s.

Spencer Bay which is overlooked by Mercury Island, a few hundred metres offshore, is a short way further on. Mercury Island owes its curious name to the fact that it vibrates when the waves crash against its rocky shores. It is one of 11 offshore islands between the mouth of the Gariep River (still known as the Orange in Namibia) about 180 km south of Walvis Bay, that were annexed to the Cape Colony in 1866 (five years after the annexation of Ichaboe Island). South Africa subsequently claimed ownership of the islands and they were reintegrated into Namibia, with Walvis Bay, only on 1 March 1994 – nearly four years after Namibia became independent.

The offshore islands, which are important roosting and breeding sites for sea birds, until recently provided rich harvests of guano, a natural fertiliser derived from bird droppings. Guano collection was stopped in 1992 as it caused a dramatic decrease in the numbers of the African penguin that nest in hollows in the guano. Their numbers have also been reduced as a result of an invasion of the islands by the Cape fur seal. This prompted the Ministry of Marine Resources to station an official on Mercury Island (probably one of the remotest corners of Namibia) to chase the seals off the island, which is home to 18 000 African penguin, the largest colony in the world. The island also has 4 500 Cape gannet.

A short climb up a ridge rewards you with spectacular views of a small bay nestling at the foot of Dolphin Head, the highest point along the 2 400-km stretch of coast between Table Mountain and Namibe in southern Angola. The rusty remains on the beach far below belong to the *Otavi* which ran aground in 1945 with a cargo of guano collected at Mercury Island. A large colony of Cape fur seals appears to be guarding the wave-battered hull of the wreck.

From here you head north, passing through magnificent rocky outcrops. At one point there is a long descent at an awkward angle that should be tackled with the right momentum. A steep climb up a high dune follows before you make your way down the dunes to the wreck of the *United Trader*. The vessel had a shipment of 700 tonnes of ammunition on board when it ran aground in the early 1970s during the sanction-busting days of South Africa's apartheid government. Unable to salvage the cargo, the government blew the ship up in 1974 and only a few pieces of mangled and twisted metal remain. It is hard to believe how far the heavy anchor chain was blasted into the dunes, while some of the smaller pieces of metal were scattered up to 5 km inland. On the return route you retrace your tracks to the base camp. The round trip is just over 60 km long.

NAMIBIA

> **ⓘ VITAL INFO**
>
> - Your vehicle must have wide (at least 15") tyres.
> - An experienced and knowledgeable guide accompanies the group. Two-way radios are supplied to maintain contact in the dunes. Recovery equipment is on hand, but otherwise you must be self-sufficient.

The sightseeing trip to the south leads along a rocky section of the coast which can be negotiated only at low tide. The rest of the trip is not without challenges. Long sections are through soft, loose sand where you drive at an angle along the dune slopes. About 20 km after leaving the base camp you arrive at the old Saddle Hill South diamond mine. Abandoned pieces of heavy mining equipment, bulldozers and buildings buried up to their roofs in sand are reminders of the intrepid Mose Kahan who mined diamonds here from 1945 to 1960. From here you follow the onward route back to the base camp, which you reach some 40 kilometres after setting off.

After breakfast on the last day you head back to Lüderitz, following more or less the same route. The new vistas presented by the return route, and the drive across the dunes in the opposite direction, however, ensure that the return journey is as enjoyable as the first day's drive.

LOGISTICS AND PLANNING

Fuel: You'll need enough fuel to cover the 450-km round trip from Lüderitz. Much of the journey is through very heavy sand and, depending on your vehicle, you might get as little as 3 km a litre.
Water: Available at the Saddle Hill base camp.
Food: As this is a self-catering trip, you should stock up on food and alcoholic beverages in Lüderitz.
Best times: This trip can be done throughout the year. There is normally a cool south-westerly wind blowing off the sea which brings relief from the heat further inland. Hot easterly 'berg' winds can sometimes send temperatures soaring to above 30°C in the winter months. Fog is common along the coast in the afternoons and overnight but it usually clears by mid-morning.

Booking

Bookings for this guided trail must be made with: Coastaways Tours, PO Box 77, Lüderitz, Namibia, tel: (+264 63) 20-2002, fax: 20-2003, e-mail: lewiscwt@iway.na. Groups must consist of a minimum of three vehicles and eight persons. The maximum group size is 15 vehicles.
Shark Island camp site, Namibia Wildlife Resorts, tel: (+264 61) 23-6975, fax: 22-4900, e-mail: reservations@nwr.com.na
Kratzplatz, tel and fax: (+264 63) 20-2458, in Lüderitz.
Klein-Aus Vista, tel and fax: (+264 63) 25-8021, e-mail: ausvista@namibhorses.com

Conception Expedition

This guided trail through the central Namib presents the ultimate challenge to your driving skills and confidence. As on the Saddle Hill Trail, you descend nerve-wracking slip faces, making split-second decisions. Long-abandoned diamond mines, the rusty remains of ships and the well-known Sandwich Harbour are attractions along the coast. The trail is conducted in a concession area of the Namib-Naukluft Park with the Topnaar community whose ancestral land the expedition traverses, and who receive a fee for each vehicle.

THE NAMIB DESERT

The Kuiseb River, its delta and the Namib coastline have been the ancestral home of the Topnaar people for centuries. Also known as the ≠Aonin (people living on the edge of the Nama territory), they live in 12 settlements along the Kuiseb River and in Walvis Bay. The trail starts at one of these settlements, Homeb, and is conducted in conjunction with the Topnaar community.

The Namib is most spectacular in the central dune sea that stretches from Elizabeth Bay, south of Lüderitz, north for 480 km to Swakopmund and 140 km inland. Crescentic dunes covering a 20-km-wide strip along the coast are most impressive between Conception Bay and Sandwich Harbour. East of these dunes is a 40-km-wide belt of parallel north–south-oriented linear dunes that reach 170 m and are separated by dune streets of as much as 2.5 km wide and 50 km long.

Landscape and vegetation

As the dunes are forever shifting the only vegetation in the sand sea is clumps of hardy spiky ostrich grass (*Cladoraphis spinosa*) and Namib dune bushman grass (*Stipagrostis sabulicola*). The !nara (*Acanthosicyos horrida*) is endemic to the Namib and grows in river courses and in the dunes with roots reaching 40 m in length. This plant is a fascinating example of adaptation to desert conditions: to reduce water loss it has no leaves, photosynthesis taking place through its thorns. The !nara plays an important part in the culture and economy of the Topnaars. In the Kuiseb River Valley and the dunes south of the river !nara bushes are owned by Topnaar families, and ownership is transferred down the family line. Harvesting of the spiny fruits usually takes place from November to May. They can be eaten raw or cooked, and are dried in flat strips like a fruit roll. The dried pips are much in demand in the confectionery industry – large quantities of these 'butter pips' are sold in Walvis Bay from where they are exported to Cape Town.

Fauna

One of the attractions of the Namib Desert lies in the multitude of smaller creatures that are specially adapted to living in this harsh and inhospitable environment. Among its unique inhabitants is the Namib golden mole that 'swims' just below the surface of the sand. It spends its

NAMIBIA

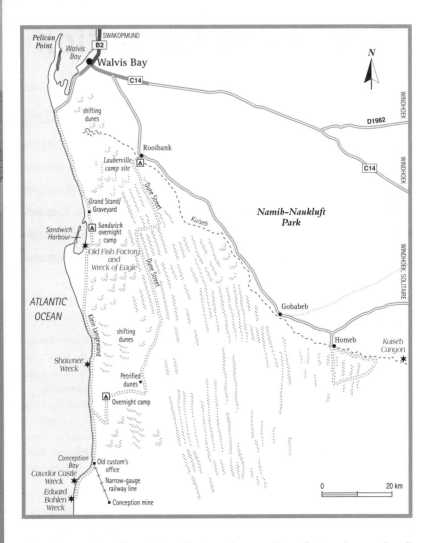

day underground, usually at the base of a clump of grass, and hunts for insect larvae and small reptiles at night. The dune hairy-footed gerbil is another small mammal endemic to the Namib. The shovel-snouted lizard is often seen foraging for seeds on dune slip faces. When surface temperatures exceed 40°C it does a thermal 'dance' by lifting a fore and hind leg in the air while supporting itself with its tail and quickly changing over to the other two legs.

Some 22 of the over 200 tok-tokkie or tenebrionid beetles recorded in the Namib have become adapted to the barren dunes. The key to their survival is the wind-blown plant material, animal faeces and dead insects that collect on the dune slip faces. Another important factor in the survival of the desert species is the precipitating fog, their only source of water.

Among the rich diversity of other inhabitants of the dunes is the web-footed gecko with its almost transparent body, Peringuey's adder (also known as the sidewinder), dancing white lady and cartwheel spiders, ants and fish moths.

The Namib coast is one of the strongholds of the brown hyaena which also occurs in the Kalahari, and the black-backed jackal. Gemsbok and springbok are sometimes encountered in the dune streets south of Homeb and gemsbok are also occasionally seen at Sandwich Harbour. A colony of Cape fur seals inhabits the stretch of coastline between Conception Bay and the wreck of the *Eduard Bohlen* that ran aground when she struck a sand bar in 1909.

Birding
In the dunes there is little birdlife, but you might see the dune lark which is endemic to the dunes between Walvis Bay and Lüderitz.

Sandwich Harbour and Walvis Bay are both wetlands of international importance. Sandwich Harbour is one of only four promontories along the Namib coast that offer suitable conditions for large numbers of shore birds. In summer the wetlands attract upwards of 145 000 birds, mainly migrants from the northern hemisphere, and in winter the area supports over 53 000 birds. In January 1998 a record 236 000 coastal shorebirds were counted, the largest single concentration in southern Africa. The birds are found mainly on the mudflats to the south of the lagoon.

The wetlands of Walvis Bay consist of the Walvis Bay Lagoon, the salt works, the beach and inter-tidal areas of Pelican Point, which forms the western arm of Walvis Bay, and the sewage reticulation works. The wetlands support up to 100 000 birds in summer and 50 000 in winter, as well as significant numbers of globally near-threatened species such as lesser flamingo, African black oystercatcher and Damara tern.

Specials: Damara tern, African black oystercatcher, chestnut-banded plover.
Water and wading birds: greater and lesser flamingos, great white pelican, avocet, black-winged stilt, black-necked grebe and white-fronted plover.
Migrants: curlew sandpiper, Caspian, common and Sandwich terns, bar-tailed godwit, turnstone, sanderling, common whimbrel, grey plover and red knot.
Other species: Hartlaub's, grey-headed and Cape gulls, swift tern, Cape cormorant.

Facilities
Lauberville camp, the first overnight stop, has four prefabricated buildings with beds and mattresses (no bedding), hot showers, flush toilets and electricity. You can also camp here. There are no facilities at the overnight stops on the second and third nights.

Getting there
Departure can be either from Windhoek or Walvis Bay. The start of the trail at Homeb is 290 km from Windhoek and 125 km from Walvis Bay.

THE ROUTE – 730 km Windhoek to Walvis Bay; 540 km Walvis Bay return
On the first day of the trail you head for Homeb, the Topnaar settlement on the banks of the Kuiseb River. You are briefed here on sand driving and other aspects of the trail, and then you set off to explore the dunes south of the Kuiseb. The reddish-orange of these dunes contrasts sharply with the colour of those at the coast where the fog water has leached the iron oxides to make the dunes light cream to almost white.

The route initially follows a wide dune street with coarse pebble sand, but you have to cross over the dunes, and this is where you will face your most serious challenge. Once across the dunes, the route takes you back to the Kuiseb River where you 'slide' down a dune into the river.

The Kuiseb River plays an important role in arresting the northward march of the dunes. Sand blown into the wide valley is periodically flushed downstream into the Ugab Delta, the

NAMIBIA

only place where the dunes have breached the river. Years may go by without the floodwaters reaching the Kuiseb, but in some years it flows for over 100 days. In 2000 the dam wall across the northern arm of the river could not contain the flood, and the river broke through the dunes to reach the sea for the first time since 1961.

Follow the river course downstream back to Homeb where you join a gravel road which you follow for 83 km to the overnight stop at Lauberville. Ancient palm trees and a plaque nearby mark the site of the mission station established by Reverend Heinrich Scheppmann of the Rhenish Mission Society at Rooibank in 1845.

On the second day the route initially follows a dune street until you get to Wake-Up Call where you have to make your way through the dunes. After negotiating this challenge, you continue along another dune street, and about 20 km after setting off the route swings west. You now have to traverse three linear dunes but this is easier than it sounds. You weave through several small dunes and down slip faces before reaching the dune crests. The route continues south along a wide dune street before swinging south-west where some petrified dunes can be seen. These dunes underlie the present sand sea and are indicative of a much earlier sand sea dating back 20 to 40 million years.

As you get closer to the camp you enter the crescentic dune belt with its apparently haphazard arrangement. The overnight stop is made in the dunes to avoid the dense banks of fog that are common overnight, but even so the fog sometimes penetrates deep into the desert.

Day three's route takes you over long flat dunes that are up to 1.5 km wide with fairly small slip faces to the coast, and then south to Conception, where diamonds were discovered in 1909 after the proclamation of the *Sperrgebiet* prohibited the pegging of new diamond claims south of 26 degrees latitude. At Conception Bay the remains of a customs post and police station can be seen. Opened in 1909, the station was moved the following year to Conception Water, about 11 km inland.

To the south lies the wreck of the *Eduard Bohlen*, which ran aground in 1909 while the captain was trying to position her in dense fog to drop a cargo of equipment for the diamond mine. The wreck lies some 500 m from the shore, half-buried under the sand. Hardly anything remains of the *Cawdor Castle* which ran aground about 4 km north of the *Eduard Bohlen* in 1926.

From the *Eduard Bohlen* the route skirts the mudflats and follows the old narrow-gauge railway line, built in 1912 to transport equipment landed at the coast to the mine at Conception Water. Weather-beaten houses and rusted pieces of machinery are bleak reminders of the diamond mining days. World War I interrupted mining activities and in 1929 Consolidated Diamond Mines, a subsidiary of De Beers, bought the diamond mining companies.

From Conception you head north up the coast. After about 27 km you reach the wreck of the *Shawnee*, an American trawler that ran aground in 1976. The Klein Langewand ('Little Long Wall') begins just north of the wreck and is a smaller version of the Langewand further south. Rising 170 m above the ocean, the dunes form a solid 'wall' right up to the coast. Since at high tide the waves lap the base of the dune, this 13-km-long section can be negotiated only at low tide.

A short way beyond the end of the Klein Langewand the trail leads you up and through the coastal dunes. The remainder of the day is a roller-coaster ride as you tackle one high slip face after another. There are several between 70 and 100 m high, but fortunately by the time you have to tackle them you will have mastered the technique of slip face driving. The route heads to Sandwich Harbour where you visit the remains of a factory where fish were salted and cured in the mid-1800s. Nearby is the wreck of the *Eagle*, beached here in 1861 after she was declared unseaworthy. The hull was initially used as a storeroom for dried fish.

Conception Expedition

>  VITAL **INFO**
> - You should have at least 15" tyres deflated to 1 Kpa for sand driving. Your vehicles need points to attach tow-ropes for recovery.
> - To slide down a slip face engage first or second gear low range, to let the en gine compression do the braking. Keep your feet away from the clutch as the vehicle could run out of control if you depress it. If you feel the vehicle moving sideways, accelerate gently to straighten.

The dunes have nearly swamped the wreck, testimony to the changes that have taken place in the coastline over the last century. Sandwich Harbour has changed markedly over the past 20 years and the northern wetlands with their freshwater pools and reed beds have shrunk from 1 km wide to under 200 m. At the same time a sand spit has moved eastwards and closed off the lagoon. It is difficult to believe that this was once a deep-water anchorage for sailing vessels, from the end of the 1700s for almost a century.

Before reaching the overnight stop in the dunes above Sandwich Harbour you will 'slide' down several more slip faces, including a final 70-m slide into the camp site.

From the overnight stop the route leads northwards through the coastal dunes. The name 'the Graveyard' only hints at the enormous slip faces that have to be negotiated. Grand Stand is the ultimate challenge to your driving skills today, but there is a chicken run if your vehicle does not have the power to climb up the very steep dunes. After about 12 km of driving through the dunes you descend to the beach from where it is an easy 34-km drive along the coastline to Paaltjies, originally the southern boundary of the Walvis Bay enclave where the trail ends.

LOGISTICS AND PLANNING

Fuel: The distance from Windhoek to Walvis Bay where the trail ends is about 730 km. Since 280 km is over soft sand you should carry fuel to cover about 940 km at normal consumption.
Water: You will need at least 40 litres. You can refill at Lauberville camp at the end of the first day.
Food: This is a fully catered trail except for alcoholic beverages and cold drinks.
Equipment: Pots, pans, braai grids, tables, chemical toilets and showers are provided, but you must bring your own tent, chair, bedroll, sleeping bag, cutlery, mug and plate.
Best times: Trails are conducted all year and the searing desert temperatures that are the rule further inland are usually moderated by the cool south-westerly wind blowing off the Atlantic Ocean. Hot easterly winds can cause temperatures to soar to 40°C between May and August and occasionally whip up sandstorms. Rain falls rarely, the average annual rainfall at Walvis Bay being only 10 mm. Along the coast dense banks of fog occur on average every three days, usually rolling in off the coast in the afternoon and clearing up by mid-morning the following day.

Booking

Trails are conducted for groups consisting of at least 12 people and a maximum of 10 vehicles. Bookings must be made through Uri Adventures. The trail price includes expert guidance, communication radios, recovery equipment and meals, but a self-catering option is also available.
Permits: Uri Adventures, PO Box 1591, Windhoek, Namibia, tel: (+264 61) 23-1246, fax: 23-1703, e-mail: jacques@uriadventures.com

Naukluft 4x4 Trail

Towering above the sand desert to the west and the farmlands to the east, the rugged Naukluft massif, which is part of Namibia's Great Escarpment, is a challenge to all, even experienced drivers. The 74.5-km-long journey takes two days, following trails blazed by pioneering farmers who once eked out an existence here. The rugged mountain appears inhospitable, and so its flat plateau comes as a complete surprise. It provided ideal grazing for the farmers of decades ago and today attracts herds of springbok after good rains. Along the way you will be treated to inspiring views, and the crystal-clear perennial pools tucked away in some of the kloofs are another of the secrets of this harsh environment.

THE PARK
The Naukluft Mountain Zebra Park was established in 1968 as a sanctuary for the Hartmann's mountain zebra after the then Administration of South West Africa bought the farm Naukluft (named after a narrow kloof in the south-east of the mountains). More farms were later bought, including a number to the west of the massif, to form a 21-km-wide corridor along which gemsbok could migrate between the escarpment and the dune sea. It became part of the Namib-Naukluft Park.

The park came into existence in 1979 when a large tract of Diamond Area II south of the Kuiseb River and unoccupied state land were amalgamated with the Namib Desert Park north of the Kuiseb River. In 1986 the Namib-Naukluft Park was enlarged again and it is now the third largest conservation area in Africa, after the Selous National Park in Tanzania and Botswana's Central Kalahari Game Reserve.

Landscape and vegetation
Rugged mountains with sheer cliffs, deeply incised valleys and undulating mountain plateaux are the main features of the Naukluft.

Particularly impressive among Naukluft's spectacular tufa formations are the huge ones at the pools in the Naukluft, about 30 minutes' walk from the camp site. These porous limestone formations were created by the evaporation of calcium carbonate-rich water filtering through the dolomite rocks. The size of some of these formations provides evidence of a much wetter climate in the geologically recent past.

As the park is situated on the edge of the Namib Desert, its average rainfall is very low – less than 200 mm a year – but several of its deep gorges have perennial springs. Namaqua and

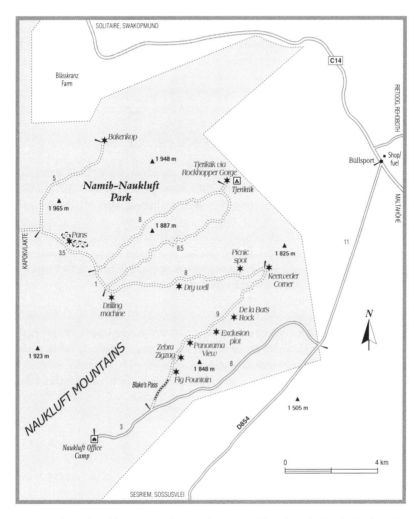

common cluster figs, false ebony and sweet thorn trees thrive along the kloofs. On the rocky slopes may be seen quiver trees, *Euphorbia virosa*, blue-leafed corkwood and moringa trees.

Occasional stands of resurrection bush (*Myrothamnus flabellifolius*), like soldiers on a parade ground, are conspicuous on exposed slopes. During dry periods the branches and leaves of this small bushy shrub fold inward and appear to be dead. But within hours of good rains they unfurl and sprout bright green leaves – hence the common name. Early settlers used it as a substitute for tea which explains its Afrikaans names – *teebossie* (also called *bergboegoe*).

Typical Karoo-like species such as the kapokbos (*Eriocephalus ericoides*) dominate the vegetation on the plateaux. Scattered mountain thorn, Namibian resin tree and shepherd's tree also grow here, while clumps of buffalo-thorn can be found on the margins of seasonal pans.

Game-viewing and fauna

Family groups of Hartmann's mountain zebra occur throughout the park. Gemsbok and springbok are more likely to be seen on the plains to the west of the mountain but at times they migrate onto the plateau. Kudu favour the densely wooded kloofs and mountain slopes with

NAMIBIA

cover, and are fairly common. Look out in rocky areas for troops of baboons, the rock dassie and the dainty klipspringer which usually occur in pairs or small family groups. The park has a healthy population of leopard but this shy and nocturnal species is seldom seen. Spotted hyaena, another of the nocturnal predators, make their way from the plains into the mountains occasionally, and cheetah, which favour the plains at the foot of the mountain, are seen from time to time alongside roads in the area. Black-backed jackal, caracal and African wild cat are among the smaller predators you may spot.

Birding
Birdlife at Naukluft is not prolific (just over 200 species have been recorded here), but birding can still be exciting since the mountains lie at the southern limit of distribution of endemic escarpment species such as the Herero chat, white-tailed shrike, Monteiro's hornbill and Rüppell's korhaan.
Raptors: Verreaux's eagle, augur buzzard, southern pale chanting goshawk, lanner falcon.
Other species: rosy-faced lovebird, Ludwig's bustard, pale-winged starling, sabota and long-billed larks, African red-eye bulbul, mountain wheatear, bokmakierie, dusky sunbird, Layard's titbabbler, black-headed canary and double-banded courser.

Facilities
Tjeriktik Camp has four A-shaped stone shelters with built-in cement bunks but you must bring your own sleeping bag and mattress. Other amenities include a communal fireplace, cold showers and toilets. Refuse bins are not provided.

You can stay before or after the trail at the **Naukluft camp site**. It has shady sites, braai places, hot showers and flush toilets. Bookings must be made well in advance through Namibia Wildlife Resorts.

CAMPING FACILITIES AND ACCOMMODATION:
Tsauchab River Camping, 65 km south-west of the Naukluft office on the D854. It has shady camp sites.
Betesda Rest Camp, situated 92 km south-west of the Naukluft office on the D854. It has shady camp sites.
Solitaire Country Lodge, at Solitaire, 78 km from Naukluft office. Bungalows, camp site, shop, tyre repairs and fuel.
Büllsport Guest Farm, 22 km from Naukluft office on the D854. En-suite rooms, farm shop and fuel.

Activities
Don't miss the **crystal-clear pools** in the Naukluft River, which are approximately 30 minutes' walk upstream from the camp site.
- The **Olive Trail** is named after the abundance of wild olive trees growing along the route. It features a deep narrow gorge where chains have been anchored to the rocky walls to assist hikers at a difficult spot. It takes between 4 and 5 hours to hike the 10-km trail.
- The **Waterkloof Trail** is more demanding since it climbs steeply to the plateau before looping back along the Naukluft River with its irresistible pools. The 17-km-long trail takes six to seven hours.
- If you are fit and time is not a consideration, you can tackle the **Naukluft Hiking Trail**. This 120-km-long trail takes eight days, but shorter four-day options are possible.

Naukluft 4x4 Trail

Reservations are not required for the day walks, but the Naukluft Hiking Trail must be booked through Namibia Wildlife Resorts (*see* Booking on page 119).

Getting there

The turnoff to Naukluft is signposted 11 km south-west of Büllsport on the D854, and it is 11 km from the gate to the office. From Windhoek head south on the tarred B1 and take the road signposted to Klein Aub, 4 km south of Rehoboth. The remaining 150 km is a good gravel road via Rietoog and Büllsport. Approaching from the south, turn west to Maltahöhe (4 km south of Mariental); continue on tar for 110 km to Maltahöhe, followed by 130 km on gravel.

THE ROUTE – 130 km Büllsport return

Points of interest along the trail have been marked but unfortunately the trail booklet is no longer available. Brief information about most of these points is provided in the route description and indicated with the corresponding marker. The numbers provided in brackets below correspond to the marked points of interest on the trail.

From the Naukluft office drive back towards the entrance gate for about 3 km before turning left onto a 4x4 track. Engage four-wheel drive low range here as you'll soon reach the bottom of Blake's Pass (1) named after Robbie Blake who built the rough track to the plateau in the late 1940s. The Fig Fountain (2), a popular drinking spot for Hartmann's mountain zebra and other animals, where you might hear the shrill metallic call of rosy-faced lovebirds, is a short way on. If you scan the cliffs to the west you'll see the distinctive enormous nests of Verreaux's eagles high up on the rocky ledges. The painted white footprints indicate the route that trailists follow on the Olive Trail.

A short but very steep ascent awaits you at Zebra Zigzag (3). As rocks on the track are often dislodged by zebra we advise you to stop to remove those that might cause wheel spin, and to negotiate the incline in low range first gear.

With the first major obstacle behind you, it's an easy 2-km drive to Panorama View (4) with its stunning views of the plains far below and the distant tabletop Zaris Mountain range with its different coloured layers. The track clings to the mountain slopes as you make your way to

HARTMANN'S MOUNTAIN ZEBRA

Hartmann's mountain zebra are endemic to Namibia and the south-western corner of Angola, occurring mainly along the escarpment and rocky river valleys extending into the Namib. They differ slightly from the closely related Cape mountain zebra which inhabit isolated mountainous areas in South Africa's Eastern and Western Cape provinces. The most significant difference is that the black and white stripes on the rump of Hartmann's mountain zebra are more even in width. Hartmann's mountain zebra stand about 23 cm taller and are about 50 kg heavier than the Cape mountain zebra. Hartmann's mountain zebra are specially protected in Namibia and may be hunted only with a permit issued by the Namibian Ministry of Environment and Tourism.

NAMIBIA

a fenced exclusion plot (5) where researchers measure the amount of food produced by plants and De la Bat's Rock (6), a popular photographic stop. This large dolomite boulder (with its colourful striped patterns) was named in honour of Namibia's first Director of Nature Conservation, Bernabé de la Bat.

At Keerweder Corner (7) the track makes a hairpin bend, and after less than 1 km you reach a picnic spot (8) with railway sleeper benches that affords views far into the distance. Further along you pass an old dry well (9), that was dug laboriously and in vain, with hand tools, at some time in the past.

After just over 1.5 km a drilling machine (10) bears testimony to the ingenuity of farmer Robbie Blake who built the track up to the plateau to drill for water for his livestock. Piece by piece over a two-week period the machine was transported up the mountain on a modified army surplus truck spanned together with a Willy's Jeep to assist it up the steeper slopes. At dangerous places a rope was tied around the truck driver's waist and someone holding the other end of the rope would walk next to the truck, from which the driver's door had been removed. The plan was that, if the truck fell off the track, the driver could be pulled to safety.

Here the track turns off to the right down the appropriately named Rockhopper Gorge (11). Negotiate this in low range while letting the vehicle 'walk' slowly over the rocks. Further on the track crosses a ridge; from here it is a short drive to Tjeriktik Camp, 28.5 km from the start, a leisurely 4-hour drive. Tjeriktik is the onomatopoeic Afrikaans name for the tit-babbler, a dull blueish-grey bird with a black-streaked white throat that is easily identified by its bright chestnut undertail colour.

Soon after setting off on the second day you pass the site of an old stock kraal and a well, and then you reach a riverbed. Large boulders can present a challenge to your driving skills, so this section should be driven with care. On leaving the riverbed the track clings to the mountain slopes as it climbs steeply up the appropriately named Four Passes.

About 8 km after leaving Tjeriktik you join the track to Bakenkop (12), and a short way on you pass a number of pans (13). They originated as rolling places for zebras taking 'dust baths' and gradually grew deeper and bigger. Over time trees grew around them, and after good rains they can hold water for several months, attracting a variety of water birds and animals. The turnoff to Kapokvlakte (14), named after the abundance of kapokbos (*Eriocephalus ericoides*) growing on the vast flat expanse of the plateau, is the next junction.

The trail heads across Kapokvlakte to the 1 960-m-high Bakenkop (15) from where you look down into the deep valley carved through the escarpment by the Tsondab River some 760 m below. As there is only one track onto the plateau you have to retrace your trail over familiar

KAPOKBOS

This bush was given its Afrikaans name kapokbos owing to the resemblance of the white woolly seed fibres to those of the *kapokboom*, a species indigenous to India. In the 16th century the Dutch East India Company exported the 'kapok' (white silky fibres) from India to Holland where it was used as a filling for cushions. The Dutch settlers at the Cape used the seed fibres of the kapokbos as a substitute. The plants flower after rains and soon afterwards their seed capsules transform the plateau into a large white carpet.

Naukluft 4x4 Trail

VITAL INFO

- Report at the Naukluft office for a briefing and equipment check before setting off on the trail.
- Ensure that wide low profile tyres are not under-inflated as the sidewalls are more likely to be damaged than standard 'bakkie' tyres in the rocky terrain.
- Black mambas are plentiful in Naukluft and don't seem to hibernate. If you do see any, treat them with due respect!

terrain except for a 1 km stretch between the Tjeriktik junction and the drilling machine. But the magnificent scenery provides a totally different perspective when you travel in the opposite direction. On your way down the pass watch out for vehicles coming up onto the plateau.

LOGISTICS AND PLANNING

Fuel: You can refuel at Büllsport farm and Solitaire, respectively 22 and 78 km from the Naukluft office.

Water: Drinking water is available at the overnight camp.

Food: Food and alcohol can be bought at supermarkets and liquor outlets in Windhoek, Mariental and Swakopmund, depending on your approach route.

Firewood: Take wood or charcoal for your overnight stop since the collection of wood is not allowed.

Best times: The trail can be done throughout the year, but the moderate temperatures of spring and autumn are the most pleasant. Daytime temperatures in winter are comfortable but at night it can be freezing cold on the plateau, with temperatures dropping to below freezing point. Snowfalls occur very occasionally. Summer days are generally hot but can be cool when there is a fresh south-westerly wind. February to April has the highest rainfall and after heavy rains the tracks can be partially washed away, necessitating the temporary closure of the trail.

Booking

Naukluft 4x4 Trail and Camp Site: Reservations must be made through Namibia Wildlife Resorts, Private Bag 13267, Windhoek, Namibia, tel: (+264 61) 23-6975, fax: 22-4900, e-mail reservations@nwr.com.na. Groups are limited to a maximum of four vehicles and 16 people.
Tsauchab River Camping, tel and fax: (+264 63) 29-3416, e-mail: tsauchab@triponline.net
Betesda Rest Camp, tel: (+264 63) 69-3253, fax: 69-3252, e-mail: betesda@iway.na
Solitaire Country Lodge, tel: (+264 61) 24-0375, fax: 25-6598, e-mail: afrideca@mweb.com.na
Büllsport Guest Farm, tel: (+264 63) 69-3371, fax: 69-3372, e-mail: buellsport@natron.net

The winding Four Passes route is negotiated on the second day of the Naukluft 4x4 Trail.

NAMIBIA

Kaokoveld

Rugged mountains, deep river valleys, boulder-strewn slopes and semi-desert plains merge in the north-western corner of Namibia to create a wild and unspoiled wilderness, the Kaokoveld. This is home to the Himba who follow the same way of life as they have done for centuries. Here, too, the famous desert-dwelling elephant can be found along with black rhino, giraffe, gemsbok, springbok and a rich diversity of endemic reptiles.

THE REGION

Kaokoveld, the geographical term for the north-west of Namibia, consists of Kaokoland which stretches southwards from the Kunene to the Hoanib River and from the Hoanib River to the Ugab River in what was formerly known as Damaraland. In terms of the political or regional boundaries, it is known as the Kunene Region.

The people

The Himba are Herero-speaking pastoralists who remained behind in north-western Namibia when most of their kin moved to central Namibia around 1750. They live in semi-permanent settlements that are dotted throughout the area, and are constantly on the move in search of grazing for their cattle.

The rich gleaming ochre colour of the women's skin is created by a mixture of butterfat, powdered oxides and herbs which they apply to protect their skin against the harsh sun. The women wear leather aprons, and leather headdresses (or the absence thereof) indicate their marital status. Married women wear a headdress known as the *erembe* which is worn inside out by widows, while newly married women wear a bridal headdress (*ekori*) for at least a month after their wedding.

The men are tall and well built and are often compared with the Maasai of East Africa. Boys and young men wear a plait (*ondatu*) until they get permission to marry; at this stage it is split into two and covered with a headdress. Men wear the headdress permanently once they get permission to marry and it may only be removed during the mourning period of a close relative, after which the head is covered again.

Their dome-shaped homes are made from mopane saplings covered with a mixture of mud and cow dung. In settlements such as Purros their homes are easily distinguished from Herero homes which are square or rectangular with a thatched roof.

Small groups of Herero people also live in Kaokoland, while Sesfontein has a population of Topnaars (*see* Conception Expedition, page 109). Damara people live in widely scattered small settlements in the area south of the Hoanib River.

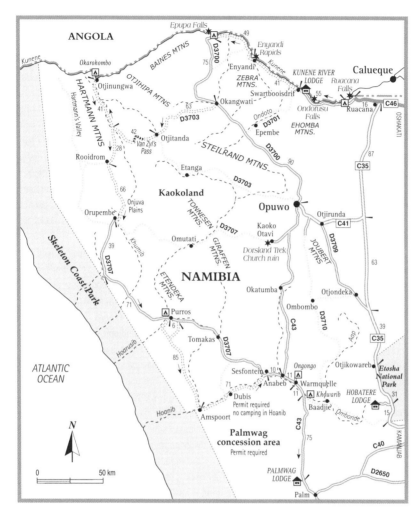

Vegetation

The vegetation of this remote wilderness region ranges from the extensive mopaneveld that is found in the eastern highlands to semi-desert plains that are transformed into grasslands after good summer rains.

Lush riverine forests of sandpaper and common cluster figs, jackal-berry, buffalo-thorn and real fan palms (locally known as makalani palms) grace the banks of the Kunene River. Ancient camel thorn and ana trees grow along the ephemeral rivers that flow westwards.

The bottle tree with its straight trunk which seems to grow out of the rock, is unlikely to escape your attention. It is endemic to the area and is closely related to the elephant's trunk (which is also known as halfmens or *noordpool*) of the Richtersveld (*see* Richtersveld National Park, page 183).

Conspicuous between November and May are the beautiful pink to mauve flowers of *Adenium boehmianum* which is also endemic. Other noteworthy species include *Hoodia parviflora* with its light-orange flowers and several corkwood (*Commiphora*) species that have a restricted distribution in north-western Namibia.

121

Fauna and game-viewing

The famous desert-dwelling elephant, black rhino and giraffe are the main game-viewing drawcards for most visitors to Kaokoveld. Were it not for the dedication of conservationists Garth Owen-Smith, Blythe Loutit, Ina Britz and others, the black rhino and elephant would have been wiped out completely.

During Namibia's liberation struggle large numbers of animals were indiscriminately shot by members of the South African Defence Force. The arming of the Himba people with rifles for 'self-protection' invariably also resulted in poaching for food, ivory and rhino horn. By 1983 only a few black rhino still survived in Kaokoland, while the population south of the Hoanib River was down to 23. Of an estimated 300 elephant in Kaokoland in 1970 only 71 were left by the mid-1980s.

Realising that poaching could be brought under control only by involving local communities, concerned conservationists formed the Save The Rhino Fund and put a system of community game guards into place. This initiative was so successful that it has become a model for other community conservation projects.

The elephant (*Loxodonta africana*) of north-western Namibia is the same species as other elephants of southern Africa but is one of only two groups of desert-dwelling elephants in the world; the other population is in Mali, North Africa. They have a smaller body mass and much larger feet than elephant living in more favourable habitats. The elephant move mainly up and down the river valleys with their riverine forests and ephemeral springs, but occasionally migrate north or south between the valleys. Around 600 elephant inhabit the north-west.

You might also come across the equally famous black rhino which belongs to the western sub-species, *Diceros bicornis bicornis*. They occur south of the Hoanib River in family groups consisting of a female, young calf and sub-adult. The males are solitary.

Black-faced impala are endemic to Kaokoland and south-western Angola where they number less than 500. Their most striking feature is the distinctive purplish-black facial blaze, while their coats are darker than those of the common impala. In the 1970s some 260 animals were translocated to the Etosha National Park where the population now exceeds 1 500.

The Kaokoland rock dassie is also endemic to the area. It is paler than other rock dassies and the patch of long hair in the centre of its back is white or pale yellow and not black. Originally classified as a species in its own right, it has been reclassified as a sub-species of the widely-spread rock dassie.

Giraffe occur mainly along the river valleys where they browse the camel thorn trees, but are occasionally seen on rocky slopes and crossing the plains. In the Kaokoveld there are numerous springs, but giraffe have not been seen drinking, presumably obtaining their water requirements from the vegetation.

Over the last few years the gemsbok and springbok populations have increased significantly and it is not uncommon to come across herds several hundred strong. Other species you might encounter include Hartmann's mountain zebra, kudu, steenbok, klipspringer and the diminutive Damara dik-dik.

A few hippo have managed to survive against all odds in the Kunene River. This river is also home to the Cape clawless otter and the water mongoose.

Lion range through the area and a pride has taken up residence in the Palmwag area, while leopard, cheetah and spotted hyaena also occur. Other carnivores you might chance upon include African wild cat, black-backed jackal, bat-eared fox and aardwolf.

North-western Namibia has an incredibly rich diversity of endemic reptiles. Among the more than three dozen endemics are Anchieta's dwarf python which is about a third of the length of the southern African python. Since the Kunene River is home to water monitor and Nile crocodile, you should always be careful when you are in the vicinity of the river.

Birding
There are several noteworthy ticks among the region's 275 bird species. The Cinderella waxbill and collared palm-thrush can be seen in southern Africa only along the Kunene River which lies at the southern limit of their distribution.

Endemics and near-endemics of north-western Namibia include the bare-cheeked babbler, Herero chat, Monteiro's hornbill, white-tailed shrike, Rüppell's parrot, violet wood-hoopoe and Carp's tit. Several species with a restricted distribution elsewhere in Namibia can also be ticked here as they use the Kunene River as a flyway. Among these are the white-browed coucal, swamp boubou, yellow-bellied greenbul, African mourning dove and Meves's starling.
Raptors: augur buzzard, lappet-faced vulture.
Other species: ostrich, red-billed francolin, pied kingfisher, southern yellow-billed hornbill, grey lourie, northern black korhaan, Rüppell's korhaan and pied crow.

Facilities
Hippo Pools, 16.5 km west of Ruacana town. Camp site under mopane trees next to Hippo Pool.
Kunene River Lodge, 67 km west of Ruacana town. Magnificent setting under lush riverine forest. Camp sites with braai places, hot showers, flush toilets, restaurant.
Epupa Falls camp site, at Epupa Falls. Beautiful camp sites under makalani palms, braai places, cold showers, flush toilets.
Okarohombo camp site, on banks of Kunene River at the head of the Marienfluss. Camp sites, braai places, water tap, cold showers and flush toilets.
Purros camp site, at Purros on the banks of the Hoarusib River. Shady camp sites, braai places, water tap, cold showers and flush toilets.
Fort Sesfontein in Sesfontein. En-suite rooms, restaurant, swimming pool, camp sites with hot showers and flush toilets.
Ongongo camp site, 27 km east of Sesfontein. Camp site close to sparkling mountain pool, braai facilities, cold showers, toilets.
Khowarib camp site, 33 km south-east of Sesfontein. Camp sites on banks of Khowarib Schlucht, traditional Himba and Damara huts, cold showers and toilets.
Palmwag Lodge, 106.5 km south of Sesfontein overlooking a spring in the Uniab River. Camp sites, braai places, showers, flush toilets, reed and thatch bungalows, restaurant, swimming pool.

EPUPA HYDRO-ELECTRIC SCHEME
Plans to build Namibia's second hydro-electric power plant on the Kunene River, the second plant on the Kunene – and for that matter in Namibia – were announced in 1990. A feasibility study recommended two possible sites: one at Epupa and the other at the Baines Mountains further downstream. The Namibian government favoured the site at Epupa which would flood the falls and push back up to 80 km upstream of the dam wall. The Angolan government, on the other hand, preferred the Baines site. As the two governments have been unable to agree on the site, the project appears to have been shelved, at least for the time being.

NAMIBIA

Activities
Kunene River Lodge offers **trips in inflatables** down the Ondoruso rapids and **quad bike trips** of the surrounding areas.

Visit the Purros and Anmire **traditional villages** to gain a fascinating insight into the culture and lifestyle of the Himba and Damara people respectively.

Getting there
From Windhoek follow the B1 north to Tsumeb and continue through Ondangwa and Oshakati to Ruacana village. The distance is 890 km.

THE ROUTE – 950–1 000 km Ruacana to Palmwag via Marienfluss and Purros

Ruacana village was originally established to house the construction workers who built the Ruacana hydro-electric power plant in the 1970s. During Namibia's liberation struggle it became a heavily fortified South African Defence Force military base surrounded by security fences and landmines. From Ruacana village retrace your tracks to the main tar road (C46), turn left and after about 6.4 km you will be greeted by a magnificent view of the Kunene River Valley, and a weir, which forms a large inland lake. The inlet tunnel for the Ruacana hydro-electric power station is situated at the weir.

You reach the turnoff to a viewpoint overlooking the Ruacana Falls 7.4 km further. Here the Kunene River plunges over a 700-m-wide V-shaped rock shelf into a 120-m-deep gorge. Since the building of a weir 1 km upstream and the Calueque Dam some 40 km further upstream, water only pours over the 'falls' when the Kunene River comes down in flood. At the falls the river swings west, for some 350 km forming the boundary between Namibia and Angola.

The surge bayhead which looks like a giant cement reservoir, two buildings and transmission lines are the only signs of the Ruacana hydro-electric power station which is located in three huge underground caverns.

At Hippo Pool, a short way on, the tar gives way to graded road which is usually in good condition up to Swartbooisdrif. The road climbs steeply up a hill and the enormous tufa formations to the left provide evidence of a much wetter period. Following the course of the Kunene you have occasional glimpses of the river. Look north, about 42 km after joining the gravel road, and you will notice that the river changes course suddenly. A short detour brings you to Ondorusu Gorge, one of the gems along the Kunene River. Here the river swings north and, after dropping over the Ondorusu Falls, turns west to thunder through a narrow gorge down a series of rapids. The falls disappear completely under the seething mass of water when the Kunene River is in flood. Large bottle trees are perched like sentinels on the rocky slopes on the Angolan side of the river.

Retrace your tracks to the main road and turn right. After 8.6 km you will reach Kunene River Lodge. This is one of the best places to tick the rare bare-cheeked babbler.

Although the distance from Kunene River Lodge to Epupa is a mere 96 km, the next leg will take you the better part of a day, so an early start is advisable. Swartbooisfdrif where the Dorsland Trekkers crossed into Namibia on their return from Angola in 1928 and 1929 (*see* box, page 132) is 4.1 km from the lodge. A 500-m detour south along a gravel road brings you to the top of the hills where a monument to these hardy Trekkers was built following their return from Angola.

Retrace your tracks and turn left (west) to continue to Epupa. The road soon deteriorates into a rough track which at places leads steeply up and down rocky passes as you skirt the northern foothills of the Zebra Mountains. Engage low range and gently tackle the steep ascents and descents with their loose rocks. The range owes its name to the alternating dark bands of dolerite and vegetation on its slopes.

About 7 km after the last rocky pass you reach the Himba settlement of Enyandi where the Kunene River splits into several channels with challenging rapids. Here the track winds further inland before meeting briefly with the river at Otjihandjavero settlement. At Otjimbapa the track to Okangwati splits off to the left, but you continue in a north-westerly direction for just under 18 km to Oronditi. Here the track swings inland and becomes rockier, best negotiated at slow speed in low range.

You will find the Epupa Falls about 33 km beyond the Okangwati turnoff. Here the Kunene River splits into several channels around rock islands with stately makalani palms, and leaps over a series of spectacular cascades and minor falls into a scenic gorge where baobabs cling to the cliff edges. The main fall on the southern bank drops 36 m into a deep narrow gorge which merges further downstream with a bigger gorge. To appreciate the breathtaking scenery fully you have to follow a footpath along the slopes of the hills above the gorge until the entire panorama is revealed. The rocks at Epupa are the oldest in Namibia, dating to some 2.1 billion years ago.

Head south along the D3700 from Epupa Falls for 700 m and turn right to reach a viewpoint 400 m off the road (used by the South African Defence Force as a guard post). It enjoys a bird's-eye view over the falls and the magnificent forest of makalani palms lining the banks of the Kunene River. Back on the D3700 the track wends its way between the Omuhonga and Omavanda mountains; just north of Okangwati you cross the Omuhonga River with its magnificent fringe of ana trees.

Okangwati, a former SADF military base, is about 75 km from Epupa. From here you can travel via Opuwo and Kaoko Otavi to the Khumib River (a distance of about 280 km), or you can head west to Van Zyl's Pass and the Marienfluss (the route we describe here) and join up later with the Khumib River.

From the western outskirts of Okangwati the track heads south-west and after about 4 km you cross a dry riverbed where it splits. The split to the left goes via Otjiyandjasemo hot springs before it rejoins the Etengwa track, while the main track continues to Etengwa for 27 km. Further on you pass Okauwa and a few kilometres beyond Ovireva Dam the condition of the track deteriorates as it makes its way through a rocky gorge before reaching Otjitanda. A short way beyond Otjitanda a track to Etanga splits off to the left, but you must bear to the right here, continuing to Otjihende. The track soon starts twisting and turning as it makes its way to the 1 323-m-high top of Van Zyl's Pass where there is a viewpoint to the right of the track with great views of the Namib plains far below.

Van Zyl's Pass, the most challenging section along the route, was named after Ben van Zyl, the 'Bantu' Commissioner for the Kaokoveld in the 1960s. Together with his right-hand man Jeremiah and teams of Himba, he built numerous tracks in Kaokoland.

The pass should be descended in low range first gear as the engine compression will act as a brake. You will drop some 770 m in altitude as you make your way down, and after passing through a valley you emerge onto the southern edge of the Marienfluss. Keep right where the track splits and continue for 17 km to the Marienfluss junction where you turn right.

For the next 41 km the track winds along the spectacular Marienfluss Valley to Otjinungwa and the Okarohombo camp site on the banks of the Kunene River.

The Hartmann Mountains to the west (and Hartmann's mountain zebra) were named after the German geologist Dr Georg Hartmann who undertook several surveys in north-western

NAMIBIA

Namibia between 1894 and 1900. To the east of the valley, which is up to 9 km wide, the rugged Otjihipa Mountains form a formidable barrier rising over 1 500 m above the valley floor.

After good rains the sandy valley is transformed into grasslands that attract herds of gemsbok and springbok as well as flocks of ostriches.

The 'fairy circles' – circular patches without any vegetation – are intriguing. Their origin remains a mystery despite several research projects.

From the Kunene River, backtrack for 41 km, and at the Van Zyl's Pass junction you keep right, continuing for about 28 km to Rooidrom, a well-known landmark. The track now heads south over the Rooidrom Pass and 51 km later you emerge onto the Onjuva Plains and the Orupembe/Otjihaa track. Turn right here and after 15 km you reach the settlement of Orupembe from where a graded track continues for 110 km to Purros. For most of the way the road traverses spectacular open plains set against the backdrop of the Etendeka Mountains to the east. These spectacular flat-topped mountains were formed some 130 million years ago when lava flows formed horizontal sheets of up to 2 km thick, but much of this has since been eroded away.

The 162-km leg from Purros to Sesfontein via the Hoarusib River will take you nearly a full day. After crossing the Hoarusib River, make your way along its southern bank to Purros settlement, cross the Orupembe/Sesfontein road and, less than 1 km on, climb into the river. After about 15 km you reach a spring and a magnificent poort which is impassable when the water table is high. In such an event you will have to backtrack to the graded road and follow it towards Sesfontein for about 6 km and turn right onto a track which links up with the Hoarusib Poort track from the north.

Exactly 2.8 km beyond the poort in the Hoarusib River you will see a track leading to the left out of the valley. Take this track and keep right at the split that you reach 6.4 km further on. The track traverses wide-open plains for 61 km until you reach Amspoort, a narrow rocky gorge in the Hoanib River. Look out here for a track heading east; follow it for about 1 km and then make your way into the river.

Elephant are frequently encountered in the valley and should be treated with the necessary respect. Unfortunately irresponsible visitors sometimes antagonise the elephants and there have been isolated incidents where vehicles have been charged. Never approach too closely and don't leave your vehicle. If you do stop to take photographs make sure that you can make a quick getaway.

There is also a healthy population of giraffe in the valley and seeing them against the backdrop of rugged mountain slopes is a unique experience. They are very tame and are often encountered resting in the shade of the acacia trees.

About 36 km from Amspoort you pass through a narrow rocky gateway. Here a track branches off to the left to follow the Ganamub Canyon to the Purros/Sesfontein road. Another 11.5 km along the Hoanib Canyon brings you to the Palmwag concession control gate where you must pay a fee.

The route leaves the river and further along splits into numerous tracks with axle-deep powdery silt. When you reach the silt, stop and close all windows as the fine powder is thrown in waves over the front windscreen if you drive too fast. Driving slowly is the best way to get through, and remember to keep clear of the vehicle ahead of you to avoid the silt.

Approximately 15.6 km beyond the control gate you join up with the Purros/Sesfontein road, and 7 km on you reach Sesfontein, named after the six fountains surfacing here. Sesfontein's history dates back to 1896 when the German authorities established a control post to

Kaokoveld

prevent the spread of foot-and-mouth disease. A German military station was built in 1901 and converted to a fort from 1905 to 1906 which housed 40 soldiers and 25 horses.

As you head east along the C43, the turnoff to Ongongo is signposted at Warmquelle, 21.6 km beyond Sesfontein. Warmquelle owes its German name to the hot spring that surfaces at the base of the hills. Also to be seen here are the remains of an aqueduct built in 1910/11 to water the extensive gardens, laid down by Dr C A Schlettwein, which can still be seen. From the turnoff it is 5.7 km along a rough track to Ongongo where a mountain stream plunges several metres over a tufa waterfall into a crystal-clear pool; a complete surprise in such a harsh and forbidding rocky landscape.

Continuing along the C43 you cross the Hoanib River 11 km beyond the Ongongo turnoff. A short way on, a signposted turnoff points the way to the camp site situated on the banks of the Khowarib Schlucht. The very first road which linked Outjo and Sesfontein partly followed the spectacular 25-km-long gorge. A visit to the nearby Anmire traditional village will give you an insight into the culture of the Damara people inhabiting this harsh landscape.

Following the C43 south, the good gravel road traverses plains, low hills, boulder-strewn slopes and river valleys. Some 56.5 km beyond the Khowarib turnoff, a signpost points the way to the Auob Canyon, 11.3 km along a rough track.

Still further south you pass the main access route into the Palmwag concession area and 3.2 km later you reach the turnoff to Palmwag Lodge. The lodge is an oasis in the barren landscape and owes its name to the makalani palms surrounding a small spring in the Uniab River. Desert-dwelling elephant frequently drink at the spring and also walk through the camp at night, so take care!

The Palmwag area is famous for its desert-dwelling black rhino; you can go in search of them by following the numerous tracks criss-crossing the concession area. A worthwhile excursion is to head to Van Zyl's Gat. Here the Uniab River has carved through the rock to form a deep pool which holds water for several months after the river has flooded. The inviting pool is especially welcoming on a sweltering hot day.

LOGISTICS AND PLANNING

Fuel: You will need fuel to cover about 950 to 1 000 km from Ruacana village to Sesfontein.
Water: There is water along the route, but you should keep your stocks of drinking water fully topped up at all times.
Food: You will need to stock up on food as there are no food stores between Ruacana and even beyond Palmwag where the route description ends, except at Okangwati where very basic supplies, cold drinks and alcoholic beverages can be bought.
Best times: The cooler winter months between May and August/September are the best time to visit the area. Daytime temperatures are pleasant but minimum temperatures of 5°C can be expected in midwinter. Summer maximum temperatures of above 35°C are especially common in the Kunene Valley. Most of the region's rainfall is recorded between January and March/April and varies from 350 mm in the eastern highlands to 50 mm on the plains in the west. After heavy thunderstorms the tracks can be difficult to negotiate. The malaria risk is higher in the summer months.

Maps

The *Shell Map of Kaokoland* is a general tourist map of the area but lacks detail on the tracks. Interesting information about the flora, fauna and other aspects is provided on the reverse.

NAMIBIA

ⓘ VITAL INFO

- Tracks scar the landscape for decades and are unsightly. Always remain on existing tracks and don't blaze your own.
- Van Zyl's Pass should be done only from east to west; it is not advisable to tow a trailer because of the steep and very rocky descent.
- Never camp near a waterhole as you might prevent animals that have walked long distances from quenching their thirst.
- Camping in the bed of the Hoanib River which falls in the Palmwag concession area is strictly prohibited as this could place unnecessary strain on the animals in the area.
- Flash floods are dangerous and unexpected as you will usually not be aware of heavy rains in the catchment area. We strongly advise against camping in riverbeds during the summer months.
- Avoid bonfires to conserve wood. Take enough firewood with you if you're headed for the Marienfluss as it is in short supply at Okarohombo camp site, or cook with gas.

The 1:250 000 topographical maps (1714 Oshakati, 1712 Swartbooisdrift, 1812 Opuwo and 1912 Sesfontein), which show most of the established major tracks, settlements and springs, are obtainable from the Office of the Surveyor-General, Ministry of Lands, Resettlement and Rehabilitation, Private Bag 13182, Windhoek, Namibia, tel: (+264 61) 24-5056. The office is situated on the corner of Robert Mugabe Avenue and Lazarette Street.

Booking
Permits: Not required, except for the Palmwag concession area which includes the Hoanib River. The permit can be obtained at two control points along the river, or at Palmwag.
Accommodation: Except at Kunene River Lodge, Fort Sesfontein and Palmwag it is not possible to make reservations, and camp sites are allocated on a first-come-first-served basis.
Kunene River Lodge, tel: (+264 65) 27-4300, fax: 27-4301, e-mail: info@kuneneriverlodge.com
Fort Sesfontein in Sesfontein, tel: (+264 65) 27-5534, fax: 27-5533, e-mail: fort.sesfontein@mweb.com.na
Palmwag Lodge, tel: (+264 64) 40-4459, fax: 40-4664, e-mail: reservations@palmwag.com.na

The Hoarusib River is a linear oasis in the barren Kaokoveld.

Nyae Nyae

The Nyae Nyae area has been the ancestral home of the Ju/'hoan Bushmen for many centuries. Formerly known as Eastern Bushmanland, it is a vast wilderness of woodlands, enormous baobabs, seasonal pans attracting thousands of water birds, elephant, roan, wild dog and numerous other game species. While you are sitting around your campfire at night you might hear the distant roar of a lion or encounter some of the numerous creatures that make their homes in and around the baobabs where the camp sites are located.

THE CONSERVANCY

In 1998 Nyae Nyae became the first communal area in Namibia to be declared a conservancy, and the rights to manage wildlife and other natural resources were transferred to the community. The conservancy stretches from the Namibian/Botswanan border westwards for 86 km and about 93 km from north to south.

The Nyae Nyae area is the home of Bushmen who speak Ju/'hoan, the central of three dialects of the !Kung Bushmen of Namibia and Botswana. Their traditional area once stretched from Rundu southwards for about 300 km and eastwards to Lake Ngami in Botswana, but they now live on less than a third of their ancestral lands. Don't expect to find Bushmen in loincloths or leather aprons as they are often portrayed on postcards and in coffee-table books. Theirs is a society in transition and, although hunting and gathering still play an important role in their lifestyle, they also keep small numbers of cattle and plant crops during the rainy season.

Tsumkwe, the administrative town, has the largest concentration of people but there are about 32 small communities, ranging in size from small extended families of a dozen people to 150. About 3 000 people make up the Ju/'hoan population.

Landscape and vegetation

Kalahari dunes with low vegetation are characteristic of the western part of Nyae Nyae. Typical trees here include Kalahari apple-leaf, wild teak, wild syringa, silver cluster-leaf and a variety of bushwillow (*Combretum*) species. Further east the sandveld gives way to calcrete and clay interspersed with patches of sand. A variety of acacias, bushwillows, leadwood and purple-pod cluster-leaf (also known as Lowveld cluster-leaf) dominates the vegetation.

Numerous small and large seasonal pans, some covered in grass and others saline, such as Nyae Nyae, dot the panveld north and south of Tsumkwe. After good summer rains up to a fifth of the area is under water. The pans hold water until deep into the winter and, as the surface water dries up, large numbers of animals move to the panveld. The pans are rich in phosphates and the salt eaten by the animals supplements this mineral deficiency in the natural grazing.

NAMIBIA

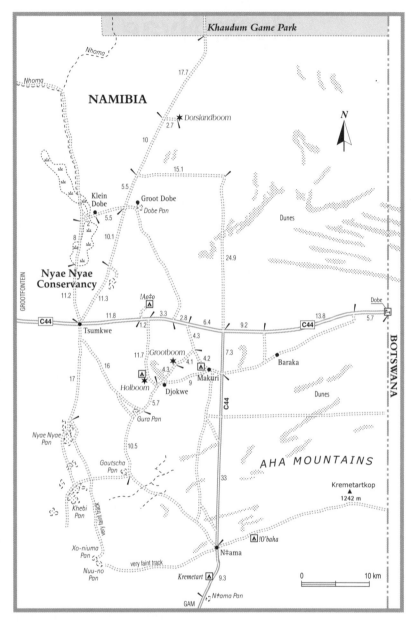

Fauna and game-viewing

A variety of animals occurs in Nyae Nyae, but the dense bush limits visibility over much of the area. There is always the chance of an unexpected sighting though: on one trip we encountered elephant, roan and wild dog on the C44 gravel road within 20 minutes of each other.

Elephant move into the area in large numbers during the rainy season and Makurivlei is usually a good place to see them. Herds of eland, gemsbok and giraffe occur in the western sandveld, and blue wildebeest, springbok, red hartebeest, roan and kudu favour the woodlands and panveld area.

Nyae Nyae

Lion, cheetah and packs of wild dog follow the movements of their prey, while the shy and nocturnal leopard is territorial. Brown and spotted hyaenas, as well as most of the smaller predators such as black-backed jackal, African wild cat and caracal, also occur.

Birding
Large numbers of water birds move onto the pans after the summer rains; flocks of over 6 000 lesser and greater flamingos can be seen at times on Nyae Nyae Pan, which also attracts Cape teal and Cape shoveller.
Specials: slaty egret (under favourable conditions), wattled crane.
Water birds: red-knobbed coot, red-billed teal, African pygmy-goose, spur-winged goose, white-backed and comb ducks, southern pochard, little grebe, whiskered tern, Allen's gallinule, ruff, great snipe.
Raptors: yellow-billed and black kites; African fish, Wahlberg's, tawny, steppe and black-chested snake eagles; amur falcon.
Other species: ostrich, grey lourie, red-billed buffalo-weaver, African grey and southern yellow-billed hornbills, Kalahari and white-browed scrub-robins, red-billed francolin, lilac-breasted roller, double-banded sandgrouse.

Facilities
Basic camp sites without any facilities are available at **Djokwe** (elephant have destroyed the basic ablutions), **Makuri**, **!Ao≠o**, **!O'baha** and **Kremetart**. It is customary to ask the headman of the village nearest the camp site for permission to camp and to pay him the fees. Firewood can be bought at the camp sites. The camp sites are under baobabs which are deciduous trees and therefore don't provide much shade in the winter months.
Tsumkwe Lodge, in Tsumkwe. Teak wood and thatched bungalows, restaurant.

Activities
We highly recommend that you try at least one of the **activities offered by the inhabitants of Makuri**. Join the women when they go out to gather veld food; track elephant with a guide; accompany the men on a traditional hunt; or attend a traditional dancing and singing session. The activities are authentic and can be arranged at Makuri.

In addition, Tsumkwe Lodge works closely with the Ju/'hoan people, and offers tourists **guided cultural tours**.

Getting there
You reach Tsumkwe, the gateway to Nyae Nyae, by taking the B8 from Grootfontein northwards for 57 km to the signposted turnoff. Turn right (east) onto the C44, a good gravel road and follow it for 223 km to Tsumkwe.

ROUTES – 800 km Grootfontein return
You can explore Nyae Nyae along numerous, mostly unsignposted, tracks which criss-cross the area. No map indicates all the tracks accurately, which can be very confusing in some areas, and keeping your sense of direction is important. If you do get disorientated use the C44 road as a landmark and head either north or south until you meet up with it.

Tracks in the panveld area are impassable during the rainy season when the more sandy terrain north of the C44 is easier to negotiate.

NAMIBIA

DORSLAND TREKKERS

No-one is sure what caused the Dorsland Trek. In May 1874 the first group of Afrikaners set off from the Crocodile River near Marico in South Africa's North West Province. A second trek began in April 1876, a third in 1877 and several smaller treks until 1906. They trekked through the thirstland of Botswana to the Dorslandboom where the first group camped in 1879. The dates carved into the trunk in 1883, 1884 and 1891 are still visible. From here they trekked through Khaudum, Etosha and Kaokoland to Swartbooisdrif on the Kunene River. From here they crossed into Angola and went north to Hamputa, where they settled. Some groups later moved deeper into Angola. In 1928/1929 when some 350 families returned to Namibia they crossed at Swartbooisdrif.

Dorslandboom

The Dorslandboom is a well-known landmark just off the track between Tsumkwe and Khaudum Game Park. To get there take the signposted turnoff to Khaudum at the four-way crossroad in Tsumkwe. Ignore the Dobe turnoff that you reach after 21.4 km and continue for another 15.5 km to a track turning off to the right (west). A 2.7-km detour brings you to this famous landmark named after the Dorsland Trekkers who camped here in 1879.

Nyae Nyae Pan and the Pannetjiesveld

The pan area south of Tsumkwe has been restocked with game and in the dry months the animals drink at an artificial waterhole on Nyae Nyae Pan's western fringes. Game-viewing is easy on the open grassy pans, but the animals are skittish and usually make off when they hear a vehicle. The area is managed as a wildlife protected area and only day visits are allowed.

Nyae Nyae Pan is the largest and most scenic pan in the area. It is about 4 km long and after good summer rains its shimmering white saline surface is transformed into a vast expanse of water which attracts thousands of water birds at times. It is best to retrace your tracks from Nyae Nyae Pan to Tsumkwe as the track linking it to Gautscha Pan is not often used. As a result it is overgrown with small acacia scrub and getting a puncture is a common occurrence.

Grootboom and Holboom

The Grootboom and the Holboom are well-known attractions of the area. From Tsumkwe head east along the C44 for 13 km to the signposted turnoff to Djokwe. Turn right (south) and after following a sandy track for 10.7 km you will reach the Holboom, an enormous baobab that owes its Afrikaans name to the huge hollow in the base of its stem. Camping is not permitted at the Holboom, but there is a camp site nearby with a hide overlooking a small seasonal pan.

Continue for 1 km to a junction where you turn left (east) and you soon pass the settlement of Djokwe. A short way on a track splits off to the left to reach the Grootboom after 4.3 km. The Grootboom, a number of trunks that have merged, has a circumference of over 30 m at the base. The track continues in a north-easterly direction and after 4.1 km links up with the Makuri track. Turn right at the junction and after 4.2 km you will reach the small settlement of Makuri. After rains Makurivlei attracts large numbers of waterfowl, and you can also expect to see many elephant in this area. The camp site is situated a short distance from the small settlement.

Aha Hills
The sand plateau of the Nyae Nyae area is broken in the south-east where the Aha Hills rise up to 100 m above the woodlands. These hills extend from western Botswana westwards for 30 km into Namibia. To get there take the C44 east from Tsumkwe for 25.5 km to the signposted turnoff to Gam. Turn right (south) here and follow the gravel C43 for about 41 km to N≠ama where the track to Aha Hills splits off to the north-east. You may camp at nearby !O'baha.

Linking routes
A visit to Nyae Nyae can be extended to the Khaudum Game Park (*see* page 134) to the north. You can link up with Tsodilo Hills & Gcwihaba Cave (*see* page 91) by crossing into Botswana via the Dobe border post, 54 km east of Tsumkwe along the C44. It is open from 08h00 to 16h30.

LOGISTICS AND PLANNING
Fuel: Fill up in Grootfontein. In Tsumkwe fuel is available only for emergencies.
Water: Usually available from settlements near the camp sites.
Food: Depending on your approach route, stock up on food and alcoholic beverages in Windhoek, Grootfontein, Rundu or Katima Mulilo. One of the shops in Tsumkwe is fairly well stocked, but only basic necessities are available between Rundu and Katima Mulilo.
Best times: The cool dry months between late April and August have the best climate, but the most rewarding time for game-viewing is just before the start of the rainy season. Birding is usually best between November and April, depending on when, where and how much it has rained.

Maps
An A4 sketch map is available at the Nyae Nyae conservancy office in Tsumkwe. Maps can also be obtained from Tsumkwe Lodge.

Booking
Nyae Nyae is a communal conservancy; before entering the area you must report at the office to pay entrance fees. It is 400 m west of the four-way cross road in Tsumkwe to the south of the road.
Tsumkwe Lodge, in Tsumkwe: tel: (+264 67) 24-4028, fax: 24-4027, e-mail: tsumkwel@iway.na

---

 VITAL INFO

- Respect the culture and customs of the Ju/'hoan Bushmen whose land you'll be traversing.
- Different spelling forms are used for the names of the various settlements, depending on which map you use, but invariably the names are fairly similar.
- Do not sleep outside as potentially dangerous animals such as lion, hyaena and elephant can walk through the camp sites at night.
- A second spare wheel and a puncture repair kit are essential as punctures caused by thorns are common.

NAMIBIA

Khaudum Game Park

Set among the sandveld of the northern Kalahari, Khaudum is a wilderness of woodlands, interrupted in the north and south by grass-covered fossil river valleys. Except for the boundary with Botswana in the east there are no fences, which gives the animals unrestricted movement even through the camps. Herds of several hundred elephant, lion, wild dog and roan are among the top game-viewing attractions, but patience is needed as it is not easy to see animals in the dense bush and long grass after the summer rains. The essence of a visit to Khaudum is its wilderness atmosphere and its sense of isolation.

Landscape and vegetation

Khaudum is in the northern Kalahari and, although low east–west trending dunes dominate the landscape in the north of the park, their undulating nature and the woodlands make them hardly noticeable. The dunes were formed by east winds, dominant in north-eastern Namibia, and later stabilised by vegetation. Wide dune streets separate the dunes. Unlike the reddish sands of the southern Kalahari, the sand over large areas of the Kavango is characteristically white or grey because of the relatively high rainfall and the leaching of iron oxides from the sand.

Several fossil drainage lines, known as *omuramba* (plural *omiramba*) in Otjiherero, cross Khaudum. The Nhoma and Chadum *omiramba* are in the south while the Khaudum and Cwiba *omiramba* pass through the north of the park. They once discharged water into the Okavango Delta, and radiocarbon dating of molluscs in the Xaudum Valley in Botswana indicates that there was standing water there some 14 000 years ago. But like the fossil rivers in the central Kalahari they no longer flow and are fed only by local rainfall. During the rainy season the accumulations of peat in the *omuramba* act as a sponge which gradually releases water into depressions in the riverbeds during the dry months.

The northern Kalahari vegetation is characterised by tree savanna and woodland. Dominant trees in the deep sands in the north of the park include wild teak, wild syringa, copalwood and Zambezi teak. In August eye-catching yellow sprays of the peeling plane are highly visible. The red puffs of *Combretum platypetalum*, a scraggly dwarf shrub of the undergrowth, also provide colour. Acacia woodlands of camel and umbrella thorn fringe the *omiramba*, growing around pans and in the clay between dunes. Short and tall grasslands cover the floors of the *omiramba*, while reed beds extend along the Khaudum Omuramba for 30 km.

The vegetation in the south of the park differs markedly from that in the north, being typically short open woodlands under 5 m high. Extensive stands of almost exclusively purple-pod cluster-leaf (also known as Lowveld cluster-leaf) occur on calcrete ridges north and south of Sikereti. Other typical species are the trumpet flower (*Catophractes alexandri*), Kalahari apple-leaf, shepherd's tree and bushwillow (*Combretum*) species.

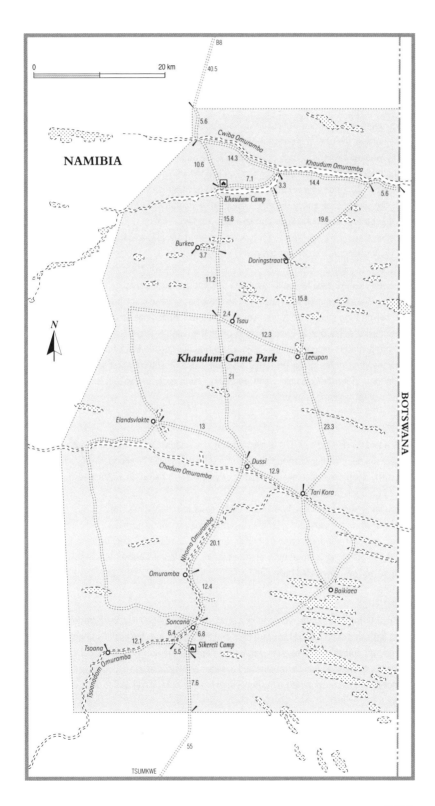

NAMIBIA

Fauna and game-viewing
The numerous small pans and hollows fill up after the first summer rains, providing enough water for the animals to disperse widely throughout the park and adjacent areas. But, once these water sources have dried up, the animals are forced to drink at the pumped waterholes spread throughout the park.

Khaudum is the heartland of Namibia's roan population and good sightings are often made in the north of the park. This greyish-brown antelope with horns that sweep backwards favours lightly wooded savanna, usually grazing during the mid-morning and just before dark.

The total elephant population of Khaudum and the adjoining communal areas is estimated at about 1 100. Large concentrations can be found at waterholes in the dry winter months, but after the summer rains they disperse widely, some migrating as far north as Angola before heading back to Khaudum. Kudu and steenbok are fairly common, as are gemsbok and blue wildebeest. You are most likely to track down giraffe in the acacia woodlands. Eland, tsessebe and reedbuck occur, but are less frequently encountered.

The park provides sanctuary to the only viable lion population in Namibia (estimated at 50 animals) outside the Etosha National Park. Packs of wild dog sometimes range through the south of the park. Consider yourself fortunate if you do come across these magnificent animals that have been persecuted almost to extinction over much of their former range. Since the park is unfenced the animals are shot by subsistence farmers when they venture into the adjoining areas.

Other predators include cheetah, leopard, spotted hyaena and black-backed jackal, as well as a variety of smaller, mainly nocturnal, predators. The side-striped jackal, which has a limited distribution in northern Namibia and Botswana, north-eastern KwaZulu-Natal and eastern Mpumalanga, also occurs here.

Birding
With a bird checklist of over 320 species, birding in Khaudum can be rewarding, especially during the summer months when the number of residents is swelled by up to 70 migrant species.
Specials: sharp-tailed starling, Bradfield's hornbill, Meyer's parrot, Dickinson's kestrel, rufous-bellied tit, black-faced babbler.
Migrants: yellow-billed kite, Wahlberg's eagle, amur falcon, Abdim's stork.
Raptors: white-backed vulture, bateleur, southern pale chanting goshawk.
Other species: southern ground-hornbill, Burchell's sandgrouse, lilac-breasted and purple rollers, red-billed francolin, crimson-breasted shrike, grey lourie, Kalahari scrub-robin, southern black tit and swallow-tailed bee-eater.

Facilities
Sikereti Camp in the south is shaded by a grove of tall purple-pod (Lowveld) cluster-leaf trees. It has basic thatch and wood huts with beds and mattresses, hot showers (if you stoke the donkey geyser), toilets and camp sites. **Khaudum Camp** in the north nestles under tall trees on the banks of the Khaudum Omuramba and has the same facilities. No bedding, crockery, cutlery or cooking utensils are provided in the huts, which have become dilapidated, so don't expect much.

Getting there
From the south, Khaudum can be approached from Grootfontein via Tsumkwe, where you take the signposted turnoff at the four-way junction. Ignore the turnoff to Groot Dobe after 21.4 km, and continue straight for another 15.5 km where a turnoff to the right leads

to Holboom, the Dorslandtrek baobab (see Nyae Nyae, page 132). The southern boundary of the park lies 17.7 km beyond the turnoff and Sikereti Camp is another 7.6 km on.

Approaching from the north, the turnoff to the park is signposted on the B8 about 112 km east of Rundu where you turn right (south). The track is initially fairly easy to negotiate, but as you continue south deep loose sand necessitates the use of low range and you are unlikely to average more than 10 km an hour. You reach the turnoff to the park after about 40.5 km and about 5.6 km on, the Cwiba Omuramba. About 700 m beyond the *omuramba* take the track turning south and continue for 12 km through deep sand to Khaudum Camp.

ROUTES – 820 km Grootfontein to Rundu via Tsumkwe;
800 km Grootfontein to Divundu via Tsumkwe

You can explore the park along a network of tracks covering over 300 km between several waterholes and the two camps. Tracks vary from hard surfaces with underlying calcrete in the south to clay in and along the *omiramba* which can be difficult to negotiate in the wet season. The sand in the north of the park is the deepest and softest you will find anywhere in Namibia outside the Namib, but after rains the tracks are compacted and driving is easy.

Sikereti Camp is a convenient base for game drives to Tsoana Waterhole in the west where you can expect to see large breeding herds of elephant in the dry season. Soncana Waterhole, 7 km north of Sikereti, can be very rewarding at times. You can park under shady acacias while watching the waterhole.

You have a choice of three almost parallel routes from Sikereti to Khaudum Camp. Driving conditions south of the Chadom Omuramba are generally fairly easy, requiring only occasional use of four-wheel drive. The westernmost route leads via Elandsvlakte and as there is usually not much game it is not recommended. The 24-km stretch between Tsau and Khaudum Camp on the centre route winds through deep loose sand which necessitates constant use of low range. Because of this it is not recommended. If you opt to do this route, set aside the better part of a day (allowing for game-viewing) to complete the 71-km stretch.

The eastern route between Sikereti and Khaudum Camp has the easiest driving conditions and also offers good game-viewing possibilities. From Sikereti the track heads in a north-easterly direction to Baikiaea Waterhole. The waterhole shares the scientific name of the Zambezi teak (*Baikiaea plurijuga*) which is a characteristic species of tall dry woodlands and favours dune crests.

You then cross the dunes to Tari Kora Waterhole where you can continue directly to Leeupan or take a detour via Dussi and Tsau waterholes before heading east to Leeupan. Beyond Leeupan the track becomes sandier and the woodlands here are interspersed with expansive grasslands. Doringstraat Waterhole (named after the acacias fringing the dune street) is 15.8 km beyond Leeupan. From here the track heads almost dead straight in a north-easterly direction to reach the Khaudum Omuramba after 19.6 km. You follow the southern bank of the

ROAN TRANSLOCATIONS

In 1970 just over 70 roan were translocated by air to the west of the Etosha. An airstrip had to be built in the Khaudum Omuramba. The animals were flown to Etosha in three groups in a chartered Hercules cargo plane – the first airlifts in the world of such a large number of sedated animals over such a long distance.

NAMIBIA

> ### ⓘ VITAL INFO
>
> - A minimum of two vehicles is advisable when visiting the park.
> - We recommend low flotation tyres which should be deflated to make driving in the deep sand easier.
> - Check regularly and remove grass that has accumulated underneath the vehicle as it could set your vehicle on fire.
> - Hyaena, elephant, lion and other potentially dangerous animals could pass through the unfenced camps at night. Pack food away and take care when walking to the ablutions after dark.
> - Take enough wood for your campfires as collecting wood in the park is not permitted.

fossil river westwards and after 14 km the track crosses over to the northern bank of the Khaudum Omuramba, where you turn left. Continue for 11 km to Khaudum Camp, situated under tall shady trees on a high dune overlooking the *omuramba* and the woodlands stretching into the distance.

The small waterhole in the *omuramba* just below Khaudum Camp attracts a variety of game including roan and elephant. Some 19.5 km to the south lies Burkea Waterhole, named after the wild syringa (*Burkea africana*) which favours deep sand and is conspicuous in the area.

Another option from Khaudum Camp is to travel eastwards along the *omuramba* to the Namibian/Botswanan border where years ago there was a Bushman settlement. Along the way there are several *gorras* (waterholes) that have been dug by elephant to get to the subterranean water in the *omuramba*. In Botswana the Khaudum is known as the Xaudum before its name changes to the Ncamaseri which links up with the Okavango Delta just north of the settlement of the same name. The return trip is 62 km.

LOGISTICS AND PLANNING

Fuel: Not available at Tsumkwe. Carry enough to cover at least 600 km if you travel from Tsumkwe to the B8 linking Rundu and Divundu or in the opposite direction.

Water: Elephant sometimes damage water installations, which leaves camps without water. Be self-sufficient.

Food: Depending on your approach route stock up on food and alcoholic beverages in Windhoek, Grootfontein, Rundu or Katima Mulilo. One of the shops in Tsumkwe is fairly well stocked but only basic necessities are available between Rundu and Katima Mulilo.

Best times: The cool dry months have the best climate but the most rewarding time for game-viewing is just before the start of the rainy season. Not only are the animals forced to drink at the artificial waterholes but visibility is also better as the deciduous trees have shed their leaves and the tall grasses have been flattened by the game and wind. A disadvantage of this period is the danger of veld fires.

Booking

Reservations must be made through Namibia Wildlife Resorts, Private Bag 13267, Windhoek, Namibia, tel: (+264 61) 23-6975, fax: 22-4900, e-mail: reservations@nwr.com.na.

North-Eastern Parks

The lush woodlands, floodplains, marshes and perennial rivers of North-Eastern Namibia contrast sharply with the country's arid western reaches. Bird-life in this well-watered region is prolific, and red lechwe, sitatunga, reedbuck and oribi are among the mammals restricted to this area. Only basic facilities are provided in the parks except at Popa Falls which has wood and thatch bungalows and camp sites with ablutions. You will camp next to pools inhabited by hippo, which adds to the wild atmosphere of the area. As few people visit this remote corner of Namibia, you will enjoy solitude interrupted only by the grunt of a hippo or the distant roar of a lion.

Landscape and vegetation
Dunes covered in tall woodlands, large rivers fringed by magnificent riverine forests, floodplain grasslands, seasonally inundated channels and mopane woodlands all merge in the north-east of Namibia to create an ever-changing mosaic of landscapes. This is described in more detail in the Route section.

Fauna and game-viewing
In Namibia, red lechwe, sitatunga and reedbuck occur only in the north-east of the country. Apart from a few in the Kunene River, hippo are also restricted to this area.

Once a wildlife paradise, eastern Caprivi experienced a significant decline in its game populations in the 1980s as a result of illegal hunting. Red lechwe, for example, decreased from almost 13 000 in 1980 to a mere 2 679 by 1986.

Game numbers are increasing slowly again following the proclamation of the Mudumu and Mamili (Rupara) national parks in 1990 and, more recently, the establishment of communal conservancies in eastern Caprivi. But it will take decades for game numbers to increase to their former levels. Information about animals in the various parks is provided in the Route description.

Birding
With a checklist of over 450 species, north-eastern Namibia is a birder's paradise. Mahango Game Park is undoubtedly the top birding spot in Namibia, boasting some 440 species.
Specials: wattled crane, rock pratincole (exposed rocks at Popa Falls), slaty egret, greater swamp warbler, Bradfield's hornbill, rosy-throated longclaw, brown firefinch, southern brown-throated weaver.
Raptors: African fish, martial, tawny, and western banded snake eagles; bateleur; African marsh-harrier; Dickinson's kestrel; southern pale and dark chanting goshawks; white-backed vulture.

NAMIBIA

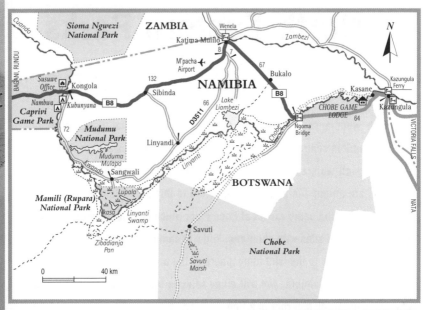

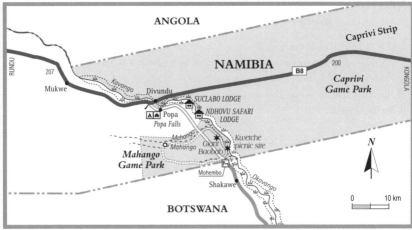

Migrants: yellow-billed and black kites, African hobby, steppe eagle, African open-bill.
Other species: coppery-tailed and black coucals, long-toed and African wattled lapwings, lesser jacana, sharp-tailed starling, tropical and swamp boubous, rufous-naped lark, comb duck, Meyer's parrot, African mourning dove, saddle-billed and marabou storks, great white and small numbers of pink-backed pelicans when Mamili (Rupara) is inundated.

Facilities

Popa Falls Rest Camp, at Popa Falls. Wood and thatch bungalows with en-suite facilities, braai places, communal kitchen. Bedding is provided but no cooking utensils, pots, cutlery or crockery. Camp sites with hot showers. There is no restaurant.
N//goabaca camp site, no reservations possible. Signposted just east of the police checkpoint at Divundu bridge. Community camp site on the northern banks of the Kavango River with

North-Eastern Parks

excellent views of the Popa Falls rapids. Camp sites with braai places, hot showers, flush toilets.
Caprivi Game Park (Bwabwata National Park), no reservations. The Nambwa camp site on the western banks of the Kwando is managed by the Mayuni community. There are no facilities at present.
Kubunyana Camp, no reservations. Signposted 7 km south of Kongola village along the C49. The camp is 4 km on. Well-run community camp on the eastern banks of the Kwando River. Camp sites with braai places, hot showers, permanent tented camp.
Mudumu and Mamili (Rupara) national parks, entry permits include camping which is allowed at designated sites (no facilities).

Activities
A visit to the **Lizauli Traditional Village**, signposted 6 km north of Mudumu National Park's northern boundary, will give you insight into the culture of the people of Caprivi. There are guided tours of the village.

THE ROUTE – 850 km Katima Mulilo to Mahango Game Park and Divundu

Divundu, where the route starts, is reached by following the B8 from Rundu eastwards for 220 km. Alternatively, if you are travelling from Khaudum Game Park, you will link up with the B8 some 88 km west of Divundu.

At Divundu, turn off the B8 onto the gravel C48 and after 5.3 km you reach the turnoff to Popa Falls Rest Camp which nestles under tall riverine forest on the southern banks of the Kavango River (known as as the Okavango in neighbouring Botswana). 'Rapids' would be a more apt description than 'falls' as the highest cascade is a mere 2.5 m high while the total drop is about 4 m. You will see only a small section of the rapids which extend for over 1 km across the width of the river as it rushes through numerous channels separated by small rocky vegetated islands. When the level of the river is low you can jump across some of the smaller channels near the southern bank to get a better view of the rapids. Popa has been earmarked for a hydro-electric scheme which has drawn fierce criticism from environmentalists, but the falls will not be inundated should the project go ahead.

Popa is a convenient base for exploring Mahango Game Park which lies at the north-eastern end of the Okavango Delta's panhandle. The park is open only for day visits and the gate is just over 15 km south-east of Popa on the C48 which divides the park in two. You are permitted to walk in the park, but always bear in mind that there could be potentially dangerous animals such as elephant, lone buffalo bulls and occasionally lion.

The most rewarding route is the 27.5-km-long drive which turns off the C48 about 300 m beyond the entrance gate. After initially following the Mahango Omuramba the road winds along the edge of the floodplain where you have a chance of seeing bushbuck in the riverine forest and herds of red lechwe on the floodplains.

Mahango is famous for its large population of elephant and in the dry season they concentrate in large numbers along the Kavango River, which is home to a healthy population of hippo. Sable, roan, kudu, buffalo, reedbuck and tsessebe are among the other species you are most likely to see. Predators are not common, but lion occasionally pass through the park.

Further along you reach a short deviation to a large baobab overlooking the floodplains which is excellent for a tea or lunch stop. Kwetche picnic spot is a short way on and with a fair amount of luck you might spot the elusive sitatunga in the papyrus reeds fringing the river. The palmveld in the area is unlikely to escape your attention.

The road loops back through teak scrub to join the C48 just over 3 km beyond Kwetche. A sandy track to Singwerengwere starts immediately opposite the junction. After initially following the edge of the Tinderevu Omuramba, the track climbs into the dunes and passes through tall woodlands of wild and Zambezi teak, wild syringa, copalwood and manketti trees.

About 20 km from the start you reach Singwerengwere waterhole and hide where with patience you might see animals drinking. The track continues through stands of buffalo-thorn, African weeping wattle and silver cluster-leaf with large camel thorn trees conspicuous at the base of the dunes. About 10 km beyond the waterhole you link up with the C48.

Heading east from Popa on the B8, you cross over the Kavango River into west Caprivi, a 200-km-long geographical curiosity that became part of the former German South West Africa in 1890, together with east Caprivi, in an exchange of territory between Germany and Britain. Germany received the Caprivi Strip and the island of Helgoland in exchange for the island of Zanzibar and parts of Botswana which was then known as Bechuanaland.

The Caprivi Strip has enjoyed protection since 1963 when a nature reserve was proclaimed that later became known as the Caprivi Game Park. During Namibia's liberation struggle it became a South African Defence Force military zone, and access became possible only after independence in 1990.

The park is inhabited by between 3 000 and 4 000 people, most of them Barakwena Bushmen, although there are also some Vasekele Bushmen who fled from Angola during that country's civil war. Most of the men were conscripted into the South African Defence Force during Namibia's liberation struggle to serve as trackers, but after independence they were left in limbo. They live in settlements throughout the park with the largest concentrations around former military bases such as Omega and Bagani.

The park's name is set to change to the Bwabwata National Park; this will incorporate the Mahango Game Park and core conservation areas along the Kavango River in the west and the Golden Triangle, which adjoins the Kwando River in the east and currently falls outside of the park. Two areas inhabited by the Barakwena Bushmen will be deproclaimed while the remainder of the park will be managed as multiple use areas. People living at various settlements will be allowed to plant crops but only those living in the deproclaimed areas will be allowed to practise stock farming. The communities will also be given tourism rights in the park.

Access is currently limited to the eastern section of the Caprivi Strip where the Ministry has an office at Susuwe. The turnoff to Susuwe office is signposted to the left (north) just before you cross over the Kwando River. From the B8 it is 3 km to the office and from here you can continue northwards to Chisu close to the Namibian border with Angola. The drive could be rewarding during the dry summer months when the animals concentrate along the river.

Turn right (south) off the B8 onto a track that winds up into the dunes. After about 6 km you pass the ruins of an old SADF military base, Fort Doppies, and a short way on the track winds down to the edge of the Kwando floodplains. Nambwa, a delightful spot set among lush riverine trees alongside a channel of the Kwando River, is about 12 km after you turn off the B8.

While the Kwando River floodplains and the adjacent floodplain grasslands support red lechwe, impala, kudu, sable, Burchell's zebra, tsessebe and giraffe favour the woodlands and the riverine fringes. Large herds of buffalo are also found here, and during the dry season it is not unusual to see concentrations of several hundred elephant on the Kwando floodplains and at Horseshoe Bend, 5 km south of Nambwa, where there is also a resident population of hippo. Numerous other species of game gather at the water's edge to quench their thirst during the dry months.

The area has a large leopard population. Although lions are present, you are more likely to see their spoor or hear them at night than set eyes on them. Wild dog, spotted hyaena and smaller carnivores such as black-backed jackal, caracal and genet also occur. Be wary of crocodiles along the Kwando River and seemingly tranquil channels and waterways.

A network of tracks criss-crosses the area, but the most rewarding game-viewing routes are along the Kwando floodplains. Some of the tracks in the woodlands are overgrown as they are seldom used and are not recommended.

From Nambwa retrace your tracks to the B8 and head east across the Kwando River, which separates west and east Caprivi, to Kongola village, where you turn right (south) onto the C49. About 35 km beyond the turnoff you reach the northern boundary of the Mudumu National Park, which is bounded for 15 km in the west by the Kwando River, and extends eastwards for about 40 km. Mopane woodlands dominate Mudumu's vegetation, except in the east where silver cluster-leaf woodlands occur in the deep Kalahari sands.

The turnoff to the Nakatwa permit office is 7.7 km beyond the park boundary, and 4.7 km later you reach the turnoff to Vubu camp site which overlooks a quiet backwater of the Kwando River. Only basic facilities are available.

Mudumu is sanctuary to several hundred elephant, and impala, Burchell's zebra and kudu are fairly common. Sable, roan, tsessebe, red lechwe and reedbuck occur in smaller numbers, but predators are uncommon. This is one of the few places in Namibia where you can see oribi, a species favouring rank grass with bush cover. The area west of the C49 and the riverfront can be explored along several tracks and is by far the most productive area for game-viewing.

Further along the C49, you reach the turnoff to Sangwali village just over 71 km from Kongola. Sangwali, under 2 km beyond the turnoff, is a beautiful traditional village with homesteads surrounded by reed screens. Ignore the track that splits off to the right just beyond the SheShe Crafts Market and continue straight. You will cross three usually dry river channels and arrive at the Mamili National Park gate just under 13 km after turning off the C49. The park should be avoided after heavy summer rains when the clay tracks become impossible to negotiate. Mamili National Park was named after Chief Mamili of the Mafwe, one of the two main cultural groups in eastern Caprivi. In 1999 the chief was part of an unsuccessful plot to secede Caprivi with armed force, and he later fled Namibia. There are plans to change the park's name to Rupara National Park after one of the park's 'islands'. On maps the name is indicated as Lupala.

RIVER OF MANY NAMES

Few rivers have as many names as the Kwando/Linyanti/Chobe which rises in the south-eastern Angolan highlands as the Cuando. On entering Namibia it is known as Kwando, and some 15 km south of the Kongola Bridge which links west and east Caprivi it forms the border between Namibia and Botswana, where it is known as the Mashi. Still further downstream it makes an almost 90-degree turn as it swings north-east to follow the line of the Gomare fault. Now known as the Linyanti, it disappears underground before it reaches Lake Liambezi. Downstream of Lake Liambezi, it is known as the Chobe which eventually joins the Zambezi River at Impalila Island, the country's north-easternmost corner where the borders of Namibia, Zambia, Zimbabwe and Botswana meet.

NAMIBIA

The park, which lies in the triangle where the Kwando River swings north-east, is a mosaic of floodplain grasslands, seasonally inundated channels, reedbeds, patches of woodlands and two large 'islands', Nkasa and Lupala. When the level of the river is high water spills across the floodplains and along a network of channels, inundating large areas, except for Nkasa, Lupala and the numerous termitaria islands (*see* box below).

Several tracks traverse the park, but access can be limited when water from the Kwando spills over into the channels. In early 2002 large areas of the floodplains and channels were inundated for the first time in well over a decade, and access to the southern section of the park was impossible until September.

The park has a large population of buffalo and elephant, but after the first summer rains the elephant migrate out of the area. Hippo and crocodile live in the Kwando River but when the area is inundated they leave the river for pools and channels. The floodplains are home to numerous red lechwe, and impala, reedbuck, kudu, bushbuck and steenbok are among the other animals you might see. Lions are present but are seldom encountered, although we once found them about 200 m from our camp site. Spotted hyaena, leopard and black-backed jackal occur but are also not often seen.

There are camp sites on the Kwando River near Liadura Forest, at Shibumu Pool which sometimes has a population of hippo and at Mparamure along the Kwando River in the east. There are absolutely no facilities, fireplaces being the only signs of camp sites. Liadura, the most popular destination, is situated on a small termitaria island with views of the floodplains all around and the Linyanti area of Botswana's Chobe National Park. Game is frequently seen drinking on the Botswana side of the river and a resident hippo population lives in a pool nearby.

Linking routes

From Mamili (Rupara) National Park you can either retrace your tracks along the D3511 to Kongola and travel west to link up with the Khaudum Game Park (*see* page 134) or continue to Katima Mulilo and the Ngoma border post where you enter the Chobe National Park (*see* page 83). Another option is to enter Botswana through the Mohembo border post and to visit the Tsodilo Hills & Gcwihaba Cave (*see* page 91).

TERMITARIA ISLANDS

Termitaria islands develop around termite mounds which raise the level of their immediate surroundings. As more termite mounds are built and rain washes small particles of clay off them, the area steadily increases in size. Over a long period of time trees, grass and plants establish themselves and bind the soil together. Termitaria islands are common in wetlands, but are not inundated by floods. Typical trees include knob thorn, apple-leaf and leadwood.

LOGISTICS AND PLANNING

Fuel: Available at Divundu, Kongola (not reliable) and Katima Mulilo.
Water: Can be obtained at Susuwe, Nakatwa and Shisinze offices.
Food: Stock up on food and alcoholic beverages before you leave the highways. There are supermarkets in Rundu and Katima Mulilo, and the shop at Kongola has a fair range of basic groceries and canned foods.

North-Eastern Parks

VITAL INFO

- Don't drive through flooded channels in Mamili (Rupara) National Park unless you have probed the depth, as there could be concealed holes large enough to swallow your vehicle. Remember that crocodiles could be lurking about.
- Sleeping under the stars without a tent is dangerous as the camp sites are unfenced.
- Access to Susuwe Island Lodge just north of Nambwa camp site and Lianshulu Lodge in the Mudumu National Park is strictly for guests only; don't expect a warm welcome if you're thinking of just dropping in.

Firewood: Take your own firewood, charcoal or gas as the collection of firewood is not permitted in any of the parks.

Best times: The dry months leading up to the first rains, usually in November, are the best time for game-viewing since the animals concentrate along the Kavango and Kwando/Linyanti rivers. After the rains the animals disperse widely as there are numerous seasonal pans where they can drink. For birding, the months between November (depending on the start of the rains) and March are best.

Maps

The maps in the Caprivi Tourist Guide that are handed out by the Ministry of Environment and Tourism are inadequate and outdated. The *Caprivi Tourist Map* (sponsored by Namibia Breweries) is in full colour with information on one side and map sections of the various parks on the other. New tracks in Mamili (Rupara) and the Caprivi Game Park (Bwabwata National Park) are not indicated, so it is essential to take note of where you are driving and use your GPS to track your route.

Booking

Permits for Caprivi Game Park (Bwabwata National Park), Mudumu and Mamili national parks can be obtained free of charge from the Ministry of Environment and Tourism's office in Katima Mulilo, tel: (+264 66) 25-3027, fax: 25-3322, or the offices at Susuwe (Caprivi Game Park), Nakatwa (Mudumu National Park) and Shisinze (Mamili (Rupara) National Park).

Reservations are not possible at Nambwa Camp Site in the Caprivi Game Park (Bwabwata National Park), Kubunyana Camp and N//goabaca Camp Site.

Popa Falls Rest Camp, Namibia Wildlife Resorts, Private Bag 13267, Windhoek, Namibia, tel: (+264 61) 23-6975, fax: 22-4900, e-mail: reservations@nwr.com.na

Main picture: Lesotho's remote Highlands.
Inset picture: The spiral aloe is one of southern Africa's most endangered aloes.

Lesotho

LESOTHO

Endless jagged mountains with snow-capped peaks, deep river valleys, blanket-wrapped people, stone houses with smoke rising from dung fires and goatherds with their flocks high in the mountains. This is the face of Lesotho, the Kingdom in the Sky.

Over 75% of Lesotho lies on the Highlands (above 1 800 m) which are dominated by the mighty Maloti Mountain range. No point in the country is lower than 1 000 m above sea level, while the 3 483-m-high Thabana Ntlenyana in the east is the highest peak south of Kilimanjaro. The vegetation is typically grassland (drab and brown in winter, but lush green after the summer rains) and at higher altitudes hardy alpine grasses and plants survive the icy winter months.

Under 0.5% of the country is protected by its two national parks and one nature reserve. Some of the most scenic mountain landscapes are in Sehlabathebe National Park in the south-east. A tract of rugged mountains in the Front Range of the Malotis in the north is protected by Ts'ehlanyane National Park. Bokong Nature Reserve, also in the north, is one of the highest nature reserves in Africa.

An exciting development which will ensure sound management and boost tourism is the proposed Maloti–Drakensberg Transfrontier Conservation and Development Area of the mountains along the north-eastern and eastern border between Lesotho and South Africa. The project was taken a step further when in June 2001 the two governments signed an in-principle agreement to establish the transfrontier conservation and development area.

Outside the conservation areas is a multitude of remote valleys, high waterfalls and towering peaks that makes Lesotho a paradise for outdoor enthusiasts and adventure seekers. Pull on a pair of walking shoes or saddle up a Basotho pony and go out to experience the country, its people and its animals. For birders there are several montane endemics such as the rare orange-breasted rockjumper.

Dinosaurs left their footprints in the mud of what was a vast inland lake that covered much of the interior of South Africa and Lesotho aeons ago and there are thousands of rock art sites throughout the country.

Meeting the local people will add another dimension to your visit especially in the remote mountain villages. A cheerful 'Dumela' greeting will always evoke a smile and a warm response as the Basotho (singular is Mosotho) are known for their peace-loving friendliness. This is reflected in the country's motto: 'Khotso, Pula, Nala' which translates as Peace, Rain, Prosperity.

Moshoeshoe forged the Basotho nation in the 1820s by uniting various small Sesotho-speaking groups and some Nguni people during the Difaqane (when large numbers of people were displaced on the highveld). Moshoeshoe moved from his original stronghold at Butha-Buthe to Thaba Bosiu in 1824. In the 1850s he became involved in a major struggle with the Free State Boers over the ownership of land west of the Mohokare (Caledon) River and resisted several attacks on his stronghold. In 1868 he requested British protection and Basotholand was annexed as a British colony. Lesotho became independent on 4 October 1966, since when it has been a kingdom with a constitutional monarch.

The iconic Basotho blanket plays an important role in family life and social traditions and few other nations have developed the blanket culture to the same

Overview

degree. While blankets are worn for everyday use, some are donned only on special occasions. From time to time you will see the distinctive conical Basotho hat.

In the mountains, the sure-footed Basotho pony remains the most common form of transport and it can gallop at full speed on narrow bridle paths and down seemingly impossible slopes. If you come across riders while you are driving, slow down until you are well past them.

An extended tour of Lesotho is now largely on tar and gravel roads although there are still some challenging tracks for the adventurous traveller. Along the two routes we describe here you will be lured ever deeper into the mountains to remote settlements and villages. And you will enjoy far-reaching vistas of mountain range upon mountain range fading into the hazy distance. High up in the mountains the air is crisp and the only sound is the wind sweeping through the grass or a goatherd playing a thumb piano.

Daytime summer temperatures in the Lowlands reach 30°C, but in the Highlands they are several degrees lower and evenings can be chilly, even in midsummer. Most of the rain falls between October and April and is usually accompanied by heavy afternoon thunderstorms and lightning.

Winter days are sunny and crisp but at night temperatures drop below freezing and frost is not uncommon. Snow can fall in any month in the Malotis, but is more common between May and September when even the Lowlands can be covered in snow. These snowfalls can make areas inaccessible for weeks.

Be prepared for any weather conditions as you could experience all four seasons in one day. Violent thunderstorms or dense cloud cover can develop within a few hours during a day starting with clear blue skies. Pack clothing for hot and cold weather conditions irrespective of the season.

Each season has its own attraction. In spring the brown grasslands are brought to life by a colourful array of flowers. When fields are tilled, the rich brown and black soil provides a striking contrast to the flush of new growth. The grasslands are a luxuriant green in summer and clear mountain streams flow everywhere. Autumn is harvest time and the grass turns brown. The first snowfalls can start in the Malotis now too. In winter the snow-capped high mountain peaks provide ample justification for Lesotho's popular nickname, the 'Switzerland of Africa'.

Viewpoint overlooking the Sequnyane River just below the Mohale Dam.

LESOTHO

ⓘ VITAL INFO

- Drive carefully at all times but especially in the mountains where oncoming vehicles often take bends on the wrong side of the road. Keep an eye out for people and animals on the roadsides.
- To avoid damage that might be caused by icing-up of your vehicle's radiator, it is advisable to fill it with anti-freeze.
- Summer thunderstorms can cause landslides, and washaways on gravel roads and river crossings off the beaten track might be risky or difficult. Heavy snow can block passes and tracks, sometimes for several weeks.
- Be aware of the danger of lightning during summer thunderstorms when you are camping. If there is a storm in your vicinity, stay in your car with the windows closed until the storm is over. If you are in your tent do not touch the sides and stay clear of metal objects. Avoid exposed ridges and lone trees, as well as riverbeds where there is a possibility of flash floods. Pitch your tent on a slight slope so that the runoff will flow past it.
- Ask a local resident to take you to the *Morena* (Chief) to obtain permission to camp in his/her area (it could be a woman as in the case of the Chieftainess of Nohana) if there are no designated camp sites. You will find people willing to help and it gives you peace of mind if other people know you are there with the *Morena*'s permission.
- Children asking for sweets are a constant nuisance. This is a legacy of the early 19th century French missionaries who handed out sweets to encourage people to attend church. Unfortunately some tourists also oblige. When asked for sweets it's best to respond with a firm but kind 'No'.

BORDER POSTS AND FORMALITIES
There are 12 border posts at various points on the border between South Africa and Lesotho. Maseru and Ficksburg bridges are open 24 hours a day. Some of the smaller border posts are open only between 08h00 and 16h00.

IMMIGRATION
Citizens of SADC countries (excluding Mozambique), Commonwealth countries (excluding Nigeria, Ghana, India and Pakistan) and EU countries do not need a visa, only a valid passport. Entry is for 30 days.

CUSTOMS
Lesotho is a member of the Southern African Customs Union and no duty is payable on your own used personal effects and vehicles. All other goods (including food) from outside the Common Customs Area consisting of South Africa,

Overview

Lesotho, Swaziland, Botswana and Namibia – which shares its customs duties from a common pool – must be reported. A permit is required to import maize, maize products, eggs and alcohol.

Road-user charges
At Maseru Bridge you will have to pay a R5.00 road user toll. The system works like a parking garage but is a little more complex. At the first boom you collect your ticket, then you pay at the cashier a little further on and after completing immigration and customs formalities you go through the final boom.

Currency and banks
Lesotho's currency is the Loti (plural Maloti), which is divided into 100 lisente and is on a par with the South African Rand. The Maloti cannot be converted to other currencies outside Lesotho. South African Rand is accepted. Take enough cash for the duration of your journey when you leave Maseru as it could be time-consuming and frustrating trying to cash foreign currency outside Maseru.

Maps
The two-part 1:250 000 Map of Lesotho published by the Lesotho Government is essential to find your way around, as villages and towns in the rural areas are not signposted. This map and other topographical maps are available from the Department of Lands, Surveys and Physical Planning in Lerotholi Road, Maseru. The postal address is PO Box 7332, Maseru 100, Lesotho, tel: (+266) 2232-2818.

In Lesotho the Gariep (Orange) River is known as the Senqu.

Katse Dam is the main storage reservoir of the Lesotho Highlands Water Project.

LESOTHO

The Mountain Road & Roof of Africa

Two of northern Lesotho's famous routes are combined in this circular tour which goes from the spectacular sandstone outcrops of the Lowlands, to deep in the heart of the craggy Maloti Mountains, over 13 breathtaking mountain passes. You pass many remote mountain villages and beautiful stone homesteads where people herd flocks of angora goats and tend fields of maize in the valleys. While almost 60% of the journey is on tarred road, this does not preclude one from seeing the best scenery this country has to offer. Nowhere else in southern Africa do you traverse 13 mountain passes which are as remote and awe-inspiring as on this route. Two dams of the Lesotho Highlands Water Project, rock paintings and a national park in the foothills of the Malotis are added attractions.

Facilities

Lodges and guest houses to suit most requirements are available on this route.
Mohale Lodge, near Mohale Dam, has en-suite rooms, restaurant and canteen-style breakfast.
Marakabei Guest House, 110 km east of Maseru on the Mountain Road, offers accommodation in traditional rondavels, and meals.
Katse Lodge, close to Katse Dam, 110 km east of Hlotse (Leribe), has rooms with en-suite facilities, restaurant, canteen-style breakfast.
New Oxbow Lodge, 60 km east of Butha-Buthe, has rooms with en-suite facilities, restaurant.
Liphofung Cultural and Historical Site, east of Butha-Buthe, has a camp site with ablutions.
Ts'ehlanyane National Park, 37 km south-east of Butha-Buthe, has camp sites with braai places and ablutions, a secluded bush camp with two eight-bed rondavels, braai area and deck and hostel-style accommodation.

Activities

Contact the Lesotho Highlands Development Authority to arrange **tours** of the Katse, Mohale and Muela dams.
You can book **Basotho pony rides** at Liphofung and Ts'ehlanyane.
There is a **39-km hiking trail** from Ts'ehlanyane National Park to Bokong Nature Reserve and **shorter walks** in both conservation areas.
The Oxbow area is a popular **winter skiing** destination.

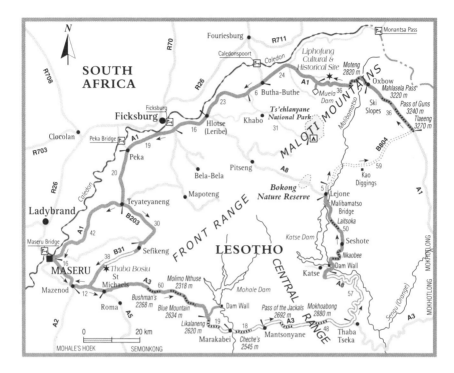

THE TOUR – 710 km Maseru return

The well-known Basotho Hat Craft Centre in Maseru is the starting point for this circular tour which consists of 400 km tar, 205 km gravel and 59 km 4x4 terrain.

Head out of Maseru along Kingsway Bypass and drive through the gentle hills of the Lowlands along the Mafeteng road for 16 km before turning left onto the Roma/Mohale Dam road. Ignore the Roma turnoff to the right 12 km on and continue straight along the Mountain Road which is a beautiful tar road to Mohale Dam. Looming ahead is the formidable barrier of the Malotis' Front Range. Soon you begin to leave the Lowlands behind as you start the steep climb to the 2 268-m-high top of the Bushman's Pass.

Blue Mountain Pass

From the summit the road plunges for 6 km to the Makhaleng Valley in a series of sweeping curves and just before ascending Molimo Nthuse Pass you will pass through a police security checkpoint. Early travellers needed every assistance to overcome the steep gradients before the pass was tarred, and the Basotho name appropriately means 'God Help Me'. Beyond the 2 318-m-high Molimo Nthuse, the road climbs ever higher as it makes its way to the 2 634-m-high top of the Blue Mountain Pass.

Mohale Dam

After hugging the steep slopes which afford beautiful views of the deep valleys of alpine grassland, the road descends steeply to the Likalaneng River. You see the signpost at the turnoff to the Mohale Dam Camp (where accommodation is available) 88 km from Maseru.

To visit the dam's information centre, continue for 2 km to the signposted turnoff and turn left after 4.4 km. About 500 m further there is a point from which to view the magnificent

LESOTHO

surrounding countryside and the marvellous road engineering. The information centre is just over 2 km further and overlooks the concrete-faced rockfill dam wall which is 145 m high and 620 m long along its crest. The wall is 600 m wide at the base and contains 7.5 million cubic metres of basalt rockfill. Water started flowing into the dam towards the end of 2002.

Backtrack to the main road and turn left onto a gravel road; after 200 m you have to stop at another police checkpoint.

Frazer's Store

You will get a taste of what the Mountain Road was like years ago although it is much improved. Since this is now gravel, the journey further is in marked contrast to the tarred road up to Mohale Dam. Although it is an all-weather road, it can be quite rutted at times. The passes only have strips of tar in very steep places and this makes these sections very slow. Just 2 km further the road begins to twist and turn up the Likalaneng Pass and then it descends to Marakabei in the Senquyane River Valley.

Take a detour to Frazer's Store (where Basotho men arrive on ponies or donkeys to buy supplies) for a cold drink and a view of rural life. Beyond Marakabei lies the Central Range of the Malotis. After crossing the Senqunyane River (Mohale Dam lies further upstream) you soon begin making your way up Cheche's Pass (2 545 m).

Pass of the Jackals

By now you will have realised why Lesotho is called the Mountain Kingdom as you negotiate one mountainous pass after another. From Cheche's Pass the road goes down to Mantsonyane where you turn sharp left just before reaching the village.

After following a valley for a short distance, the road climbs steeply to the 2 692-m-high summit of the Pass of the Jackals. The road twists and turns to the summit of the 2 880-m-high Mokhoabong Pass before descending to remote Thaba Tseka which was inaccessible by road until 1969.

Katse Dam

Turn left at the signposted turnoff to Katse Dam on the western outskirts of Thaba Tseka. The road winds over fairly level terrain above the cliffs of the Semenanyane River Valley. You will pass some lovely villages with sandstone and thatch houses before reaching the tar road at Katse Dam about 57 km beyond Thaba Tseka.

You can visit the Katse Dam information centre and be taken on a guided tour of the dam. To get there, turn left and continue to the Lesotho Highlands Development Authority building. Completed in 1997, the dam has a 185-m-high double curvature concrete wall with a crest length of 710 m. The wall contains 2.3 million tonnes of concrete. It is linked via the Muela Dam and 80 km of tunnels to the Vaal Dam catchment area which received its first inflow of water from the project in January 1998.

If you turn right you will get a good view of the dam wall before the road winds out of the valley to a viewpoint overlooking the dam itself.

You then continue up the Nkaobee Pass (2 510 m) from where you drop down into the Matsoku Valley. The roller-coaster ride continues as you head up the Laitsoka Pass (2 650 m) and down again to the Malibamatso Bridge across Katse Dam. A short way beyond the bridge you pass the intake tower where water enters the transfer tunnel to Muela Dam. The dam is 77 m deep here.

The Mountain Road & Roof of Africa

> ## BOKONG NATURE RESERVE
> One of the highest nature reserves in Africa, Bokong is at the top of the Mafika Lisiu Pass, west of Lejone, over 3 000 m above sea level. It protects alpine wetlands, grasslands and heathlands. Among its attractions are the Lepaqoa Waterfall and colonies of the Slogget's rat, commonly known as the ice rat. The visitors' centre is spectacularly sited on the edge of a 100-m-high cliff overlooking the Lepaqoa Valley. You can explore the reserve along a network of trails ranging from a 45-minute interpretative trail to full day hikes. A 39-km-long trail links the reserve to Ts'ehlanyane National Park to the north.

Lejone village is 13.6 km beyond the bridge. As you enter the village, look out for an Adit 6 signpost; here you turn right onto a gravel road which deteriorates into a rough track after 5 km. Engage four-wheel drive when you hit the first short but steep hill as the remaining 59 km is over rugged 4x4 terrain. The track winds along the slopes above the upper reaches of Katse Dam. About 17.8 km after it leaves the tar road there is a sharp turn to the right and the track winds down to cross the Malibamatso River in which Katse Dam was built. A foot bridge ensures that the inhabitants of the area are not cut off when the river is in flood but there is no causeway at the crossing and you will find it impassable if the river is high.

On the far side, the track now winds up the valley carved by the Kao River; you cross this river twice (there are no causeways here either) and 4 km beyond the first crossing a track is signposted to Mabote to the left. Although some maps show that this track can be followed to the tarred road between Butha-Buthe and Hlotse, this is not the case. A short way beyond the turnoff you cross the Kao River once more and the track worsens.

The real 4x4 adventure
You have reached the start of the real 4x4 adventure (this section cannot be done in a 2x4).

Be sure to take the track to the right when you reach Kao to skirt the diamond diggings. Diamonds were discovered here in the late 1950s and the area was initially opened to Basotho concession holders. As they could not exploit the diamonds deep below surface level, full-scale mining operations were later conducted, but the mine was not profitable and was abandoned – heavy machinery, equipment and all. Kao then reverted to Basotho concession holders who continue to search for diamonds, using the most basic methods.

Beyond Kao the track deteriorates even further and there are several short but steep rocky ascents and descents where you should take care. About 11 km after Kao you emerge onto a high plateau, over 3 000 m above sea level, and for the next 10 km the track is easily negotiated – sheer bliss. As you descend to the Matsoku River the track deteriorates again; after passing a few houses you wind up to join the Butha-Buthe/Mokhotlong tar road where you turn left.

Roof of Africa
You are now on the Roof of Africa made famous by the first Trans-Lesotho rally, an event that soon earned the reputation of being one of the toughest in the world. The inaugural Roof of Africa rally was held between Johannesburg and Durban's beachfront in 1966. Part of the challenge was to set the shortest time across Lesotho from Butha-Buthe to Sani Pass.

LESOTHO

Tlaeeng Pass

Soon you reach the top of Tlaeeng Pass (3 270 m), which is the highest point in southern Africa that is accessible by road. As you sweep around the bends you will be stunned by the views of the deep valleys and high mountain peaks. The road then winds along the 3 240-m-high Pass of Guns and further on you reach the Mahlasela Pass (3 220 m). In winter the mountains here are often blanketed in snow and this is one of only two destinations in southern Africa where you can ski. It is a steady descent from the summit of Mahlasela Pass to the New Oxbow Lodge ski resort.

Moteng Pass

From Oxbow Lodge the road climbs steeply out of the valley, and about 9 km from the lodge you reach a viewpoint at the top of the 2 820-m-high Moteng Pass. Stop here and walk up the small hill to the left of the parking area. There is a lovely view of the pass and the Lowlands in the distance.

With the exception of Sani Pass, the Moteng Pass is by far the most spectacular of Lesotho's many tortuous mountain roads. It sweeps down the Front Range of the Malotis in a series of spectacular U-bends. After 17 km it reaches the turnoff to Liphofung cultural and historical site, a Lesotho Highlands Development Authority (LHDA) project managed by the local community.

The Sesotho name Liphofung means 'place of the eland' and well-preserved rock paintings depicting the eland (as well as other animals and humans in various postures) in the magnificent sandstone caves can be visited under the supervision of a well-informed guide. He will give you valuable insight into the paintings and show you around the small cultural village. A shop and ablution facilities are available.

Muela Dam

Having left the Highlands, the road to Butha-Buthe (where King Moshoeshoe I had his first stronghold) continues down the Hololo Valley. About 8 km beyond Liphofung a signpost points to the turnoff to Muela Dam and hydro-electric scheme situated about 6 km off the main road. Water is transferred from Katse Dam along a 45-km-long tunnel to the Muela power station and the Muela Dam, which in turn is linked to the Vaal River catchment area (the Ash River) via two tunnels of 37 km and 22 km.

The valley opens up gradually and you now travel across hilly country punctuated by sandstone plateaux with sheer cliffs. About 6 km beyond the turnoff to Caledonpoort Border Post

LESOTHO HIGHLANDS WATER PROJECT

The Lesotho Highlands Water Project transfers water from the upper Senqu River basin through a series of dams and tunnels to Gauteng. The first phase included the construction of the Katse Dam (the main storage reservoir for the project) and a tunnel linking it to a smaller dam, Muela, in the foothills of the Malotis' Front Range. From Muela the water is transferred along a tunnel to the Vaal River catchment area. Mohale Dam also formed part of the first phase and is linked to Katse by a 32-km-long tunnel. Three more dams are proposed and when the ambitious project is completed in 2027 it will have 240 km of tunnels.

The Mountain Road & Roof of Africa

in Butha-Buthe a signpost to the left points the way to the settlement of Khabo and Ts'ehlanyane National Park. A 31-km journey on a good gravel road brings you to the entrance gate of the park in the foothills of the Malotis' Front Range.

Ts'ehlanyane

Set against a backdrop of rugged mountain scenery, Ts'ehlanyane is another LHDA project providing protection to some of the best-preserved stands of oldwood, a species typical in kloofs and along streams at high altitudes. Here they are unusually dense, almost forming woodlands. The berg bamboo (*Arundinaria tesellata*) along the rivers and streams is the habitat of the bamboo sylph (*Metisella syrinx*), a darkish brown butterfly with small yellow flecks on the wings. It is usually best seen in January and February.

From Ts'ehlanyane, retrace your tracks for just over 31 km to the tar road. Turn left and follow the A1 to Hlotse (also referred to as Leribe), Kolonyama and Teyateyaneng, two towns renowned for their handicrafts. You can buy beautiful woven rugs, tapestries and other handicrafts at a number of good craft shops.

Either continue along the A1 to Maseru for 42 km or take a detour to Sefikeng from where a gravel road goes to Thaba Bosiu. Guided tours of Lesotho's most important historical site can be arranged at the tourism office at the foot of the mountain. You join the tarred road at the tourism office; after 9 km it joins the Mountain Road. Here you turn right and after 6.6 km right again, continuing for 16 km to Maseru.

LOGISTICS AND PLANNING

Fuel: Take enough to travel from Maseru to Butha-Buthe, roughly 550 km. Although it is available en route at Marakabei and Thaba Tseka, stocks can be unreliable.
Water: Available at Ts'ehlanyane but we suggest you take your own. (When we were there, leaf litter had entered the water system, making the water unsuitable for drinking, but this could have been a temporary problem.)
Food: You can buy groceries and alcoholic beverages at shops in Maseru. Frazer's Store in Marakabei has a fair range of groceries, and basic foodstuffs can be bought at stores along the way.
Firewood: Take your own firewood, charcoal or gas if you plan to camp.
Best times: Spring and autumn are generally the best seasons for a visit but remember that there's always a possibility of snow.

Booking

Mohale Lodge: tel: (+266) 2293-6432
Marakabei Guest House: tel: (+266) 585-0303
Katse Lodge: tel: (+266) 2291-0202
New Oxbow Lodge: tel: (+27 51) 933-2247
Liphofung Cultural and Historical Site: tel: (+266) 2246-0723
Ts'ehlanyane National Park: tel: (+266) 2246-0723
Katse, Mohale and Muela dam tours: tel: (+266) 2291-0276 for Katse, 2293-6217 for Mohale and 2248-1211 for Muela.

LESOTHO

Trans-Maloti

This journey takes you along the scenic Senqu Valley Road to Sehlabathebe National Park in the remote south-east of Lesotho. You follow the Trans-Maloti Track over the spectacular Matebeng Pass along one of the few remaining 4x4 tracks in Lesotho and continue to Sani Pass, which is one of the highlights of the route. Unlike the Highlands in the north, the landscape of southern Lesotho is characterised by sandstone outcrops and a patchwork of cultivated fields set amid rolling hills. You pass many villages and isolated settlements in this densely populated part of the country.

Facilities

Along this route there are several recommended accommodation establishments that range from backpackers' dormitories to self-catering chalets or bungalows.

The Trading Post, in Roma, 33 km from Maseru, offers self-catering accommodation in an old sandstone house and rondavels.

Semonkong Lodge, 122 km from Maseru and 13 km from Maletsunyane Falls, has rustic stone and thatch bungalows, backpackers' dormitories and a restaurant which serves delicious home-cooked meals (trout if you are lucky). A communal kitchen is available for self-caterers.

Malealea Lodge, 121 km from Maseru, has options that range from rustic chalets with en-suite showers and en-suite farmhouse rooms to backpackers' accommodation and camp sites.

Bethel Business and Community Development Centre has a fully-equipped guest flat, dormitory with bunks, kitchen and dining room facilities, meals on request.

Nohana does not have a camp site, but Chieftainess Christina is more than pleased to let you stay in her village for a small fee.

In order to camp at **Seforong Gorge** (where there are no facilities), you need to obtain permission from Chief Hareeng.

Sehlabathebe Lodge in Sehlabathebe National Park has rooms with separate and en-suite bathrooms, fully equipped kitchen, lounge with fireplace. Self-catering only.

Molumong Guesthouse and Backpackers is 7 km south of the Mokhotlong/Sani Pass road and offers self-catering accommodation in a former trading post.

Sani Top Chalet on the very edge of the Drakensberg Escarpment has rooms with shared bathrooms, backpackers' accommodation and a restaurant.

Activities

For **4x4 day excursions** into the surrounding mountains use The Trading Post, Semonkong Lodge and Malealea Lodge as a base. Semonkong, Malealea and Sani Top Chalet offer **pony treks** ranging from a few hours to extended overnight trails.

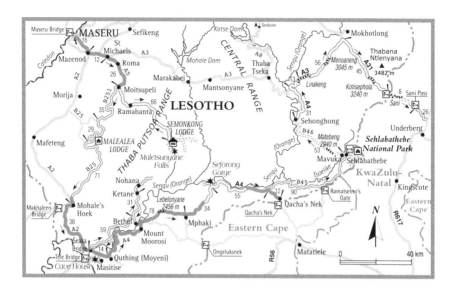

Sani Top Chalet is a good base for **hikes to Thabana Ntlenyana**, the highest point south of Kilimanjaro (a tough full day's hike there and back) and the nearby Hodgson's Peaks (three-and-a-half hours return).

THE TOUR – 1 400 km Maseru to Himeville

From the well-known Basotho Hat in the centre of Maseru follow the Kingsway Bypass and continue along the road to Mafeteng for 16 km where you turn left for Roma. The road traverses the cultivated fields and grasslands of the Lowlands for 12 km to St Michaels where the Mountain Road (see The Mountain Road & Roof of Africa, page 152) continues straight. Turn right here and as you head for Roma the white sandstone cliffs that are so characteristic of the Lowlands become more prominent.

The Trading Post on the right-hand side of the road is a good alternative to staying in Maseru, and the owners Ashley and Jennifer Thorn are helpful. Ashley is a veteran of the Roof of Africa Rally and can advise you first-hand on day routes in the area.

Situated in a picturesque sandstone valley, Roma is an important religious and educational centre. The first Roman Catholic Mission in Lesotho was established here in 1862, and today there are three seminaries.

Roma also houses the National University of Lesotho – which has its origins in the Pius XII College dating back to 1945 – and several primary and secondary schools.

Beyond Roma the road ascends steeply out of the Lowlands to cross the Front Range of the Malotis. As you get to the top of Ngakana Pass two prominent peaks come into view. Their Sesotho name Thabana li-Mele, which means 'the mountains that are like breasts', refers to their shape.

The road winds up and down to cross several rivers and streams until you finally run out of tar at Moitsupeli.

Turn left onto a gravel road and after 14 km you will reach the settlement of Ramabanta where you cross the Makhaleng River. Nowadays you hardly notice the river-crossing but in 1973 an intrepid explorer friend of ours, who was returning from Semonkong to Maseru, was stuck on the 'wrong' side for 18 days!

LESOTHO

Maletsunyane Falls

Beyond Ramabanta the road climbs out of the Makhaleng Valley and soon snakes its way up the Thaba Putsoa Range which has tarred sections in steep places. About 40 km after leaving the tar you reach the summit where you are greeted by expansive views of the valley formed by the Maletsunyane River. The road makes its way down along the mountain slopes into the valley and 19 km beyond the summit you reach the turnoff to the Maletsunyane Falls, 8.5 km away.

Semonkong, a Sesotho name that means 'place of smoke', a reference to the clouds of spray from the falls, lies 2.5 km further. This remote mountain settlement only became accessible by road in 1971, when, if road conditions were really good, the journey from Maseru took an entire day. Today it is a leisurely three-hour drive.

Semonkong Lodge is a good base from which to set off to the falls, and your hosts Jonathan and Armel, are extremely knowledgeable and helpful. Instead of driving, ride a pony, which you can hire at the lodge or hike along the river to the falls.

If you have time and energy you can walk down to the pool beneath the falls, but arrange a guide at the lodge first. The 192-m-high falls, the second highest in southern Africa, are also known as Le Bihan Falls after a French Catholic missionary who visited the falls in 1881, the first white person to do so.

From Semonkong, backtrack to the tar at Moitsupeli. Instead of turning right continue straight on a gravel road (signposted Maseru via Koro Koro) for 1.6 km where you turn left onto a track. Spectacular sandstone outcrops dominate the scenery to your right; the Makhalaneng River has incised a deep valley to the left. The terrain becomes more undulating, and 33.6 km after you leave the tar road a signboard indicates a left turn to Malealea Lodge, another 33 km on.

Botsoela Waterfalls

The road twists and turns as it makes its way above the deep Mamaebana and Makhalaneng valleys. About 18 km beyond the last turnoff you reach a viewpoint overlooking the valley spread out below the Gates of Paradise. Malealea Lodge lies across the valley to the southwest amid a clump of trees; by road it is another 14 km.

A narrow pass takes you down to the Botsoela River. A 500-m walk downstream will reveal a lovely view of the twin Botsoela Waterfalls and gorge. Follow the right-hand bank of the river to the top of the gorge where you cross over (beware of slippery wet rocks) for the best views of the falls and gorge.

The track climbs out of the valley and at the T-junction you turn left, continuing for another 9.1 km to a road which joins in from the right. Keep straight to reach Malealea Lodge 3 km further. A former trading post, Malealea has a rustic charm and at times can be a hive of activity with pony treks. Owners Di and Mick Jones always find time to chat, advise on what there is to do and show true mountain hospitality.

Gates of Paradise

Make an early start to reach Nohana as it is a long day's journey; not in distance, but in time.

Just over 3 km out of Malealea take the road to the left and soon you'll begin to climb to the Gates of Paradise from where there are stunning views of the surrounding valleys and mountains. The plaque inscribed 'Wayfarer! Pause and look upon a Gate of Paradise' was erected by Malealea's first owner, Mervyn Smith, who lived here from the early 1900s until his death in 1951.

About 7.7 km after leaving Malealea you reach a T-junction where you turn left, passing maize fields and villages before descending to the Makhaleng Valley. The prominent pyramid-shaped peak

> ### SPIRAL ALOE
>
> The striking and unusual spiral aloe (*Aloe polyphylla*) is one of the most endangered aloes in Lesotho. Its common name refers to the leaves which are arranged either clockwise or anti-clockwise, while the species name *polyphylla* means 'many leaves'. This aloe is endemic to Lesotho where it is restricted to steep barren basalt slopes at altitudes above 2 200 m. It has beautiful pale red to salmon-pink flowers, usually in September and October. Much sought-after by collectors, these aloes have decreased significantly in number during the last two decades and several sites have been destroyed completely. Semonkong Lodge has a few cultivated specimens. The owners and staff will also direct you to where they grow in their natural state. Do not be tempted to buy these aloes from people selling them along the road. It is a protected species.

to the south-east used to be a landmark for Jewish pedlars who traded there in years gone by. In time it became known as Masemouse, a corruption of the Afrikaans word *smous* (pedlar).

The road winds steeply out of the valley and then follows a wavy course parallel to the Mokhele Range and the Makhaleng River Valley to reach Mohale's Hoek, 71 km beyond Malealea. Unlike the scenery in the Highlands further north, the southern part of Lesotho is characterised by striking sandstone outcrops, and the landscape is more arid.

From Mohale's Hoek you have the luxury of a tarred road for 38 km to the Nohana turnoff, or 144 km if you're headed for Seforong Gorge.

Ketane Falls

The 103-km detour to Ha Jobo, 12 km beyond Nohana will take you at least four hours, and there is no option but to backtrack to the main tarred road as the gravel road comes to an abrupt end a short way further up the valley. A road is being built to Semonkong and, once it has been completed, travellers will be able to take a much shorter route to Nohana. The scenery is stunning but, to make the journey really worthwhile, you should combine it with an overnight hike to the Ketane Falls. The 122-m-high falls, the second highest in Lesotho, cascade over two steps into a delightful pool. There are also some rock paintings, but these are best explored if you get directions from the Christian mission at Ha Jobo.

Soon after turning off tar onto the gravel road to Nohana you pass the four-span Seaka Bridge which was erected in 1959 across the Senqu River.

Bethel Mission Station

The gravel road winds in and out of several valleys and there are some lovely views of the Senqu below. Ignore the turnoff to the left 37.7 km after turning off the tar road. Further on, a steep descent to the Tlaling River is followed by a long climb to the settlement of Phamong.

About 59 km after leaving the tar road you reach the turnoff to the Bethel Mission Station and the Bethel Business and Community Development Centre. An enterprising Canadian, Ivan Yaholnitsky, who has been living in Lesotho since 1986, has built up a solar 'village' and offers accommodation – an ideal spot to break your journey to or from Nohana.

LESOTHO

At the junction to Bethel, the road to Nohana continues to the left and deteriorates almost immediately. After about 2 km, straight ahead you will see the contact between the sandstone and the dark basalt. The road hugs the slopes as it skirts a ridge; you are now enfolded by the mountains.

About 14 km beyond the Bethel turnoff, the sandstone cliffs of the valley ahead come into view. A woolshed 16.5 km beyond the Bethel turnoff is a crucial landmark: turn right 600 m beyond it. The road descends steeply through a break in the cliffs to the Qobokoane River and winds along the Ketane Valley as it makes its way up to Ketane. With under 2 km to go to Ketane a sandstone outcrop with a hole eroded through it comes into view on your left. From here 3.7 km remains to the turnoff to Chieftainess Christina Nohana's homestead.

> **VITAL INFO**
>
> After heavy rain the Matebeng River is likely to be impassable and snow could block the Matebeng Pass any time of the year (most likely in winter). If you are caught, retrace your tracks from Sehlabathebe for 89 km to the tar road and leave Lesotho through the Qacha's Nek border post.

Cave House

Beyond Nohana the road winds along the Ketane Valley and there are lovely views of the river which you follow upstream. About 8 km from Nohana there is an inconspicuous turnoff to a bridge over the Ketane River to the right, 200 m beyond the 11-km marker.

If you turn right here, cross the bridge and turn sharp right again, you will reach the Youth with a Mission station, where Mark and Ronel Beckett are based, 900 m beyond the bridge. They accommodate visitors travelling in a single vehicle or a small group but as they are sometimes away it is best to contact them by e-mail in advance: QRV@intekom.co.za.

From here, backtrack for 103 km to the tar road, where you turn left, continuing for 9.2 km to a signpost to the Masitise Primary School. Ask at the school to view the historic Cave House built in 1866 by the Reverend D F Ellenberger of the Paris Evangelical Mission. The ingenious missionary enclosed the natural recess of the cave with sandstone blocks and lived here for 17 years. An imprint of a dinosaur footprint can be seen on the roof of the cave.

Back at the tar road you turn right, continuing to a turnoff opposite the Leloalang Industrial Training School. Take the turnoff to the left and continue to the river to view the dinosaur footprints on the opposite bank. Quthing (Moyeni) is a short way on and we advise you to refuel here for the remainder of the journey.

Seforong Gorge

A short way beyond Quthing the road meanders along the Senqu River Valley with spectacular views of the river and the sandstone cliffs. After passing Mount Moorosi you cross the Quthing River and wind steeply up the spectacular Lebelonyane Pass (2 456 m). Every time you think you're at the top, the road ahead goes even higher. A roller-coaster ride takes you down to Mphaki and about 15 km further the tar road ends. After 19 km on gravel turn left when you see the signpost for Hareeng High School, and drive for 4 km to the school where you should ask one of the students (they speak English) or villagers to take you to Chief Hareeng Tsepho for permission to camp at Seforong Gorge and to get directions.

The gorge is one of Lesotho's undiscovered gems. The Seforong River has carved through the sandstone cliffs to a depth of 230 m, on its journey north to join the Senqu River. The sheer cliffs provide nesting sites for bald ibis and Cape vulture. During the Difaqane wars they served as a refuge. You can camp on the flat spot just above the gorge. Walk along the Seforong River through the gorge to its junction with the Senqu River to appreciate the magnificent scenery.

Making for Sehlabathebe

Once you have backtracked to the main road, turn left. The road soon makes its way up a steep pass to cross a ridge and winds down to the scenic Senqu River Valley. The long fingers of development are visible in the tarred roads stretching westwards from Qacha's Nek as far as Tebellong. You reach Tebellong 35.7 km beyond the Seforong turnoff. Along the Senqu Valley the 2 853-m-high Maseepho dominates the scenery to the north.

Nineteen kilometres beyond Tebellong Hospital, an important landmark, keep a sharp lookout for the unsignposted turnoff to the left which will take you to Sehlabathebe National Park. You're now back on gravel and after crossing the Sejabatho River the road ascends steeply before levelling off. After 15.5 km it reaches a split to St Francis School. Keep left. The road twists vigorously as it makes its way to the remote border post of Ramatseliso's Gate, 45 km beyond the last split.

The scenery changes dramatically and the road traverses rounded grassy hills with outcrops of white sandstone against the backdrop of Thaba li-Maqoa to the north. About 29.5 km beyond Ramatseliso you reach Mavuka village, where the road to the Matebeng Pass turns off to the left. The entrance gate to Sehlabathebe is about 5 km on and the last 10 km to the lodge will take at least 45 minutes.

Sehlabathebe National Park

Sehlabathebe is one of the most wonderful places in Lesotho. Dominating its grassy meadows, white sandstone outcrops, natural rock arches and marshes are the triple peaks of the Baroaba-Bararo or the Three Bushmen. Established in 1970 as Lesotho's first national park, Sehlabathebe is home to two unique species. The endangered Drakensberg minnow (*Pseudobarbus quathlambae*) inhabits the streams. It averages 13 cm in length and its colour ranges from olive and grey-brown to deep blue with silvery white underparts. It is thought to be extinct in streams and rivers draining eastwards from the escarpment into KwaZulu-Natal. Another jewel of Sehlabathebe is a rare aquatic plant, *Aponogeton ranunculiflorus*, which is confined to rock pools in the park and a few pools on the KwaZulu-Natal side of the Drakensberg.

Extraordinary rock formations are an attraction of Sehlabathebe. The sandstone here is exposed at a higher altitude than anywhere else in the Drakensberg, and centuries of wind, rain and extremes of temperature have shaped it into fascinating caves, pillars, arches and potholes. The formations are just north of the lodge and a few hours exploring the area pass quickly.

Kepiseng

A rewarding half-day excursion is along the Tsoelikane River to Kepiseng (The Cap), a sandstone landmark. Continue to the 20-m-high Tsoelikane Waterfall where you can take a refreshing dip in the icy mountain water before heading back to the lodge. If you are interested in rock art, you can visit the rock painting sites, of which there are at least 60 in the park.

Grey rhebok and mountain reedbuck are the two large animals you are most likely to see, while large herds of eland migrate to the park in summer and can usually be seen between December and March. Oribi also occur.

LESOTHO

As the grasslands of Sehlabathebe are relatively pristine, this is the only place in Lesotho where you are almost guaranteed to tick the yellow-breasted pipit, a species confined to ungrazed grasslands over 2 500 m above sea level. Bald ibis feeding on the grasslands and lammergeier soaring overhead are two other highlights. Orange-breasted rockjumper, mountain pipit and Drakensberg siskin are three montane 'specials' that will delight birders.

Scan the rocky outcrops for ground woodpecker and sentinel rock thrush, while the grasslands might yield secretary bird, pin-tailed whydah and yellow bishop.

If you're planning to travel from Sehlabathebe to Sani Pass in one day, start very early as the 220-km journey takes at least 10 hours of hard driving – in favourable conditions! From Sehlabathebe, backtrack to Mavuka where you turn right and head up the Litsoeneng Valley. As you begin to wind up the Matebeng Pass in a series of tight switchbacks, you cannot help wondering whether a crossing is possible. With a sigh of relief you finally reach the 2 940-m-high top – about 13.4 beyond the Mavuka turnoff. Take a break to enjoy the terrific scenery and to photograph one of Lesotho's few untarred major passes.

The track now winds steeply down the side of the Matebeng River Valley and 19.4 km from the top you finally reach the valley. Passing a clump of poplars, orchards and cultivated lands, you drive through a narrow poort and continue along the bank of the river.

Ignore the well-defined track ascending the left-hand bank of the river just after passing through the poort, and continue for 2 km along the left bank until you see a bridge.

The approaches on both sides have been washed away, so the river is crossed a short way downstream. A steep ascent follows up a pass with some loose gravel and one nasty inward-sloping incline. From the top of the plateau there are splendid views of the Senqu Valley to the left. You have an easy stretch of driving before the road winds down to the Sehonghong River and then climbs steeply to the mountain village of the same name. Much to your relief you join a good gravel road at the northern end of the village. From here it is 31 km of easy driving to the Thaba Tseka/Sani Pass road. On the journey there are lovely views of the Senqu River which might one day be dammed in the vicinity of the settlement of Mashai as part of the Lesotho Highlands Water Project.

Linakeng and Menoaneng Passes

From the junction the road descends almost immediately; after 13 km it reaches Linakeng where it ascends steeply along the Linakeng Pass, only to wind down again to follow the Linakaneng River. But the roller-coaster ride is far from over and you soon begin a sustained climb to the 3 045-m-high top of the Menoaneng Pass, gaining over 1 000 m. Stop here to enjoy the superb views stretching northwards before tackling the last 20.5 km to the Mokhotlong/Sani Pass Road where you turn right.

Kotisephola Pass, Black Mountain and Thabana Ntlenyana

The road ascends steadily along the valley of the Sehonghong River and then makes a final ascent up the Kotisephola Pass (3 240 m) and across the Black Mountain which is often covered in snow. If you stop at the summit and walk up the ridge to the right, the 3 482-m-high Thabana Ntlenyana ('the beautiful little mountain') can be seen to the north-east. Were it not for the fact that it is the highest peak south of Kilimanjaro, this rather unimposing peak would attract little attention.

Further on the Sani Flats, which is a grassy meadow that extends along the escarpment, comes into view, and it is only a few kilometres from here to your final destination, Sani

Top Chalet. Perched on the very edge of the escarpment, this is the highest (licensed) pub in southern Africa and offers breathtaking views of the Little Berg far below.

The lammergeier with its wedge-shaped tail and the bald ibis are two rare bird species often seen here. Also of interest is Slogget's rat that can be found among the rocks around the chalet. These reddish brown rats, also known as ice rats, are restricted to high altitudes in Lesotho, the uKhahlamba-Drakensberg and Eastern Cape Drakensberg where they have to survive extreme temperatures when it has snowed.

Sani Pass

After passing through the Sani Pass border in Lesotho (2 865 m), you almost immediately begin descending the pass which sweeps down a steep U-shaped valley in a series of spectacular hairpin bends. As little as a decade ago these presented a formidable challenge to driver and vehicle alike but now it is an easy drive up or down. It remains a marvel of engineering, however. Over the first 1.5 km of the descent there are no fewer than 16 switchbacks.

Sani Pass was originally a bridle path used by 300 transport riders and 5 000 pack animals to transport food and provisions from KwaZulu-Natal to eastern Lesotho.

On 26 October 1948 the first motor vehicle drove up the treacherous mountain pass – an almost incredible feat. Seven years later the intrepid David Alexander pioneered the Mokhotlong Transport Company's first service from Himeville below the Berg to Mokhotlong. In those early days some of the hairpin bends could be negotiated only by reversing to and fro three times and the journey was not without risks. Just over 8 km beyond the Lesotho border post you reach the South African post from where it is a winding 26 km to the junction to Himeville and Underberg, which marks the end of a wonderful journey through Lesotho.

LOGISTICS AND PLANNING

Fuel: Fill your tank in Maseru and Moyeni. Have enough fuel to travel 610 km from Moyeni to Underberg in South Africa as fuel supplies can be unreliable in the rural areas.
Water: It is advisable to carry drinking water with you.
Food: Stock up on food and alcoholic beverages in Maseru as you will find only basic foodstuffs along the way.
Firewood: Take your own firewood, charcoal or gas for the overnight stops.
Best times: Spring and autumn are generally the best months for a visit as temperatures are comfortable. Snowfalls occur so beware.

Bookings

The Trading Post, tel and fax: (+266) 2234-0202
Semonkong Lodge, tel: (+27 51) 933-3106
Malealea Lodge, tel and fax: (+27 51) 447-3200 or 448-3001
Bethel Business and Community Development Centre: PO Box 53, Mt Moorosi 750, Lesotho, e-mail: bbcdc@uuplus.com
Nohana: No booking required
Seforong: No booking required for camp at Seforong Gorge
Sehlabathebe Lodge, in Sehlabathebe National Park: tel: (+266) 2232-3600
Molumong Guesthouse and Backpackers: tel: (+27 33) 345-7045, e-mail: molumong@worldonline.co.za
Sani Top Chalet: tel: (+27 33) 702-1158, e-mail: sanitop@futurenet.co.za

Main picture: The remote Richtersveld, north-western South Africa. Inset picture: The Drumstick is one of several interesting rock formations at Die Toon in the Richtersveld National Park.

South Africa

SOUTH AFRICA

Aptly known as 'a world in one country', South Africa is richly endowed with a mosaic of landscapes ranging from the lofty mountain peaks of the Drakensberg and the rugged scenery of the Richtersveld to the harsh Karoo with its wide expanses. Several of its conservation areas are home to the Big Five (lion, leopard, elephant, rhino and buffalo) and large herds of antelope and other mammals. The land also supports a rich diversity of birds, reptiles, amphibians, trees, shrubs and flowering plants.

The world-famous Kruger National Park, the game parks and reserves of KwaZulu-Natal and many other conservation areas throughout the country offer exceptional experiences with nature. Only three of these wildlife destinations are included in this book – the Karoo and Richtersveld national parks and the Baviaanskloof conservation area. Riemvasmaak, the fourth South African destination, does not enjoy any conservation status.

The main reason why we have included only four South African destinations in this book is the excellent state of South Africa's road infrastructure and tourism facilities. This has brought most national parks and game and nature reserves within easy reach of densely populated urban areas, and they consequently lack the essential ingredients of what we consider 'wild places': minimal development of tourism infrastructure, and a sense of wilderness, isolation and remoteness. This does not, however, detract from the experiences and activities offered by these more accessible parks and reserves, many of which can be incorporated into a journey to the wild places we have included in the book.

Cone-shaped dolerite koppies, tabletop mountains, expansive plains roamed by herds of springbok, black wildebeest, black rhino and other species are among the many attractions of the Karoo National Park which is at the heart of the Great Karoo. Part of the allure of the Karoo lies in its crisp clean air, the aromatic smell of the 'bossies', and the endless space and solitude.

The Richtersveld National Park in the Northern Cape is South Africa's only mountain desert. Among the Richtersveld's wealth of succulents are the striking elephant's trunk or *halfmens*, 17 aloe species and a wealth of mesembs (succulent members of the family *Aizoaceae*). The Richtersveld is also renowned for its stunning mountain scenery which contrasts sharply with the green ribbon of vegetation growing alongside the Gariep River, the park's northern boundary.

Several hundred kilometres upstream of the Richtersveld along the Gariep River is Riemvasmaak, a little-known wilderness. Bounded in the south by the Gariep, Riemvasmaak lies north-west of the Augrabies Falls National Park in an area characterised by tabletop mountains, deep valleys and plains. The Molopo Canyon with its sheer cliffs and hot spring is a highlight of Riemvasmaak.

The proclaimed road that winds through the Baviaanskloof conservation area in the Eastern Cape allows you to explore the rugged grandeur of this remote area with its profusion of trees, shrubs and flowering plants. A journey through this wild kloof can be combined with outdoor activities such as hiking in the wilderness areas and mountain biking.

Overview

In an exciting development, several transfrontier conservation areas have been established between South Africa and its neighbours. Among these are the Kgalagadi Transfrontier Park which links South Africa with Botswana; the Great Limpopo which links Kruger National Park with the Limpopo National Park in Mozambique and Gonarezhou National Park in Zimbabwe; Ai-Ais/Richtersveld with Namibia; the Maloti/Drakensberg with Lesotho; and the Lubombo Transfrontier Conservation Area with Swaziland and Mozambique. Several of the wild places covered in this book traverse transfrontier conservation areas in countries adjoining South Africa.

In line with the phenomenal growth in sales of recreational vehicles and the increased need of city dwellers to escape to the wilds, even if it's just for a day or a weekend, there has been a proliferation of 4x4 trails on private property countrywide. Many of these destinations provide an opportunity to 'get away from it all' within easy reach of densely populated metropolitan areas. It is impossible to do justice to all these destinations, and we recommend that you obtain a copy of *Drive Out*, an annual publication listing over 250 self-drive destinations and guided 4x4 trails throughout southern Africa.

Since South Africa has excellent road links with neighbouring countries, the wild places described in this book in neighbouring countries are easily accessible by road. Among the major road links are the Maputo Corridor between Gauteng and Maputo, and the Platinum Highway, presently under construction, which will link up with the Trans-Kalahari Highway. The latter traverses the Kalahari in Botswana and, from Buitepos on the border between Botswana and Namibia, continues to Windhoek and the coastal towns of Swakopmund and Walvis Bay.

The Karoo and Richtersveld national parks as well as Riemvasmaak are situated in arid areas known for their extremes of temperatures. Maximum summer temperatures ranging between 33 and 40°C are not uncommon and can exceed 50° in the Gariep River Valley. Minimum temperatures can drop to 5°C in midwinter when the Nuweveld Mountains in the Karoo National Park are often snow capped. Annual rainfall ranges from 125 mm in the Riemvasmaak area which lies in the summer rainfall area to 260 mm in the Karoo National Park which has rain throughout the year. Most of the Richtersveld's rainfall is recorded

The Richtersveld is South Africa's only mountain desert.

SOUTH AFRICA

in winter. The Baviaanskloof has a highly variable climate as a result of its location and topography. Its rainfall occurs throughout the year, peaking in summer.

South Africa has a great diversity of cultures and two of the destinations described in this chapter offer the possibility to interact with the local inhabitants: the Nama of the Richtersveld and the Riemvasmakers. While the Richtersvelders refused to move out of their ancestral lands to make way for the proclamation of a national park (resulting in the creation of a contractual park), the Riemvasmakers were the first people to lodge a successful land claim following the democratisation of South Africa in 1994.

BORDER POSTS AND FORMALITIES

There are 16 border posts between South Africa and Botswana. Popular entry points are the Skilpadhek/Pioneer Gate (06h00 to 22h00), Kopfontein/Tlokweng (06h00 to 22h00), Groblersbrug/Martin's Drift (08h00 to 18h00) and Ramatlabama (07h00 to 20h00).

There are 12 border posts between South Africa and Lesotho. Maseru and Ficksburg bridges are open 24 hours a day. Some of the smaller border posts are open only between 08h00 and 16h00.

Komatipoort/Ressano Garcia, on the Maputo Corridor linking Witbank and Maputo, is open from 06h00 to 19h00, Ponta do Ouro in the far south from 07h30 to 17h30 and Pafuri border post in Kruger National Park from 08h00 to 16h00.

The main points of entry into Namibia from South Africa are at Vioolsdrif/Noordoewer in the south of Namibia and Ariamsvlei/Hohlweg in the south-east of the country. Both border posts are open 24 hours.

IMMIGRATION

You will need a valid passport and, depending on your nationality, a visa. Enquiries about visas can be directed to South African diplomatic representatives abroad. Visitors requiring visas and who intend travelling to countries neighbouring South Africa and back are advised to apply for multiple entry visas.

CUSTOMS

There is no duty on new or used personal effects and sporting and recreational equipment imported for use during your stay in South Africa. The duty-free allowance for visitors includes 2 litres of wine, 1 litre of spirits and alcoholic beverages, 400 cigarettes, and new or used goods with a total value not exceeding R1 250 per person.

VEHICLE DOCUMENTATION

Have your vehicle registration document handy at border posts where you might be asked for the original vehicle registration document.

DRIVING

The wearing of seat belts (including passengers in the rear seats) is compulsory and you must have an International Driving Permit (obtainable from the Automobile Association) or a valid driver's licence with you while driving.

Overview

Unless otherwise indicated, the speed limit in urban areas is 60 km an hour and 120 km on national roads.

CURRENCY AND BANKS
The South African Rand is divided into 100 cents and is also legal tender in Lesotho, Swaziland and Namibia. Banks and ATMs (auto teller machines) are available throughout the country and even in small towns cashing money, exchanging foreign currency or withdrawing cash from an ATM should not be a problem. Although credit cards are widely accepted, you cannot pay for fuel with credit and debit cards. Only petrol/garage cards are accepted for fuel.

IMPORTANT INFORMATION
Riemvasmaak falls in a malaria epidemic area and it is advisable to consult a doctor or travel clinic about the most effective prophylaxis, especially when visiting the area in summer.

The quality of South Africa's drinking water is very high and tap water is safe to drink throughout the country.

MAPS
Maps of the roads and tracks in the four destinations are available and are sufficient when used in conjunction with the route markers provided in the Richtersveld National Park, Riemvasmaak and the Karoo 4x4 Trail.

A good road map or road atlas will be useful to get to the start of the destinations. The Map Studio *Road Atlas of South Africa* (currently in its 17th edition) will be a useful investment.

The Northern Cape is home to a rich diversity of aloes and other succulents.

SOUTH AFRICA

Karoo 4x4 Trail

Vast plains shimmering in dancing heat waves, wide open space merging with the horizon, low Karoo bushes and solitude – all of these images come readily to mind when you mention the name Karoo. For many travellers it is just a place to pass through as quickly as possible, one that is best avoided during the heat of the day. The 80-km-long 4x4 trail in the Karoo National Park situated near Beaufort West in the Western Cape will soon dispel any such misconceptions as you make your way across plains that abound in antelope, as you pass through lush vegetated valleys and struggle up steep inclines, to viewpoints that afford far-reaching vistas of the magnificent landscape accompanied by the distinctive aroma of Karoo bushes.

THE PARK

The Karoo National Park was established in 1979 to preserve a representative sample of the Karoo biome that covers vast areas of South Africa. The nucleus of the original park consisted of a large area of commonage donated by the Beaufort West Municipality and two farms bought with money made available by the state and additional funds raised by the SA Nature Foundation (now WWF South Africa). Since then the park has been enlarged several times through the acquisition of neighbouring farms. The long-term aim is to expand the park from its current 86 000 ha to at least 100 000 ha.

Although rehabilitating the overgrazed farmland is a long and slow process, remarkable recovery of the vegetation in the original section of the park has been achieved in just under a quarter of a century.

Landscape and vegetation

Dominating the park's landscape are the majestic Nuweveld Mountains with their steep slopes and dolerite cliffs. Bulthoudersbank, the highest point in the park, rises over 1 000 m above the plains which characteristically cover 80% of the Karoo. Tabletop mountains, cone-shaped peaks and deep ravines add to the park's scenic allure.

In spite of the Karoo's harsh climate, an amazingly rich variety of hardy grasses, succulents, dwarf shrubs and trees occurs here. 'Karoo bossies' is a collective name for the small bushes that are so characteristic of the plains and mountain slopes.

The early farmers gave these plants descriptive names that usually refer to a particular characteristic, among them are *koggelmandervoetkaroo* (*Limeum aethiopicum*) which resembles the foot of a lizard, good Karoo (*Pentzia incana*) because of its palatability, and *biltongbos* (*Pteronia glomerata*).

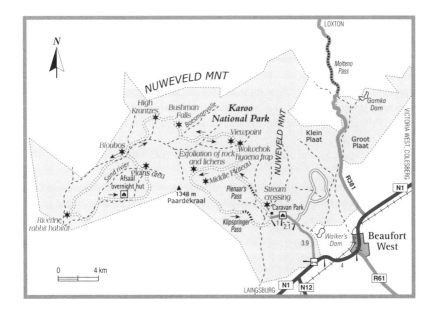

Typical trees and shrubs found in the Karoo National Park include the yellow pomegranate which is covered in a spectacular mass of flowers after rains, honey thorn (also known as the *kriedoring*), cancer bush (*Sutherlandia frutescens*) and Karoo cross-berry (*Grewia robusta*). Sweet thorns occur on the banks of river washes. Broom's aloe (*Aloe broomii*) with its long slender flower heads is conspicuous on rocky slopes from late August to early October.

A single stand of the star tree, which is endemic to the mountains around Sutherland and Calvinia, occurs on the plateau in the park. It grows as a shrub or small tree with needle-like leaves and owes its common name to the star-like appearance of the rosette-shaped leaves. In 1985, when the Springbok Hiking Trail was the only facility in the park, we were fortunate to see this rare plant on the trail.

Fauna and game-viewing

The Karoo plains were once the habitat of vast herds of migrating springbok: the traveller George Thompson reported seeing '... prodigious flocks of springboks spread over the plains as far as the eye could see' near Beaufort West in June 1823. Thompson estimated that he had seen about 100 000 springbok in the course of an 80-km journey.

It didn't take the Dutch farmers, who began settling in the Karoo in the 1750s, long to wipe out the teeming herds of antelope and baboon; mountain reedbuck, grey rhebok, klipspringer and a variety of smaller mammals were all that remained.

In 1977, when the establishment of the park was still in its initial stages, springbok and black wildebeest were released, and red hartebeest, gemsbok and Cape mountain zebra were reintroduced during the following year. Buffalo have also been introduced from the Addo Elephant National Park in the Eastern Cape.

Lion, leopard and wild dog will be brought in once the park has been expanded to its long-term aim of at least 100 000 ha.

Bat-eared fox, black-backed jackal, caracal, Cape clawless otter and honey badger count among the small mammals that occur in the park.

SOUTH AFRICA

Birding
To date some 170 bird species have been recorded in the park. The cliffs and rocky habitats support the highest concentration of Verreaux's eagles in southern Africa outside of the Matobo Hills area in Zimbabwe. This is largely due to the abundance of rock dassies (the main prey of Verreaux's eagle) and the many suitable nesting and roosting sites on the cliffs of the Nuweveld Mountains. Research has shown that a single pair of Verreaux's eagles catches at least 135 dassies a year and they therefore play an important role in keeping the dassie population in check.

Raptors: jackal, augur and steppe buzzards; booted and martial eagles; lesser kestrel; peregrine falcon.

Other species: ostrich, southern tchagra, Namaqua sandgrouse, cinnamon-breasted warbler, Karoo chat, Karoo korhaan, Ludwig's bustard, blue crane, Cape penduline tit, ground woodpecker, Namaqua warbler, and Karoo long-billed and Karoo larks.

Facilities
A century-old stone shepherd's cottage has been restored to serve as the overnight hut on the trail. It is equipped with six bunk beds, a single bed, gas lamp and fireplace.

In the **Karoo Rest Camp** facilities range from fully equipped and serviced chalets and cottages built in the Cape-Dutch style to camp sites with communal hot showers and flush toilets. Other amenities include a well-stocked shop, restaurant, swimming pool and information centre. Reservations must be made through SA National Parks (*see* details on page 176).

Activities
Enquire about guided night drives at park reception.
- The **Fossil Trail** gives you a fascinating insight into the geological forces that fashioned the Karoo and the era when dinosaurs roamed what was once a huge inland lake. Several fossil specimens can be seen along the trail – some reconstructed and others displayed as they were found. Numbered signs indicate points of interest that are explained in a trail pamphlet.
- Walk the 800-m-long **Bossie Trail** to familiarise yourself with the fascinating Karoo vegetation. Over 60 typical Karoo plants along the trail have been labelled with their common and scientific names.

RIVERINE RABBIT

In 1994 six riverine rabbits, which is southern Africa's most endangered mammal species, were released into an enclosure in the Sand River area after they had been successfully bred in captivity at the De Wildt breeding centre situated near Hartbeespoort Dam in North West Province. Overgrazing of the dense vegetation fringing the rivers and streams in the central Karoo had resulted in a dramatic population decline. The riverine rabbit was feared extinct until 1979, when one was seen near Victoria West. After an extensive search a few animals were caught and taken to De Wildt for a breeding programme in 1987. Although the animals initially seemed to have settled down in their new home, the project was not successful.

Karoo 4x4 Trail

BLACK RHINO

Part of the trail winds through the rhino camp in the Sand River area where three black rhino of the western sub-species were released in 1993, some 215 years after the last rhino was shot in the vicinity of the park. The translocation formed part of a project to prevent inbreeding and to separate the black rhino gene pools. A bull and a cow were transferred from Vaalbos National Park near Barkly West and a cow was relocated from the Augrabies Falls National Park. A calf was born within 18 months of their arrival in the park.

Getting there

The turnoff to the park is signposted 4 km south of Beaufort West on the N1 to Cape Town; from here it is another 6 km to the rest camp.

THE ROUTE – 120 km Beaufort West return

A short way after leaving the rest camp the track crosses a stream in Fonteintjieskloof and you reach the foot of Pienaar's Pass. Stop here, engage low range first gear and drive carefully up the steep narrow track built along the slopes of the kloof. Construction of the track began in 1945 and it took farmer Kowie Pienaar and four workers 10 years to complete (after it was opened, the journey to and from the plateau by horse or wagon to count sheep was cut from three days to a few hours).

You reach the middle plateau once you have negotiated the pass; here you should keep an eye out for Cape mountain zebra and red hartebeest. Springbok usually occur on the plains but migrate into the mountains after rains when new growth sprouts.

Still further on you reach the 'Wolwehok' – a stone cage built to catch predators such as brown hyaena, leopard and jackal (early Afrikaans farmers commonly referred to the hyaena as a wolf). Bait was tied to a peg at the back of the cage and when the animal took the bait a mechanism that released a flat stone in front of the opening was triggered. The animal was later either speared or shot dead through a small opening in the rear of the trap.

Expansive views of the dolerite-capped Nuweveld Mountains and the plains below greet you at a nearby viewpoint. From here the pass winds down the mountain slopes to a valley where a track to the old Doornhoek homestead, which has been converted into a self-catering guest cottage, splits off to the left. The trail climbs steeply upwards to a viewpoint overlooking the Bushman Falls which are dry except after rains. The white streaks on the rock faces are formed by calcium in the urine of the rock dassie.

The trail continues its steep ascent before levelling off below the dolerite cliffs of the Nuweveld Mountains. These cliffs were formed over 180 million years ago when molten matter intruded into the overlying rock. Unlike lava it did not reach the surface and as it cooled down inside the earth's crust it was transformed into dolerite and cracked vertically. Over millions of years the softer rock was eroded away, leaving only the hard dolerite caps that are so characteristic of the Karoo koppies and mountains. They are up to 100 m high and, as they eroded, large boulders and rocks gouged deep gullies as they slid to the base of the slopes; here they formed clusters that later provided a foothold for trees and shrubs.

SOUTH AFRICA

THOMAS BAIN

Of the 24 roads and passes Thomas Bain built, his most outstanding work is without doubt the Swartberg Pass which links the Little Karoo and the village of Prince Albert in a series of sweeping curves. Among his many other famous roadworks are Cogman's Kloof, Garcia's Pass, the Passes Road between George and Knysna and the spectacular Groot River and Bloukrans passes in the Tsitsikamma. Thomas was the son of Andrew Geddes Bain whose monumental roadworks include Bain's Kloof and Michell's passes in the Western Cape.

A steep ascent to the Doringhoek River brings you to a junction where you will rejoin the trail the following day. Turn right here to follow the track which runs parallel to the Sand River before it loops back to the overnight hut.

The second day's route initially traverses the plains area before you retrace your tracks to Kruiwakloof where you turn right. For the next few kilometres you mainly follow a contour as you make your way to the junction with the tourist route where the 4x4 trail ends. From here you follow a tar road down the Klipspringer Pass, built using the dry-packed stone wall technique of Andrew Geddes Bain, and in places the retaining wall is over 9 m high. Michell's and Bain's Kloof passes in the Western Cape are among the famed road engineer's lasting memories (*see* box on his son Thomas Bain above). Construction of the Klipspringer Pass (which was completed in 1991) took over two and a half years as most of the work was done by hand.

Stop at the viewpoint overlooking the Rooivalle ('red falls'). Topsoil that is washed downstream after rains turns the water into a seething mass of red water, hence the name of the falls.

LOGISTICS AND PLANNING

Fuel: Obtainable in Beaufort West.
Food and beverages: Take enough for one night.
Firewood: Take your own firewood, charcoal or gas for the overnight stop.
Best times: Autumn and spring are generally the best seasons to visit the park. The Karoo is renowned for its extreme temperatures. In summer it is boiling hot with average maximum temperatures of about 33°C in January. In winter, the Nuweveld Mountains are often covered in a blanket of snow and minimum temperatures in June and July average about 5°C. Rainfall averages a meagre 260 mm and occurs throughout the year with a peak in February and March. August can be windy and Beaufort West holds South Africa's wind-speed record – 186 km an hour.

Maps
A map of the trail is included in the trail booklet which gives information on the various sites of interest along the route.

Bookings
Advance reservations must be made with South African National Parks, PO Box 787, Pretoria 0001, tel: (+ 27 12) 428-9111, fax: 343-0905, e-mail: reservations@parks-sa.co.za.

Riemvasmaak

This little-known corner of South Africa is situated in the sparsely-populated Northern Cape Province, not far from the town of Upington and the Augrabies Falls. The people of Riemvasmaak make their living from stock farming and irrigation agriculture, but they have seized on tourism to supplement their income. Three 4x4 routes traverse the harsh, starkly beautiful landscape of this region, which is bordered in the south by the Gariep River with its lush riverine fringe and vineyards. The spectacular Molopo Canyon with its hot spring is just one of the highlights of a visit to Riemvasmaak, but in addition there are panoramic vistas and delightful camp sites tucked away in deep valleys to attract you. As well as the 4x4 trails, active visitors can also explore the area on foot or by mountain bike.

THE REGION

Later Stone Age people and their descendants, the Bushmen, lived in the Riemvasmaak area for thousands of years, and the rock engravings that may be seen on the Perdepoort Trail are a reminder of these hunter-gatherers. Small groups of pastoral Khoikhoi also lived here later and Riemvasmaak was surveyed and set aside as grazing for the descendants of the Khoikhoi people in 1870.

Under South Africa's apartheid policy of separate development, Riemvasmaak became a so-called 'Coloured Reserve' for the descendants of the Khoikhoi people.

This wild tract of land became the new home of a group of pastoral people who migrated here in the early 1900s from southern Namibia as well as Xhosa-speaking people from Tsitsikamma in the Eastern Cape. Riemvasmaak owes its name to the practice of the Riemvasmakers to punish Bushmen stock rustlers by tying them with leather thongs to a natural stone pillar in the Molopo River. On one occasion a culprit managed to free himself and only the thongs were found at the stone pillar.

In 1973 the people of Riemvasmaak were resettled in line with the apartheid government's homelands policy. The Namibians were relocated to the area then known as Damaraland, in the mistaken belief that they were Damara, and the Xhosa were resettled in the former Ciskei (now part of the Eastern Cape). Riemvasmaak then became a military testing area for South African Air Force fighter jets and long-range artillery guns, and a large tract of land was incorporated into the Augrabies Falls National Park as a contractual park.

Following the first democratic elections in South Africa in 1994, the Riemvasmakers who had formerly been moved to Namibia and Ciskei became the first people to lodge a successful land claim. When the South African Defence Force left the area, the contractual

SOUTH AFRICA

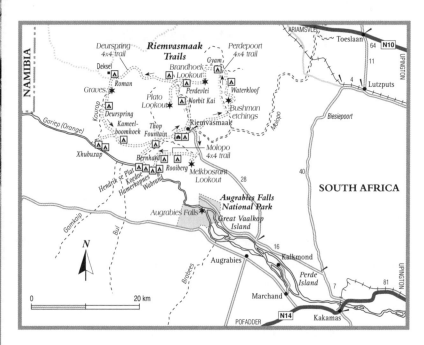

park ceased to exist. The first group of Riemvasmakers returned from Namibia in March 1995, and the Xhosa-speakers followed. While the Riemvasmakers are traditionally pastoralists living mainly in the settlement of Riemvasmaak and several outposts, the Xhosa-speakers are concentrated along the Gariep River where they farm. The total community now numbers approximately 1 200 people.

Landscape and vegetation

Eroded granite outcrops, long tabletop mountains and deep valleys characterise the landscape of Riemvasmaak in the west. In sharp contrast are the flat-topped mountains separated in the east by sandy plains, which are transformed into grasslands after rains. The Gariep River forms a natural boundary in the south, and the Molopo River has eroded a spectacular deep gorge with sheer cliffs through the landscape just west of the Riemvasmaak settlement.

The vegetation is typical of arid areas and is adapted to withstand high temperatures and little rainfall. Black thorn, shepherd's tree, stink shepherd's tree, driedoring (*Rhigozum trichotomum*), blue neat's foot and jacket plum occur widely through the area. Milkbushes (*Euphorbia*) are characteristic of the flat mountain tops, and quiver trees and Bushman poison tree (*Euphorbia avasmontana*) are conspicuous in rocky areas. The small-leafed Karoo boerbean is dominant along river courses in the rocky western reaches of the area. White karee and wild tamarisk grace the banks of the Gariep River. Grassy plains extend over the sandy eastern section of the area.

Fauna and game-viewing

Game is scarce and, although fair numbers of kudu occur in the wooded kloofs, they are seldom seen. Small family groups of klipspringer and rock dassies inhabit rocky areas, and steenbok also occur.

Predators are represented by black-backed jackal, caracal and leopard.

Riemvasmaak

Birding
Birding enthusiasts will have ample time to indulge as the trails are all short.
Raptors: Verreaux's eagle, jackal buzzard, rock kestrel, lanner falcon, black-shouldered kite and African harrier-hawk.
Water birds (along the Gariep River): Pied and giant kingfishers, Goliath and black-headed herons, Egyptian goose, African darter.
Others: Namaqua and double-banded sandgrouse, three-banded courser, Ludwig's bustard, Karoo korhaan, ant-eating chat, mountain wheatear, common scimitarbill, pale-winged starling, hamerkop and Cape francolin.

Facilities
Four stone and reed chalets are set among the rocky slopes of the spectacular Molopo Canyon with its sheer cliffs. They sleep from four to eight people and have a kitchenette, cold shower, wash basin and braai area.

There are also **camp sites without facilities** and a communal braai area near the spring. The descent into the canyon is steep, but there is a track with a less severe gradient for 2x4 vehicles. A hot spring where water with a temperature of 39°C bubbles to the surface is close, and you can relax in two small cement pools, or in more natural surroundings further downstream. Don't be surprised, as we were, if while you are relaxing in the pools you are suddenly surrounded by goats that come to drink here.

Several **camp sites without facilities**, except a stone wall which acts as a wind break, are available along the three routes.

Activities
You can explore the area on a **mountain bike or on foot** with the option of a guide. One of the hiking highlights is the **12-km-long route from the hot springs** along the spectacular Molopo Canyon to the Gariep River. The **Huab Fall Walk** is just 1.4 km to the usually dry waterfall upstream of the Molopo Camp.

Getting there
Approaching along the N10, take the turnoff signposted Keimoes, 64 km west of Upington and 70 km east of Namibia's Ariamsvlei border post. Follow the directions to Kakamas for 55.8 km on gravel roads where you turn right (west). After 15.6 km you turn right and continue for another 28 km to the settlement of Riemvasmaak.

The route from Kakamas is signposted (Namibia/Riemvasmaak) just east of the town on the N14. Follow this road for just over 7 km, turn left (west) and the remaining 43.6 km follows the same route as described above.

ROUTES – 330 km Kakamas return
You have a choice of three routes, none of which requires more than average 4x4 driving skills, over largely rocky terrain. Distances range from 43 km to 63 km which means that each trail takes only a few hours to complete. To appreciate the area properly you should spend at least two nights out, or base yourself at the hot spring and do the trails as day routes.

Many of the tracks are negotiable by 2x4 bakkies with a high ground clearance and wide tyres, as long as you follow the recommended direction of the trails and have some experience in driving through sand and over rocky terrain. Enquire at the information office.

SOUTH AFRICA

Gneiss outcrops punctuate the landscape of Riemvasmaak.

Deurspring trail
From the Information Centre follow the road past the clinic (housed in a container). After 200 m you pass a track leading off to the left to the hot spring (signposted Place to Go). The route winds across a wide plain set against the backdrop of tabletop mountains and further on you reach the turnoff to the site of the old military base. Except for a few cement foundations and a high sand wall that surrounded the base, nothing else remains and the detour is not really worth the effort. The track now follows a valley and beyond Norbit Kai camp site you ascend a short pass to reach the On Kais Falls (dry except after rains).

You reach a T-junction and the On Kais camp site about 1 km on. The track to the right leads to Perdevlei camp site, but for the Deurspring route you must follow the track to the left which climbs steeply as it makes its way to the plateau. When you reach the turnoff to the Plato Lookout (1.1 km beyond the T-junction) turn left and continue slowly for 5 km along a bumpy track to the viewpoint overlooking the valley you have just negotiated. Retrace your tracks to the main track, where you turn left, and continue for 500 m to the junction with the Perdepoort Trail. Turn left.

The track now traverses a vast plateau with little vegetation other than clumps of milkbush. After crossing the plateau for about 9 km the track drops down steeply into the narrow upper reaches of the Kourop River Valley. At the split to Deksel (a small stock post with the unlikely Afrikaans name that means 'lid'), turn left to reach Roman Camp a short way on.

From here the trail follows the course of the valley which is hemmed in by flat-topped mountains. Just under 2 km beyond Roman Camp you reach a small cemetery of the Riemvasmaak people. Lying about 120 m to the east of the track, it must surely rank among South Africa's remotest and most desolate cemeteries. You then pass the small settlement of Deurspring ('jump through') and a short way on you reach Rolputs ('rolling well'). Surrounded by a grove of false ebony trees, this is a delightful camp site.

For a while the valley opens up but, as you continue south, you begin to wonder how the track will take you across the ridges and valleys ahead. Just over 6 km beyond Rolputs, the track descends steeply in a short rocky pass where it is advisable to engage low range first gear. Less than 2 km on a track splits off to the right. Take this track and after following a wide valley you reach a sandy riverbed where your sand driving skills will be put to the test. Turn left here and after a short section of sand you reach the banks of the Gariep River. The lush green vineyards extending all along the southern banks of the river contrast sharply with the rock and sand of the northern bank.

Backtrack to the split at the top of the valley, where the track winds through broken countryside dominated by eroded gneiss outcrops, ascending steadily to the plateau which offers extensive views of the plains south of the Gariep River. Clumps of Namaqua porkbush,

Riemvasmaak

> **ⓘ VITAL INFO**
>
> Since Riemvasmaak falls in a malaria epidemic area, we advise you to consult a doctor or a travel clinic about the most effective prophylaxis, especially when visiting the area in summer.

which is a small succulent tree with silvery grey bark, are conspicuous along this section.

Further along you reach a split with the Gariep River and Molopo River mouth to the right. Ignore this track, as it forms part of the Molopo Trail, and continue straight, descending steeply to reach Thop Fountain camp site. After heavy rains a waterfall tumbles down the smooth granite rocks at the head of the valley in which the camp site is situated.

From Thop Fountain the track climbs back to the plateau to reach the turnoff to the Tabakputs camp site (an Afrikaans name that means 'tobacco well') and after 1.3 km you reach a turnoff to Droëputs ('dry well'), a small settlement situated a few kilometres off the main track. The turnoff to the hot spring in the Molopo Gorge is 3.5 km on and Riemvasmaak is just over 1 km further.

Perdepoort trail

The beginning of the Perdepoort 4x4 trail is signposted 700 m east of the Information Office. From here the track traverses typical Kalahari plains and soft sand (engage four-wheel drive). Ignore the turnoff to the small settlement of Gyam about 9 km from the start of the trail, and continue through Perdepoort, which is a narrow pass flanked by low outcrops. About 3 km beyond the Gyam turnoff, a signpost indicates the turnoff to a rock engraving site. Follow this track past a homestead and then turn left, continuing for about 1 km until the road ends. From here a short walk will take you to the engravings etched into a large rock slab. They depict geometrics and animals but are of poor quality when compared with engravings found elsewhere in the Northern Cape Province.

Retrace your route to the main track where you turn left. The landscape now changes to flat-topped mountains interspersed by sandy plains. After 6 km on you will reach Waterkloof Camp, which is situated below exposed granite slopes that are transformed into a beautiful waterfall after rains.

Turn left when you reach a junction 2.3 km beyond Waterkloof Camp (the road continuing straight stops at the boundary of the Riemvasmaak area). A short way on you reach the turnoff to Gyam Camp which is shaded by large camel thorn trees. The trail continues across a plain before reaching a rocky ascent which must be negotiated in low range first gear. After about 600 m the track improves and heads to the Brandhoek Lookout, overlooking a wild valley to the south. The track now traverses the flat summit of the mountain to reach the turnoff to the Perdevlei Camp and the junction with the Deurspring Trail. The remainder of the route follows the onward section of the Deurspring Trail in reverse.

Molopo trail

Follow the main road to Kakamas from the information office and after 5.5 km turn right onto the signposted route. About 1.2 km further you come to the turnoff to the Melkbosrant Lookout. After 3 km the track stops just short of the summit and a short walk brings you to a vantage point overlooking Melkbosrant (named after the milkbushes dominating the landscape) and the Augrabies Falls.

SOUTH AFRICA

The main track continues across gently undulating terrain to Spaarwater until it reaches the delightful Rooiberg Camp and nearby Bernhard Camp. Two steep downhill stretches follow and the track then passes beautifully eroded rocks, where you might see klipspringer, before it comes to Klein and Groot Remvasmaak. As the Afrikaans name suggests you have to 'turn on the brakes' – engage low range first gear – to ease the vehicle down the steep rocky section.

A short way on you reach the sandy banks of the Gariep River where you have a choice of several camp sites. Hugging the edge of the Gariep River, the track climbs up a rocky pass from where there is a fine view over the river and the vineyards on its southern bank. A short section through loose sand brings you to the Molopo River and after 1 km you reach a junction. The track to the left soon joins a gravel road and after 2 km you reach Vredesvallei, an irrigation farm set up for Riemvasmaak's Xhosa-speaking people. If you continue straight instead, you will join a gravel road which climbs steadily out of the Gariep River Valley to the junction with the Molopo 4x4 Trail. From here it is 10 km along a gravel road back to Riemvasmaak.

LOGISTICS AND PLANNING

Fuel: Available at Kakamas, Upington and Ariamsvlei. You need fuel to cover about 350 km for the round trip from Kakamas, including all three trails.

Water: Bring water with you as the water from the Gariep River is unfit for consumption unless it is purified or boiled.

Food: Stock up at towns en route to Riemvasmaak as only basic necessities can be bought at Riemvasmaak.

Firewood: Bring your own firewood, charcoal or gas as firewood is scarce.

Best times: The cooler months between April and September are the best time to visit the area. In mid-summer temperatures can rise above 40°C. Rainfall averages 125 mm a year with most of the rain recorded between February and April. The rains are usually accompanied by thunderstorms.

Maps
A small map of the trail is available, but is sufficient as the routes are generally well marked.

Booking
Permits for the trail can be obtained from The Tourism Information Office, Private Bag X10, Kakamas 8870, tel: (+27 54) 431-0945, fax: 431-0506 (please mark clearly for Riemvasmaak), or through the Green Kalahari office in Upington, tel: (+27 54) 337-2885.

The harsh, but stunningly beautiful, landscape of Riemvasmaak.

Richtersveld National Park

Punctuated by the Gariep River in the north, the Richtersveld is a vast, varied desert landscape with row upon row of hills, distant peaks, deep valleys and bizarre natural rock sculptures. As you travel deeper into the mountains along river courses and gravel tracks built by early prospectors and miners, ever-changing vistas unfold and you will be rewarded with stunning views. In spite of its harsh climate, the Richtersveld is a botanical treasure-house with many rare and endangered plants. Best known among these is the *halfmens* (also known as elephant's trunk) and giant quiver trees, the outlines of which are etched against the skyline.

THE PARK

The Nama people of the Richtersveld are the descendants of Khoikhoi pastoralists who migrated from northern Botswana westwards along the Gariep River some 3 000 years ago. As the Khoikhoi migrated further west, they were forced by the increasing aridity to split into two groups. One settled north of the Gariep River, and the other south of the river – an area that became known as Little Namaqualand.

Foundations and ruins along the Richtersveld tracks are reminders of an era when prospectors and miners in search of copper and other minerals were attracted to the area. Diamonds were found at Sendelingsdrif in 1966 and mining started four years later. Since the Richtersveld is a contractual park, mining still takes place, but it affects no more than 5% of the park.

The idea to establish a national park in the Richtersveld started gathering momentum in 1972, but, as the local Nama people were not prepared to move out of their ancestral lands or to discontinue their semi-nomadic livestock farming, the park was proclaimed only in 1991.

The park is unique in the sense that it was the first contractual park that was not incorporated into an existing park. It is run in partnership with the communities at Kuboes, Eksteenfontein and Lekkersing, and one member from each community and a representative of the stock farmers serve on a management committee. Also represented on the committee are the park warden and four other staff members.

In terms of the agreement with the northern Richtersveld community, the land is leased to SA National Parks for 30 years. Although state-owned land, it was proclaimed in consultation with the Northern Richtersveld Management Board which represents the local communities. The Nama are allowed to continue livestock farming in the park with a limit of 6 600 head of livestock.

SOUTH AFRICA

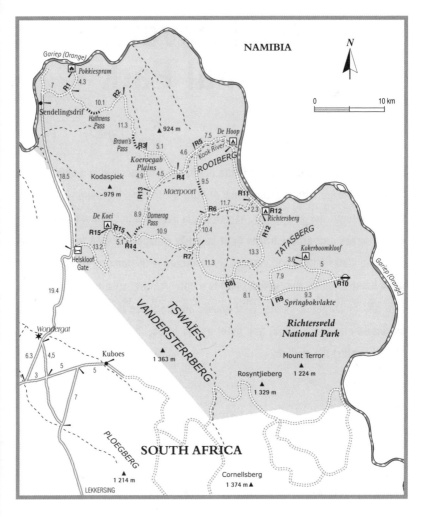

The Ai-Ais Nature Reserve and Hunsberg conservation area lie just to the north of the Gariep River which forms the boundary between South Africa and Namibia. The flora and fauna of this area are no different from that of the Richtersveld, which makes the two areas ideally suited to a transfrontier park.

In August 2001 the Namibian and South African governments signed an agreement on the establishment of such a park, and a treaty to make the park a reality is expected to be signed in 2003. The pont at Sendelingsdrif will be brought into operation to allow visitors to cross the river. Attractions in the Namibian section of the park include the Ai-Ais hot spring, the spectacular Fish River Canyon and the rugged Hunsberg which will be opened to 4x4 enthusiasts.

Landscape and vegetation

Bounded by the Gariep River in the north, the Richtersveld is South Africa's only mountain desert park; a harsh and inhospitable landscape of rugged kloofs and challenging mountain peaks rising over 1 000 m above the plains to the west. Springbokvlakte and Koeroegab Plains are the only two large plains amid the rugged mountainscape.

Richtersveld National Park

The Tatasberg (1 026 m) in the east is a mass of granite boulders towering more than 500 m above the Springbokvlakte. The nearby Die Toon is a familiar landmark with a weird collection of granite rock formations at the aptly named Giant's Playground at its northern foot. Formations have been given descriptive names such as the Drumstick, Screaming Skull, Toadstool and Queen Victoria's Profile. Intriguing names of some of the other mountains include Gorgon's Head, Mount Terror, Rosyntjieberge (raisin mountains) and Seven Sisters.

The floral wealth, especially succulents, is one of the most outstanding features of the Richtersveld. Over a third (586) of the 1 615 plant species recorded in the Richtersveld are succulents. Among the small succulents are stone plants (*Lithops*), vygies (a collective name for mesembs of various genera), plakkies (*Cotyledon*), noorsdoring (*Euphorbia*) and the squat botterboom (*Tylecodon*). The strange-looking elephant's trunk or *halfmens*, Namaqua porkbush and several corkwood species also occur here. A seasonal display of ephemeral flowering plants, commonly referred to as *gousblomme*, daisies and gazanias, provides a blaze of colour to the landscape, usually from mid-August to September, depending on the timing and spacing of the winter rains.

A variety of rare and endemic aloes flourishes in this harsh landscape. They include the giant quiver tree which reaches heights of up to 10 m, the maiden's quiver tree, Pearson's aloe (*Aloe pearsonii*) and Meyer's aloe (*Aloe meyeri*). Quiver trees are characteristic of the rocky outcrops.

Fauna and game-viewing

The harsh environment does not support large herds of game, but you might chance on some species, among them Hartmann's mountain zebra, grey rhebok, klipspringer, steenbok and common duiker. Leopard roam the mountains and are seldom seen, and brown hyaena are sighted very occasionally.

Smaller mammals to keep an eye out for include ground squirrel, black-backed jackal, Smith's red rock rabbit, dassie rat, baboon and vervet monkey.

The absence of most large mammals in the Richtersveld is amply compensated for by the rich diversity of reptiles: to date some 52 species have been recorded in the park. There are 35 skink, agama, gecko and other lizard species, and among the 15 snake species are black spitting cobra, puffadder, horned and many-horned adders. There is one chameleon species, the Namaqua chameleon, and one tortoise species.

Birding

With a checklist approaching 200 species, birding in the park can be rewarding, especially along the Gariep River.

Raptors: Verreaux's eagle, African fish eagle, jackal and augur buzzards, black-chested snake eagle and southern pale chanting goshawk.

Water birds: Pied, giant and malachite kingfishers, black-crowned night-heron, Goliath and black-headed herons, African darter, spur-winged and Egyptian geese, reed and white-breasted cormorants.

Other species: Namaqua sandgrouse, Ludwig's bustard, Karoo korhaan, double-banded courser, bokmakierie, pale-winged starling, dusky sunbird, swallow-tailed bee-eater and mountain chat.

Facilities

Arieb guesthouse cottage at the park headquarters at Sendelingsdrif has five bedrooms (with a total of 10 beds) and two bathrooms, one with shower and the other with bath.

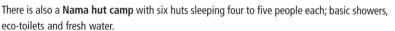

SOUTH AFRICA

There is also a **Nama hut camp** with six huts sleeping four to five people each; basic showers, eco-toilets and fresh water.

In the park there are **camp sites without any facilities** at Pokkiespram, Richtersberg, De Hoop and Kokerboomkloof.

En route to the park, overnight facilities are available at several **Richtersveld communities** where you can gain insight into the culture of the Richtersvelders and try some traditional food.

Lekkersing, 117 km south of Sendelingsdrif. Rooms in village and camp site at Koerdap, 10 km from village.

Eksteenfontein, 116 south of Sendelingsdrif. Guesthouse and camp site.

Kuboes, 85 km south of Sendelingsdrif. Community-run camp site and accommodation in traditional *matjieshuise*.

Sanddrif, off main road between Alexander Bay and Sendelingsdrif. Guesthouse accommodation.

OTHER OPTIONS

Beauvallon, A Reck Guesthouse, east of Alexander Bay on road to Sendelingsdrif.

Brandkaros, 27 km north-east of Alexander Bay on road to Sendelingsdrif. Rondavels and camp sites.

Activities

Visit the **Richtersveld Arts and Crafts Centre** at Sendelingsdrif, which was started in 1996 by women from Kuboes, Lekkersing, Eksteenfontein, Sanddrif and Port Nolloth. A variety of hand-made printed fabrics, cushion covers, sling bags and other items are on sale.

Several South African companies operate **canoeing trips** on the section of the Gariep River downstream of Noordoewer/Vioolsdrif – offering a different perspective of the Richtersveld.

Getting there

From Springbok follow the N7 for 42 km to Steinkopf and then continue along the R382 for 94 km to Port Nolloth. From here head north for 85 km to Alexander Bay, and then east on a gravel road past Beauvallon and Brandkaros. At the Sendelingsdrif turnoff, 50 km on, turn left to reach the mining settlement of Sendelingsdrif which is 43 km further.

The P2960 via Eksteenfontein (a typical Richtersveld settlement) is an alternative approach off the R382 between Steinkopf and Port Nolloth. The distance from the turnoff to Sendelingsdrif is about 156 km on gravel roads.

A spectacular approach from Vioolsdrift is to follow the road along the southern bank of the Gariep River downstream to Modderdrift Suid. From here the route leads over the Helskloof Pass to Eksteenfontein and then on to Sendelingsdrif. The total distance is about 180 km.

ROUTES – 750 km Steinkopf return via Eksteenfontein, Sendelingsdrif and Vioolsdrif
You can explore the park along several numbered routes, most of which can be traversed by a 2x4 bakkie with a high ground clearance during the dry season. The route descriptions include references to the numbered route junctions in the park.

Sendelingsdrif to Pokkiespram

From the park headquarters the track follows the road past old diamond mining works to Swartpoort for about 7 km and then veers off to the left (R1). Further on you pass through a gateway in the Pokkiespram Mountains to reach the Pokkiespram camp site 4.3 km beyond the last junction.

Richtersveld National Park

Set on the banks of the Gariep River, the camp site is ideal for visitors arriving late in the afternoon at Sendelingsdrif but can be very dusty when the wind howls down the Gariep River Valley. The sunsets here are spectacular and in the late afternoon the Lorelei Mountains north of the Gariep River are painted in rich pastel hues.

Sendelingsdrif to De Hoop

Follow the Pokkiespram route, but after 7 km (R1) turn right instead of continuing to Pokkiespram. The track now follows a river valley and then winds up the Halfmens Pass to reach the Halfmens Forest after about 5 km. A walk around the area with its large concentration of *halfmens* trees will reveal the amazing variety of plants that grow in these unlikely surroundings.

Further along, the track crosses a ridge and then continues down the western arm of the Koumas River past the Aubeep Flats before swinging sharply south to head up the eastern arm of the Koumas River. On leaving the valley, the track meanders through the mountains along Brown's Pass (built in the 1970s by an intrepid diamond prospector after whom it is named) and then traverses the northern reaches of the Koeroegab Plains.

Ignore tracks (R3 and R4) turning off to the right until you reach a windmill where the trail swings north to follow the course of the Kook River, so named because the river 'boils' down the valley after heavy rains. About 4.6 km past the windmill the track to Maerpoort splits off to the right (R5), but you continue down the narrow valley incised through the reddish-brown slopes of Rooiberg. Further along there is a short descent into the riverbed and you reach De Hoop less than 3 km on.

With its sandy banks and expansive views across the Gariep River, it is one of the most popular camp sites in the park. At the foot of the mountains near the Kook River Mouth are the foundations of the homestead of the Avenant family who farmed here from 1926 to 1959.

De Hoop to Richtersberg along the Gariep River

The Richtersberg camp site (R12) lies a mere 10.4 km upstream from De Hoop, but the thick sand on the banks of the Gariep River makes it necessary to deflate your vehicle's tyres (be prepared for a dusty drive). A short way after leaving De Hoop you pass Klein De Hoop at the mouth of the Klein Kook River, and about 8 km from De Hoop you will reach the Dabbie Xab River (R11). Richtersberg camp site lies another 2.3 km further upstream.

De Hoop to Richtersberg via Dabbie Xab River

A longer, more scenic alternative is to retrace your tracks up the Kook River for 7.5 km and then turn left (R5) to continue through Maerpoort, a narrow passage through the mountains. About 3.8 km from the turnoff you crest a rise where one of the most magnificent scenes in the Richtersveld meets your eyes – stretched out below is a small sandy plain set against the backdrop of reddish-black hills merging into towering blue mountains.

About 9.5 km beyond the turnoff you reach a junction (R6) where you turn left onto a track which follows the Dabbie Xab River to reach the Kliphek, a narrow passage through boulders, after 3.4 km. From here it is 8.4 km to the mouth of the Dabbie Xab River (R11) but it is a slow journey: the riverbed is littered with rocks, and you have to make tight turns to avoid them. There are several seeps that would be difficult to negotiate after heavy rains. The Richtersberg camp site (R12) is about 2.3 km upstream of the junction. Set on the banks of the Gariep River, this is a good birding spot.

SOUTH AFRICA

De Hoop to Richtersberg via Tatas River

Follow the De Hoop to Richtersberg route (described on page 187) to the Dabbie Xab River junction (R6) where you turn right. You have the option of a direct route of 6.5 km or a longer 10.4-km route along a river course to the R7 junction where you turn left.

Heading eastwards through spectacular mountain scenery, you cross the Ganukouriep River after 7.4 km and the road winds upwards to reach the R8 junction after almost 4 km. Turn left here and the track soon makes its way up Rooihoogte where the remains of an old prospectors' camp can be seen.

From here the track follows the course of the Tatas River Valley where Tata, the Namaqua after whom the river and the Tatasberg are named, was buried. Richtersberg camp site (R12) is 13.3 km from the R8 junction.

De Hoop to Kokerboomkloof

From De Hoop follow the route via junctions R5, R6 and R7 to R8, where you ignore the Richtersberg turnoff (described on page 187), and continue straight. After about 7 km you reach the western edge of the Springbokvlakte and if you look north-east, Die Toon, also known as Eierkop, comes into view. Less than 1 km later you reach the R9 junction where you can either take a direct route to Kokerboomkloof or a longer detour across Springbokvlakte, until you reach a sign prohibiting entry to the Grasdrif diamond prospecting area. Turn left here to continue to Kokerboomkloof.

For the more direct route, turn left at the R9 junction (while the longer route continues straight for 9.3 km to the R10 junction to Kokerboomkloof) and follow the track which winds gently uphill. After 5.7 km you will reach a turnoff to the right where there is a short steep ascent to a viewpoint. The Springbokvlakte lies way below your feet against the backdrop of saw-edged peaks with names like Mount Terror (1 224 m), Devil's Tooth and the Rosyntjieberg (1 329 m). Often dry and barren, the vast plain is transformed into lush grasslands after good rains when livestock and herders can be encountered here.

After crossing the watershed you drop down into the valley in which Kokerboomkloof lies. The camp site is named after the concentration of quiver trees growing here. Unfortunately, however, many of them have died.

Do take time to explore the northern foothills of Die Toon to look for the many fascinating rock formations that have been fashioned out of the friable granite rock by wind, rain and extremes of temperatures. They are not signposted, but a few hours spent amongst the rocks will be well rewarded.

CONTRACTUAL PARKS

Contractual parks like the Richtersveld National Park are state-owned or private land that is managed by South African National Parks in conjunction with the landowner. With the written approval of the owners, these areas may be included in existing national parks, on the understanding that the landowners may continue farming, mining and other activities, subject to certain conditions. The Postberg Nature Reserve, which forms part of the West Coast National Park, is another example of a contractual park.

Richtersveld National Park

Kokerboomkloof to Helskloof
From the camp site, backtrack to the R9, R8 and R7 junctions and then continue along the main track to the R14 junction. A 3.5-km detour to the north will take you along the Domerog Pass, named after pass-builders Johannes Domerog and Willem his son. Large concentrations of the botterboom (*Tylecodon*), easily identified by its squat stem and bright green leaves after rains, are seen on the way up. Stop just before the summit to admire the stunning views of the broad Valley below. Backtrack to the R14 junction and turn right to reach the turnoff to the De Koei camp site (R15) 5.1 km on. From here the track winds above a valley dominated by Paradysberg to the east, and you reach the summit of Helskloof after 7.2 km.

There are masses of the rare Pearson's aloe (*Aloe pearsonii*) and the dwarf quiver tree on the mountain slopes. From here you descend steeply for just under 6 km down Helskloof which presented a real challenge to early travellers but nowadays is an easy drive.

Linking routes
Although the two are nearly 1 000 km apart you can link up with Riemvasmaak (*see* p. 177) if you are approaching the Richtersveld along the N14 via Upington and Kakamas.

LOGISTICS AND PLANNING
Fuel: Available at Sendelingsdrif in the park, as well as Springbok, Alexander Bay and Noordoewer (in Namibia). Containers of fuel are sold at Eksteenfontein.
Water: Obtainable at Sendelingsdrif. Water from the Gariep River should be purified before it is used for drinking and cooking.
Food: Stock up on food and alcoholic beverages for the duration of your visit.
Firewood: Bring your own firewood for campfires and charcoal or gas for cooking.
Best times: The climate is extreme: mid-summer temperatures of up to 53°C and cold winter nights. Rainfall varies between 5 mm at the coast and 200 mm high up in the mountains and is recorded mainly in the winter. Mist, known to the Nama as *Malmokkies* or *!Huries*, often blows in from the coast and is a life-giving source of water for the desert flora. Autumn and spring have the best weather with spring seeing the bleak landscape transformed into carpets of spring flowers.

Maps
A map indicating the tracks, numbered junctions, distances and waypoint positions is available at the park headquarters. On one side of the *Conti Richtersveld National Park and Northern Namaqualand* map the routes have been indicated on aerial photographs (a useful feature) while the reverse has a detailed road map.

Booking
Book in advance with South African National Parks, PO Box 787, Pretoria 0001, South Africa, tel: (+27 12) 428-9111, fax: 343-9035, e-mail: reservations@parks-sa.co.za.
Lekkersing: tel: (+27 27) 851-8580, fax: 851-7097
Eksteenfontein: tel: (+27 27) 851-8373 or 851-8619
Kuboes: tel: (+27 27) 831-2095
Sanddrif: tel: (+27 27) 831-1426
OTHER OPTIONS:
Beauvallon, A Reck Guesthouse: tel: (+27 27) 831-1592
Brandkaros: tel: (+27 27) 831-1856

SOUTH AFRICA

Baviaanskloof

Wild river valleys, patches of indigenous forest with yellowwoods, slopes covered in spekboom and valley-bush euphorbia, stark quartzite ridges and contorted rock strata merge along the 120-km-long Baviaanskloof in the Eastern Cape. The area is a delight to professional and amateur botanists, over 1 160 plant species having been recorded. It offers peace to those wanting to escape city life. It can be explored in a sturdy 2x4 vehicle with a high ground clearance, except after rain when the steep inclines and declines will be a challenge.

THE CONSERVATION AREA

In the early 18th century white settlers began to arrive in the remote Baviaanskloof Valley, originally home to Bushmen hunter-gatherers. Here they made a living from farming with angora goats and cultivating wheat, citrus fruit and vegetables.

Most of the Baviaanskloof has enjoyed protection since 1923 when it was proclaimed a water catchment administered by the Department of Water Affairs. In 1987 it was transferred to Cape Nature Conservation and since 1994 it has been managed by Eastern Cape Conservation.

The hardships of farming in this wild area combined with the flooding of the fertile valley upstream of the Kouga Dam forced several farmers out of the valley. The land was bought and incorporated into the conservation area. Between 1987 and 1995 15 332 ha was acquired through funds raised by WWF-South Africa and other conservation organisations and 4 338 ha was bought by the state. The fourth largest conservation area in South Africa, its parallel-running Baviaanskloof and Kouga ranges form the arms of a U. Effective conservation is hampered by its unconsolidated shape and there are plans to expand the conservation area by nearly three times its existing size.

Landscape and vegetation

The rugged and spectacular Baviaanskloof forms the focal point of the area which is bounded for 120 km by the Baviaanskloof Mountains to the north and the more extensive Kouga Mountains to the south. Jagged cliff faces, contorted rock strata, quartzite ridges and deep valleys formed by the Baviaans, Kouga and Groot rivers add to the allure of the wild scenery.

The varied topography has resulted in a rich diversity of plant life and the conservation area also incorporates several major vegetation types. Patches of magnificent indigenous Knysna forest in the well-watered kloofs give way to succulent thickets with valley-bush euphorbias towering high above the scrub and spekboomveld, a dense scrub dominated by the *spekboom* (known in English as the porkbush). At higher elevations expanses of grassy fynbos and mountain fynbos are dominant. Among the fynbos plants are 45 erica and 15 protea species. The bright orange-red flowers of the bitter aloe are conspicious between May and August. Two rare cycads – the Karoo cycad (*Encephalartos lehmanii*) and Suurberg cycad – also occur here.

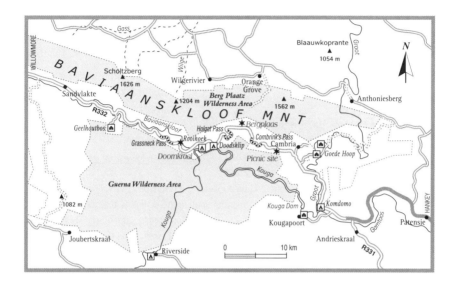

The Willowmore cedar, one of South Africa's four cedar tree species, is endemic to the Baviaanskloof and Kouga mountains. Early settlers cut down the trees for fencing and building material, and it is today restricted to the most inaccessible reaches of the conservation area and can also be seen on the farm Rus en Vrede over which the road passes. To deviate from the proclaimed road requires permission from the owners.

Fauna and game-viewing

Soon after farmers began settling in the valley all the larger animal species were exterminated. Klipspringer, kudu, grey rhebok, mountain reedbuck, bushbuck and bushpig were more fortunate, as were leopard, caracal, baboon and a variety of smaller species, and they have all managed to survive. Seven eland were released in the east of the Baviaanskloof conservation area in 1989. They were followed by 14 Cape mountain zebra from the Karoo National Park the following year – 19 years after the last one roamed the mountains. Since then herds of buffalo and red hartebeest have been reintroduced. Future plans for an expanded conservation area include the reintroduction of lion, elephant, black rhino and hippopotamus.

Birding

The diverse habitats are home to equally diverse birdlife and, with some 300 species recorded in the area, birding can be rewarding.
Raptors: Verreaux's and booted eagles, peregrine falcon.
Common species: Cape sugarbird, orange-breasted sunbird, Cape bulbul, Victorin's warbler, pale-winged starling, fork-tailed drongo, ground woodpecker, swee waxbill, Cape francolin.
Other species: Knysna lourie, protea seed-eater, sickle-winged chat, Cape rockjumper, yellow-throated woodland-warbler and forest canary.

Facilities

Komdomo in the east has camp sites with ablution facilities and picnic sites.
Geelhoutbos (west) has self-catering chalets.
Basic camp sites are available at **Doodsklip** and **Rooihoek**.
Several private accommodation establishments are in the western part of the kloof.

SOUTH AFRICA

Activities
There are numerous **unmarked hiking routes and** you can also explore the area by **mountain bike** and on **horseback**.

Getting there
From Port Elizabeth travel westwards along the N2 and take the Gamtoosmond/Loerie off ramp onto the R331. The tar road winds along the foothills of the Elands and Groot Winterhoek mountains past Loerie and then follows the Gamtoos River Valley to Hankey and Patensie, an important fruit-producing area. Dominating the skyline to the north is the Groot Winterhoek range with the distinctive 1 758-m-high Cockscomb, named after its five crests that resemble a rooster's comb. We first saw this familiar Eastern Cape landmark many years ago when we did the Gonaqua Hiking Trail in the Elandsberg further west.

About 16 km beyond Patensie you pass a rock formation resembling the profile of Queen Victoria (closer examination reveals that it consists of round stones and pebbles). Further on you reach the turnoff to the Kouga Dam which provides water to the irrigation farms lower downstream and the Nelson Mandela (Port Elizabeth) metropolitan area.

> **ⓘ VITAL INFO**
>
> The route can usually be done in a 2x4, but after rains the road can be dangerous and a 4x4 is preferable.

THE ROUTE – 320 km Port Elizabeth to Willowmore

A few kilometres beyond the turnoff to the Kouga Dam the road swings north to reach the Komdomo camp site at the entrance to the Groot River Poort, the gateway to Baviaanskloof. The kloof owes its name to the numerous baboons (*baviaan* in Dutch) that occurred here when farmers began settling in the valley. Here the road makes its way along a narrow gorge between the Coutomiet and Komdo mountains and past lichen-encrusted cliffs. After following the forested banks of the Groot River for 10 km you pass the turnoff to Goede Hoop where there used to be an old mission station.

Goede Hoop is the starting point of the 20-km-long Osseberg 4x4 trail which initially follows the forested course of the Groot River. The trail crosses the river about six times before it climbs steeply out of the valley to link up with the Steytlerville/Patensie gravel road. The trail is open to groups of a minimum of two and a maximum of eight vehicles.

Cambria, where the citrus orchards are in sharp contrast to the surrounding harsh mountains, is a short way beyond the Goede Hoop turnoff. From here the road winds up Combrink's Pass to Bergplaas, a grassland plateau which offers stunning views over the surrounding mountains and valleys. A testimony to the ingenuity of the early farmers of the valley is the cableway, no longer in use, which was built in the early 1960s across the deep gorge between Enkeldoorn and Bergplaas farms to transport livestock and agricultural produce.

As you make your way down the Holgat Mountain Pass you will see the cone-shaped Langkop, a distinctive landmark, and a short way on you reach the turnoff to the camping site with the rather morbid name of Doodsklip. According to local folklore people died here under mysterious circumstances – hence the name which means 'death stone'.

Continuing further along the valley you reach the turnoff to Rooihoek. Its main attraction is an inviting pool with white sandy beaches set against the backdrop of rugged quartzite ridges, and camp sites and basic toilet facilities are available. Hikers can set off from here to explore the Guerna Wilderness Area to the south and Berg Plaatz Wilderness Area to the north.

Baviaanskloof

Beyond Rooihoek you reach Kruisrivier at the confluence of the Baviaanskloof and Kouga rivers. Kudu, bushbuck and eland are often seen, so keep a sharp lookout for them in the area.

Further on you pass Doornkraal before coming to Droëkloof (dry kloof) where, despite its name, you can have a swim in an inviting pool at a causeway. Next you head up Grassneck Pass where the road winds steeply upwards and makes a spectacular hairpin bend just before the top. Stop at the viewpoint at the top to take in the magnificent scenery – dominating the skyline to the north-west is the 1 626-m-high Scholtzberg, the highest point in the Baviaanskloof Mountains, and to the south lies the Guerna Wilderness Area which can be explored only on horseback or foot.

A steep descent takes you to the valley of the Baviaans River where there is another pool in which to swim, at a causeway. Still further on you reach Apieskloof and Akkerdal, two old farms, and then reach the turnoff to Geelhoutbos. The five six-bedded self-catering chalets are set among a forest of Outeniqua yellowwood, white stinkwood and white ironwood trees. The nearby swimming hole is welcome on a hot day.

Beyond Geelhoutbos the valley opens up and the remaining 110 km to Willowmore traverses private farmland spread along the Baviaanskloof Valley. Tourism has proved to be a better option than farming and several accommodation establishments are situated along the valley. In the 1920s a factory to process baboon hides was established on Sandvlakte where there is a guest farm with self-catering chalets.

Still further on you reach Rus en Vrede farm, where you can embark on a rough four-wheel drive track into the Kouga Mountains, and then to the farming settlement of Studtis – the area where well-known South African author, P H Nortje, was born.

Beyond Studtis lies the Nuwekloof Pass, the last of the five passes along the route, and an excellent example of the ingenuity of the renowned pass-builder Thomas Bain who constructed the Patensie to Willowmore road between 1880 and 1890. Nuwekloof Pass marks the end of the Baviaanskloof and the remainder of the journey to Willowmore is an easy drive.

LOGISTICS AND PLANNING
Fuel: Available at Patensie. A full tank will see you through to Willowmore.
Water: Available at camp sites and Geelhoutbos.
Food: Take enough food for the duration of your visit.
Best times: Spring, early summer and autumn are generally the best times to visit. The climate is influenced by the varied topography. In mid-summer temperatures in the Baviaanskloof Valley can reach up to 45°C but high up in the mountains it is usually several degrees lower. Winter days are generally cool to cold and, in the valley, temperatures can drop to below freezing point. However, hot Berg winds can cause temperatures to soar up to 30°C in winter. The Baviaanskloof enjoys rainfall throughout the year, from 1 000 mm a year in the east to 200 mm in the valley.

Maps
A specially printed double-sided 1:50 000 topographical map of the Baviaanskloof can be bought at the Eastern Cape Nature Conservation office in Patensie.

Booking
Reservations must be made in advance with the Reserve Manager, PO Box 218, Patensie 6335, tel: (+ 27 40) 635-2115, fax: 635-2535. For inquiries, call (+27 42) 283-0882.
For details of private accommodation, consult the website: www.baviaans.co.za.

Main picture: The Karoo National Park in South Africa.
Inset picture: Sand-driving skills are a must in Namibia.

The Basics

THE BASICS

VEHICLES, ACCESSORIES AND EQUIPMENT

THE VEHICLE
Carefully consider...
- engine capacity and gear ratios;
- power, and how the vehicle can be made to use it;
- fuel: diesel or petrol, leaded or unleaded – and its availability – a major factor in the logistics of your journey;
- ground clearance, load space, carrying capacity, approach, departure and rollover angles;
- whether the vehicle suits the terrain you are planning to traverse.

The basics of 4x4 driving
- Familiarise yourself with the vehicle and its capabilities. Get the necessary skills – go to a 4x4 school if necessary.
- Hire a 4x4 if you're unsure how dedicated you are going to be to 4x4-ing as a lifestyle. They can be hired in all major centres in southern Africa – some come fully-equipped.

Where to get help choosing a 4x4
Specialist magazines such as *Leisure Wheels* and *South African 4x4* are useful sources of information on vehicles, trails, 4x4 training centres and clubs. *Drive Out*, a biannual publication, is packed with information on all aspects of 4x4-ing, including a comprehensive list of 4x4 trails in southern Africa. From time to time 4x4 trails are featured in *Getaway* magazine. Experienced 4x4 enthusiasts will be happy to share their wealth of knowledge with you and, if you enjoy social outings, you should consider joining one of the many 4x4 clubs.

Tyres
You will traverse a wide variety of road and offroad surfaces on your journeys. Make sure the tyres you choose are suitable for the terrain you will cover.

ACCESSORIES
Weigh up the usefulness of accessories against the cost and frequency of use.

Calculate...
- the distance you will cover;
- the fuel consumption under different conditions;
- the availability of fuel along the route.

Consider the benefits of...
- a built-in water tank;
- a roof rack for quick access to less obvious things than luggage – like the high-lift jack, a second spare and jerrycans;
- accessories, such as a freezer, which need an additional battery;

- a winch – good for when you get stuck in a ditch;
- a fire extinguisher – which is essential and mounted in the cab.

THE EQUIPMENT
- **Tents:** Choose a stand-alone tent or a rooftop tent. Stand-alone for the convenience of leaving it erected at the camp site; rooftop for its coolness and distance from the ground.
- **Cool box or freezer:** The latter for long trips.
- **Trailer:** Convenient for storage, but difficult to tow in rocky areas, sand and mud.

DRIVING IN DIFFICULT TERRAIN
Remember...
A four-wheel drive vehicle doesn't mean that you can go anywhere and get out of any tricky situation.

Always...
- engage four-wheel drive and lock your hubs (depending on your vehicle) before getting into trouble;
- avoid getting deeper into trouble when you are stuck in mud. Get out of the vehicle, take stock of the situation and decide what needs to be done.

IN SAND
- Reduce tyre pressure to about 1 Kpa (front) and 1.2 Kpa (rear) to increase the 'footprint'.
- Avoid giving too much power when the vehicle's speed starts decreasing.
- Avoid driving in areas with thick loose sand in the heat of the day when the sand is at its softest.
- When you want to stop, let the vehicle roll to a gentle halt rather than braking which creates a mound of sand in front of the wheels.

ON DUNES
Driving on dunes is exhilarating, but can be a nerve-wracking experience, requiring split-second decisions.
- Ensure that you are in the right gear and have the necessary speed to get to the crest.
- Avoid driving in soft loose sand with even the slightest angle.
- Driving down a slip face, engage low range, keep the vehicle in a straight line and accelerate slightly if you feel the back of the vehicle coming around.

OVER ROCKY TERRAIN
- Stop and check for obstacles that might cause serious damage.
- Engage low range first gear and use just enough power to let the vehicle clear the obstacle.

THE BASICS

- On a steep ascent, engage low range first or second gear and accelerate just enough to keep the vehicle moving steadily upwards.
- Avoid using too much power if there are loose rocks or boulders, as this will cause wheel spin.
- Engage low range first gear and let the vehicle 'walk' down a slope against its engine compression.
- Keep all four wheels on the ground at all times crossing ditches and dongas to prevent the vehicle becoming cross-axled.

IN MUD
- If possible, avoid mud.
- Or if unavoidable place a 'mat' of thin mopane or other branches over the track, or dump rocks into the rut.

THROUGH RIVERS
- Never cross a river unless you can wade through, as there can be concealed obstacles, wash-aways or holes.
- Always make sure there is an easy exit point.
- Enter the river slowly and increase the speed gradually.

IN ELEPHANT COUNTRY
- Never lose sight of the fact that animals such as elephant can be dangerous and unpredictable.
- Always adhere to the speed limit in parks and reserves.
- Stop at a safe distance from animals, for instance an elephant, and see how they behave.
- If an elephant stands its ground, edge the vehicle slightly forward and then reverse. You might need to do this more than once, but it usually works.
- Never move into a breeding herd of elephants as you could be charged.
- Never take any risks.
- Always try to drive past elephant before stopping to take photographs or watching them. This will enable you to get away quickly should an elephant decide to charge.

MAPS AND NAVIGATION
- Obtain all necessary maps before setting off rather than counting on buying them at your destination.
- A GPS (Global Positioning System) has numerous advantages and functions and for many travellers it has become an indispensable tool.
- Don't under-estimate the time it will take to get to your destination.
- Don't rely on signposts alone.
- Always ask: 'Where is the road to ...?' rather than: 'Is this the road to ...?' which might elicit a 'Yes', even if that is not the case.
- Consult aid workers, non-governmental organisations and government officials on the condition of roads and tracks in their area. They use them.

DISEASES AND OTHER DANGERS
- Consult a doctor before travelling to malaria areas about the best prophylaxis.
- Bilharzia is also widespread in large parts of southern Africa. Prevention is better than cure, so avoid washing and swimming in water, especially slow-flowing streams and stagnant pools.
- Keep your car windows closed and wear trousers and long-sleeved shirts in tsetse fly areas. The incidence of sleeping sickness (also known as trypanosomiasis) is low, but a bite from an infected tsetse fly could result in the disease.
- Check for ticks in game-rich areas, as infected ticks transmit tick bite fever.
- Be on the lookout for tampans. These are flat, reddish-brown soft ticks that live about 8 cm below the surface of the soil and emerge when they detect the carbon dioxide produced by animals and humans.
- Always keep a lookout for snakes in shrubs and bushes alongside tracks.
- Avoid scorpions and snakes when moving around the camp at night, always use a torch and wear closed shoes rather than open sandals.
- Don't confront potentially dangerous animals such as elephant and hippo. Don't set up camp in their paths or too close to the water's edge.
- It is essential to take out medical insurance and arrange membership of a medical emergency service.

ENHANCING YOUR EXPERIENCE
- Plan for a successful holiday.
- Have your vehicle serviced or thoroughly checked a few days before your planned departure date.
- Don't overload the vehicle.
- Have the necessary travel and vehicle documentation, permits and currency of the country or countries you intend visiting.
- Remember to take enough cash as garages in remote areas often accept only cash.

BUSH ETIQUETTE
- Protect the fragile environment, and show respect to other visitors by keeping noise to a minimum and not invading their privacy.
- Respect the culture and traditions of the indigenous people you encounter.
- Burn combustible material, including cigarette butts, and remove non-combustible refuse.
- Use existing fireplaces, rather than making a new one, and let the fire burn out completely, instead of burying the coals when you break up camp.
- Don't be tempted to have a bonfire. Collect only enough for a small fire which is better for cooking purposes and environmentally friendlier.
- Avoid camping at or near waterholes where free camping is permitted as you could prevent animals that have walked long distances from drinking.
- Use the 'cat method' when answering the call of nature in areas where there are no toilets. Dig a hole of no deeper than 25 cm to keep within the biological disposal layer.

THE BASICS

- Burn toilet paper before covering the hole with sand which should be lightly trampled down.
- Never relieve yourself closer than 50 m to any water body.
- Tampons and sanitary towels are best disposed of by burning them in a fire.
- Always stay on existing tracks and do not blaze your own trail. New tracks scar the landscape, often for decades.
- Never drive over dry pans as the tracks will remain visible for many years.
- If you are curious to see what is behind a ridge off the road, park your vehicle and take a walk there.
- Ask permission from the local chief or headman to set up camp in his area.
- Respect cultural and archaeological sites.
- Do not touch rock paintings or rock engravings, and don't spray water or any other liquid over them. Never remove archaeological objects or tamper with them.

PACKING
Pack systematically as this will enable you to find things easily, even if you arrive at your camp site in the dark.

ESSENTIALS

Emergency food & water	☐	Multi-purpose knife	☐
First aid kit	☐	Permits	☐
GPS/compass	☐	Torch & spare batteries	☐
Maps	☐	Travel & vehicle documentation (where required)	☐

CAMPING EQUIPMENT

Basin/bucket (for personal washing)	☐	Shower	☐
Bed roll/air mattress	☐	Sleeping bag	☐
Brush & dustpan	☐	Stretcher	☐
Chairs	☐	Table, folding	☐
Cool box	☐	Tarpaulin/groundsheet	☐
Fold-up basin (for dishes)	☐	Tent (with sewn-in floor)	☐
Freezer (if required)	☐	Tent pegs & poles	☐
Light (gas or battery powered)	☐	Washing line, 5 m thin nylon cord	☐
Pillow	☐	Washing pegs	☐
Rubber mat, small	☐	Washing powder &/or soap	☐

CLOTHING

Jersey/warm top	☐	Sleepwear	☐
Rain gear (waterproof)	☐	Socks	☐
Sandals	☐	Sunhat	☐
Shirts – long- & short-sleeved	☐	Swimming costume	☐
Shoes – walking (comfortable & sturdy)	☐	Tracksuit	☐
		Trousers	☐
Shorts	☐	Underwear	☐

PERSONAL

- Bath plug ☐
- Body lotion/moisturiser ☐
- Brush or comb ☐
- Cash & credit cards ☐
- Deodorant ☐
- Feminine hygiene products ☐
- Insect repellent ☐
- Shampoo & conditioner ☐
- Shaver ☐
- Soap ☐
- Spare spectacles ☐
- Sunglasses ☐
- Sunscreen ☐
- Tissues ☐
- Toilet paper ☐
- Toothbrush ☐
- Toothpaste ☐
- Towel ☐

MISCELLANEOUS

- Binoculars ☐
- Camera & film ☐
- Field guides & reference books ☐
- Notebook & pen ☐

VEHICLE SPARES, TOOLS AND EQUIPMENT

The following basic table can be adapted to suit your own needs and mechanical knowledge.

- Allen key set ☐
- Axe ☐
- Belts – fan & power steering ☐
- Brake fluid ☐
- Chisel ☐
- Electrical wire ☐
- Exhaust repair kit ☐
- Files – flat & round ☐
- Fire extinguisher ☐
- Fuel filter ☐
- Funnel ☐
- Fuses ☐
- Glue, quick set ☐
- Grease ☐
- Hacksaw & blades ☐
- Hammer – small & 1.8kg ☐
- Jack – high lift & bottle ☐
- Jerry cans ☐
- Jumper cables ☐
- Light bulbs ☐
- Multi-meter ☐
- Moisture repellent ☐
- Nuts, bolts & washers to fit main attachment points ☐
- Oil – engine, differential & gearbox ☐
- Petrol tank repair kit ☐
- Pliers – long-nose, circlip & fencing ☐
- Puncture repair kit ☐
- Radiator repair kit ☐
- Radiator hoses & clamps ☐
- Screwdrivers – flat head & star ☐
- Snatch rope ☐
- Spade ☐
- Spanners of all kinds ☐
- Spare keys ☐
- Spare wheels x2 ☐
- Spark plugs ☐
- Spark plug spanner ☐
- Tape – duct & insulation ☐
- Tie down straps ☐
- Tow rope ☐
- Tyre lever ☐
- Tyre pressure gauge ☐
- Tyre pump ☐
- Tyre weld ☐
- Valve caps ☐
- Valve extractor ☐
- Wheel spanner ☐
- Wire – thin & bloudraad ☐
- Wire cutters ☐
- Wrench – monkey ☐

ESSENTIAL READING

MOZAMBIQUE

Clancey, P. A. *The birds of Southern Mozambique*. African Bird Book Publishing, 1996.

Newitt, Malyn. *A History of Mozambique*. Witwatersrand University Press, 1995. The most comprehensive history book on the country.

Olivier, Willie & Olivier, Sandra. *African Adventurer's Guide to Mozambique*. Struik Publishers, 2000. General information on the country, tourist destinations, activities and self-drive routes.

Parker, V. *The Atlas of the birds of Sul do Save, Southern Mozambique*. Cape Town and Johannesburg: Avian Demography Unit and Endangered Wildlife Trust, 1999.

BOTSWANA

Clauss, Bernhard & Clauss, Renate. *Common Amphibians and Reptiles of Botswana – more than just creepy-crawlies*. Gamsberg Macmillan, 2002. Useful if you want to make a closer study of creatures often overlooked.

Comley, Peter & Meyer, Salome. *A Field Guide to the Mammals of Botswana*. Africa Window, 1994. Photographs and an informative text.

Dennis, Nigel (photographs), Knight, Michael & Joyce, Peter (text). *The Kalahari – Survival in a Thirstland Wilderness*. Struik Publishers, 1997. The superb photographs are complemented by an informative text, providing in-depth insight into the Kalahari.

Main, Mike. *African Adventurer's Guide to Botswana*. Struik Publishers, 2001. The author's extensive knowledge of Botswana makes this an informative guide to all the popular tourist destinations in Botswana. Especially useful are his route descriptions and route maps with GPS references.

Penry, H. *Bird Atlas of Botswana*. University of Natal Press, 1994.

Pickford, Peter & Pickford, Beverly. *The Miracle Rivers – The Okavango & Chobe of Botswana*. Southern Books, 1999. This well-known husband-and-wife team gives insight into the Okavango Delta system and Chobe.

Roodt, Veronica. *Trees and Shrubs of the Okavango Delta* and *Common Wild Flowers of the Okavango*. Shell Oil Botswana, 1998. Handy companions on the Delta and beyond.

Ross, Karen. *Okavango – Jewel of the Kalahari*. Struik Publishers, 2003.

Van der Walt, Peet & Le Riche, Elias. *The Kalahari and its plants*. Published by the authors, 1999. Very informative text, but the photographs are unfortunately poorly reproduced.

Van Rooyen, Noel, Bezuidenhout, Hugo & de Kock, Emmerentia. *Flowering Plants of the Kalahari Dunes*. Ekotrust, 2001.

Gemsbok Wilderness Trail

Derichs, Peter. *Kgalagadi Transfrontier Park*. Published by the author, 2001. A useful introduction to the park. It contains numerous photographs of waterholes, vegetation, animals and birdlife.

Eloff, Fritz. *Hunters of the Dunes – The Story of the Kalahari Lion*. Sunbird, 2003. This fascinating account of 40 years of research by Professor Eloff on the lions of the Kalahari is illustrated with excellent colour photographs.

Kgalagadi Transfrontier Park Travel Guide. South African National Parks, 1999. A 34-page full-colour brochure with concise, interesting information on a wide range of subjects including the vegetation, birds, small mammals, antelope and predators of the park.

Two comprehensive books on the region are unfortunately both are out of print, but you might find a copy in your library:

Mills, Gus & Haagner, Clem. *Guide to the Kalahari Gemsbok National Park*. Southern Books, 1989.

Nussey, Wilf. *The Crowded Desert – The Kalahari Gemsbok National Park*. William Waterman Publications, 1993.

Central Kalahari Game Reserve

Owens, Mark & Owens, Delia. *Cry of the Kalahari*. Harper Collins, 1985. Fascinating insight into the seven years this husband-and-wife team spent in Deception Valley while they were researching the brown hyaena; largely responsible for the area's popularity.

Moremi Game Reserve

Butchart, Duncan. *Wildlife of the Okavango*. Struik Publishers, 2000. A small, very useful guide.

Harvey, Chris & Kat, Pieter. *Prides – The Lions of Moremi*. Southern Books, 2000. Based on the study of four neighbouring lion prides in the Moremi area.

Chobe National Park

Balfour, Daryl & Balfour, Sharna. *Chobe – Africa's Untamed Wilderness*. Southern Books, 1997. This book documents the year that the Balfours spent in Chobe in words and stunning photographs.

Tsodilo Hills & Gcwihaba Cave

Main, Mike. *Kalahari – Life's variety in dune and delta*. Southern Books, 1987. Detailed information on Tsodilo Hills and Gcwihaba Cave as well as on various aspects and destinations in the Kalahari delivered in an easy-to-read manner; out of print.

NAMIBIA

Bridgeford, P & M. *Touring Sesriem and Sossusvlei*. P & M Bridgeford, 1997. Although specifically written for Sesriem and Sossusvlei, this guide is also useful in describing many aspects of the natural history of the dune sea traversed on the Conception Expedition and the Saddle Hill 4X4 Trail.

Craven, Patricia & Marais, Christine. *Damaraland Flora*. Gamsberg Publishers, 1992. Detailed descriptions with illustrations of plants likely to be seen in Damaraland.

ESSENTIAL READING

Craven, Patricia & Marais, Christine. *Namib Flora*. Gamsberg Publishers, 1986. Detailed descriptions with illustrations of plants found in the Namib.

Cubitt, Gerald (photographs) & Joyce, Peter (text). *This is Namibia*. New Holland Publishing, 1999. Combines a detailed introduction to the country as a whole with lavish photographs.

Grünert, Nicole. *Namibia. Fascination of Geology*. Klauss Hess Publishers, 2000. This travel guide explains the interesting geological features for the layman.

Olivier, Willie & Olivier, Sandra. *African Adventurer's Guide to Namibia*. Struik Publishers, 2003. Detailed information on Namibia, tourist destinations and major attractions.

Seely, M. *The Namib*. Shell Oil Namibia Limited, 1987. This guide introduces the plants, animals and envrionment of the Namib Desert.

Kaokoveld

Pickford, Peter & Pickford, Beverly (photographs) & Jacobsohn, Margaret (text). *Himba – Nomads of Namibia*. Struik Publishers, 1998. Superb photographs complement the authoritative text about the Himba culture.

Rice, Mary & Gibson, Craig. *Heat, Dust and Dreams*. Struik Publishers, 2001. The people, flora and fauna of the area are described in words and beautiful photographs.

LESOTHO

Southern Lesotho

The interesting story of the Sani Pass is described in two very good books:

Alexander, David. *Sani Pass – Riding the Dragon*. 1992, last reprinted in 2000. A vivid description of the days when Alexander's Mokhotlong Mountain Transport company pioneered the route up Sani Pass and on to Mokhotlong.

Clarke, Michael. *The Saga of Sani Pass and Mokhotlong*. 2001. The flora, fauna and early history of the area and some early pioneers and characters. A good read.

SOUTH AFRICA

Richtersveld

Cornell, Fred. *The Glamour of Prospecting*. David Philip, 1986. This autobiography gives a fascinating insight into the early days of Alexander Bay and the Richtersveld.

Reck, K. W. *Tracks and Trails of the Richtersveld*. Published by the author, 1994. A detailed account of the mining history, place names and attractions of the area. Try getting a copy at the Springbok Café in Springbok.

Williamson, Graham. *Richtersveld – The Enchanted Wilderness*. Umdaus Press, 2000. The definitive work on the Richtersveld, illustrated with beautiful colour photographs.

FIELD GUIDES AND OTHER REFERENCES

You will find the following field guides useful on your journeys to wild places.

Apps, P. (ed.) *Smithers' Mammals of Southern Africa – A Field Guide*. Struik Publishers, 2000.

Barnes, K. N. (ed.) *The Important Bird Areas of Southern Africa*. Birdlife Africa, 1998.

Branch, B. *Field guide to Snakes and other Reptiles of Southern Africa*. Struik Publishers, 1998.

Carruthers, V. (ed.) *The Wildlife of Southern Africa, A field guide to the animals and plants of the region*. Struik Publishers, 2000.

Coates Palgrave, C. *Trees of Southern Africa*. Struik Publishers, 2002.

Estes, R. D. *The Behaviour Guide to African Mammals*. Russel Friedman Books, 1997.

Estes, R. D. *The Safari Companion – A Guide to Watching African Mammals*. Russel Friedman Books, 1999.

Maclean, G. L. (ed.) *Roberts' Birds of Southern Africa*. Trustees of the John Voelcker Bird Book Fund, 1993.

Newman, K. *Newman's Birds of Southern Africa*. Struik Publishers, 2002.

Sinclair, I., Hockey, P. & Tarboton, W. *Sasol Birds of Southern Africa*. Struik Publishers, 2002.

Stuart, C. & Stuart, T. *Field Guide to Mammals of Southern Africa*. Struik Publishers, 2001.

Stuart, C. & Stuart, T. *A Field Guide to the Tracks & Signs of Southern and East African Wildlife*. Struik Publishers, 2001.

Van Wyk, B. & Van Wyk, P. *Field Guide to Trees of Southern Africa*. Struik Publishers, 1997.

Walker, C. *Signs of the Wild*. Struik Publishers, 1996.

INDEX

A

Acanthosicyos horrida 109
adder, many-horned 104
adder, Peringuey's 104, 106, 110
Adenium boehmianum 121
agama, ground 43
agama, Makgadikgadi spiny 68
Aha Hills 90, 133
Ai-Ais Nature Reserve 184
Ai-Ais/Richtersveld Transfrontier Park 169
aloe, bitter 190
Aloe broomii 173
aloe, Broom's 173
Aloe litteralis 91
Aloe meyeri 185
aloe, Meyer's 185
aloe, mopane 91
Aloe pearsonii 185, 189
aloe, Pearson's 185, 189
Aloe polyphylla 148, 161
aloes *171*
aloe, spiral *148*, 161
ana trees 31
!Ao≠o 131
apalis, Rudd's 20
Aponogeton ranunculiflorus 163
apple-leaf tree 30
Arieb guesthouse cottage 185
Arundinaria tesellata 157
Audi Camp 69, 70, 79, 82

B

babbler, bare-cheeked 123, 124
babbler, black-faced 136
Bahine National Park 27, 28
Baikiaea plurijuga 137
Baikiaea Waterhole 137
Bain, Andrew Geddes 176
Baines' Baobabs 69, 71, 73, 75, 76
Baines, Thomas 69, 76
Bain, Thomas 176, 193
Bakgalagadi people 54
bald ibis 163
bamboo sylph 157
Baobab Loop 75
Bape 58, 60
barbet, white-eared 20
bat, Commerson's leaf-nosed 93
Baviaanskloof 168, 170, 190–193, *191*
Beaufort West 172, 176
Beauvallon, A Reck Guesthouse 186, 189
bee-eater, blue-cheeked 86
bee-eater, carmine 78, 86
bee-eater, European 68, 86
beehives 26
beetle, tenebrionid 104, 110
berg bamboo 157
Berg Plaatz Wilderness Area 192

Bethel Business & Community Development Centre 158, 165
Bethel Mission Station 161
Betesda Rest Camp 116, 119
bilharzia 199
Biques Camping 33
bishop, yellow 164
Bitterpan 43
Black Mountain 164
Blue Mountain Pass 153
boerbean, Karoo 178
Bokong Nature Reserve 148, 152, 155
border posts
    Botswana 37
    Lesotho 150
    Mozambique 15
    Namibia 101–102
    South Africa 170
Bosobogolo Pan 46, 48, 49
Bossie Trail 174
Boteti River 67, 68, 70
Botsoela Waterfalls 160
botterboom 185, 189
bottle tree 121, 124
boubou, swamp 123
brakbos 104
Brandberg 100
Brandkaros 186, 189
broadbill, African 20
buffalo 73, 78, 82, 85, 142
buffalo-thorn 57
bullfrog, African 68
Büllsport Guest Farm 116, 119
bunch-of-grapes 104
Burkea africana 138
Burkea Waterhole 138
bushbuck, Chobe subsp. 36, 67, 85
bush etiquette 199–200
bushman grass, dune 104, 109
Bushman poison tree 178
bushman's candle 104
Bushmen 40–41, 55, 61, 96, 129, 131, 133, 142
Bwabwata National Park *see* Caprivi Game Park

C

camel's foot tree 31
camping equipment 200
cancer bush 173
canoeing 33, 186
Cape fur seal 107, 111
Caprivi Game Park 141, 142, 145
carrot tree 85
Casa Msika 32
Catophractes alexandri 42, 57, 71
Cave House 162

cedar, Willowmore 191
cell phones 17
Central Kalahari Game Reserve 55–60, *56*
chameleon, flap-necked 68
chameleon, Namaqua 104, 185
Chapman, James 69, 76
Chapman's Baobabs 69
chat, Herero 116, 123
cheetah 73
Chief's Island 77
Chitengo Camp 30, 32
Chobe National Park 36, 37, 83–90, *84*
cholera 17
Cladoraphis spinosa 104, 109
climate
    Botswana 37, 45, 49, 54, 60, 82, 90, 97
    Lesotho 149, 157, 165
    Mozambique 14, 23, 29, 33
    Namibia 101, 113, 119, 127, 133, 138, 145
    South Africa 169, 176, 182, 189, 193
cluster-leaf, purple-pod 134
cluster-leaf, silver 57, 66, 74
Coco Cabanas 21, 23
Combretum platypetalum 134
Commiphora 75, 104, 121
Conception Bay 112
Conception expedition 109–113, *110*
corkwood, blue-leafed 115
corkwood trees 75, 104, 121
Cotyledon 185
coucal, white-browed 123
crane, crowned 32, 63
crane, wattled 32, 63, 131, 139
Crocodile Camp Safaris 69, 70, 79, 82
crocodiles 24, 81, 123, 143
cross-berry, Karoo 173
cuckoo, great spotted 52
currency 103
    Botswana 38
    Lesotho 151
    Mozambique 16
    Namibia 103
    South Africa 171
customs
    Botswana 38
    Lesotho 150
    Mozambique 16
    Namibia 102
    South Africa 170
cycad, Karoo 190
cycad, Suurberg 190

D

Dabbie Xab River 187
Damaraland *98–99*

Damara people 124, 127
dassie, Kaokoland rock 122
dassie, rock 174, 175
Dead Tree Island *37*, 81
Deception Valley 55, 57, 58–59
De Hoop camp site 187
Deurspring Trail 180
Die Toon *168*, 185, 188
diving 21, 22, 23
Djokwe 131
dog rose, African 30
dollar bush 104
Dombo Hippo Pool 81
Domerog Pass 189
Doodsklip 191, 192
Doringstraat Waterhole 137
Dorsland Boom 132
Dorsland Trekkers 132
dove, mourning 123
Drive Out 169, 196
driving
    4x4 techniques 197–198
    Botswana 38, 39
    Lesotho 150
    Mozambique 16, 17
    Namibia 102, 103
    South Africa 170–171
Drotsky's Cabins 93, 97
duiker, common 20, 24, 51, 67
duiker, red 20, 32

E
eagle, steppe 140
eagle, Verreaux's 116, 117, 174
eagle, Wahlberg's 25, 136
ebony, false 115
egret, slaty 131, 139
Eksteenfontein 183, 186, 189
eland 42, 48, 51, 57, 91, 163, 191
elephant 20, 36, 73, 85, 141, 142
elephant, desert 122, 126, 130
elephant's trunk 185,187
Encephalartos lehmanii 190
environmental etiquette 199–200
Enyandi 125
Epupa Falls 125
Epupa Falls camp site 123
Epupa hydro-electric scheme 123
Eriocephalus ericoides 115, 118
Etendeka Mountains 126
Etosha National Park 100
Euphorbia 178, 185
Euphorbia avasmontana 178
Euphorbia virosa 115

F
'fairy circles' 126
falcon, amur 136
falcon, red-footed 68
false-thorn, paperbark 85
fig, common 115
fig, Namaqua 91
fig, Namaqua cluster 114
firefinch, brown 139
Fish River Canyon 101
flamingo, greater 63, 65, 131
flamingo, lesser 63, 65, 111, 131
fly-catcher, black-and-white 32
Fort Sesfontein 123, 128
Fossil Trail 174
fox, Cape 57
Frazer's Store 154, 157

G
gannet, Cape 107
Gariep River 180, 181, 184, 187
Gates of Paradise 160
Gcodikwe heronry 80
Gcodikwe Lagoon 80, 81
Gcwihaba Cave 36
Gcwihaba Hills 90, 91, 93, 95–97
gecko, barking 68
gecko, Tsodilo thick-toed 92
gecko, Turner's thick-toed 92
gecko, web-footed 110
Geelhoutbos 191, 193
gemsbok 73, 91, 111, 122
Gemsbok Wilderness Trail 40–45, *41*
gerbil, hairy-footed 110
giraffe 27, 42, 57, 122, 126
godwit, bar-tailed 111
golden mole, Namib 109–110
Gorongosa National Park 17, 30–33, *31*
Grassneck Pass 193
Great Limpopo Transfrontier Park 27–28, 169
greenbul, yellow-bellied 123
Green, Frederick Joseph 69
Green's Baobab 69
Grewia robusta 173
Grootboom 132
Groot Kolk 43
Gubatsa Hills 85
Guerna Wilderness Area 192, 193
Guma Lagoon Camp 93, 97
Gweta Rest Camp 69, 70

H
Ha Jobo 161
halfmens 185, 187
hartebeest, Lichtenstein's 29
hartebeest, red 29, 42, 48, 52, 57, 175
Hartmann Mountains 125–126
health 199
Helskloof 189

Herero people 37, 120
heron, purple 32, 80
Himba people 120, 124
Hippo Pools 123
hippopotomus 24, 78, 139, 142
Hoba Meteorite 100
hobby, African 140
Hodgson's Peaks 159
Holboom 132
Homeb 109, 111
honey-thorn 173
Hoodia parviflora 121
hornbill, Bradfield's 136, 139
hornbill, Monteiro's 116, 123
Huab Fall Walk 179
Hunsberg conservation area 184
hyaena, brown 27, 42, 48, 57, 110
hyaena, spotted 42, 78

I
ibis, bald 164, 165
ibis, sacred 80
ice rat 155, 165
Ihaha camp site 87
impala, black-faced 122
Inara 109
Inhambane *14*
ironwood, Lebombo 24
Island Safari Lodge 69, 70, 79, 82

J
jackal, black-backed 27, 43, 110
jackal, side-striped 136
Jensenobotrya lossowiana 104
Ju/'hoan people 96, 129, 131, 133
Julbernardia globiflora 24

K
Kalahari Gemsbok National Park *see* Kgalagadi Transfrontier Park
Kanyu Flats 71, 73
Kaokoveld 100, 103, 120–128, *121*, *128*
Kao River 155
kapokbos 115, 118
Karoo 4x4 Trail 172–176, *173*
Karoo National Park 168, 169, 172–176, *173*
Karoo Rest Camp 174
Katse Dam *151*, 152, 154–155, 156, 157
Katse Lodge 152, 157
Kaziikini Community Camp Site 79, 80, 82
Kepiseng 163
kestrel, Dickinson's 136
kestrel, lesser 68
Ketane Falls 161

INDEX

Kgalagadi Transfrontier Park 37, 169
Kgama-Kgama Pan 71, 75
Khankhe Pan 52
Khaudum 100, 103
Khaudum Camp 136, 137, 138
Khaudum Game Park 134–138, *135*
Khiding Pan 48
Khomani Bushmen 40–41
Khowarib camp site 123
Khutse Campground 52, 53
Khutse Game Reserve 50–54, *51*, *54*
Khwai floodplain 78, 80, 82
kingfisher, woodland 86
kite, black 140
kite, yellow-billed 52, 136, 140
Klein-Aus-Vista 106, 108
Klipspringer Pass 176
knot, red 111
Koanaka Hills 90
Koeroegab Plains 184
Koichab Pan 106
Kokerboomkloof 188
Kolmanskop 106
Komdomo 191, 192
korhaan, black 68
korhaan, Rüppell's 116
Kori camp site 58
Kotisephola Pass 164
Kouga Mountains 190
Kratzplatz 106, 108
Kremetart 131
Kruger National Park 24, 25, 27, 28–29
Kuboes 183, 186, 189
Kubu Island *see* Lekhubu Island
Kubunyana Camp 141, 145
Kudiakam Pan 73
Kuiseb River 109, 111–112
Kukama 58
Kunene River 124–125
Kunene River Lodge 123, 124, 128
Kwando River 143

L

Lake Manyemba 27
Lake Urema 30, 33
lammergeier 164, 165
Lang Rambuka 43, 44
lark, dune 106, 111
Lauberville camp 111, 112
Lebelonyane Pass 162
Le Bihan Falls *see* Maletsunyane Falls
lechwe, red 77, 139
Lekhubu Camp Site 59
Lekhubu Island 61, 63, 64–65
Lekkersing 183, 186, 189
Leopard Pan Camp Site 59

Lesholoago Pan 46, 48
Lesotho Highlands Water Project 156, 164
Letiahau Camp Site 59
Lianshulu Lodge 145
Limpopo National Park 24, 25, 27, 27–28
Linakeng Pass 164
Linyanti 85, 89
Linyanti camp site 87
lion 48, 57, 68, 73, 86, 122, 136
 Kalahari 42
Liphofung Cultural & Historical Site 152, 156, 157
Lithops 185
lizard, shovel-snouted 110
Lizauli Traditional Village 141
longclaw, rosy-throated 139
lovebird, rosy-faced 116, 117
Lubombo Transfrontier Conservation Area (LTFCA) 18, 169
Lüderitz 106

M

Mababe Depression 83, 84
Mabuasehube Pan 46, 47, 48
Mabuasehube Park 46–49, *47*
Mabuasehube Wilderness Trail 43, 48, 49
Mafika Lisiu Pass 155
Mahango Game Park 139, 141
mahogany, pod 18, 24
Mahurushele Pan 52
Makgadikgadi Pans *34–35*, 36, 50, 57, 61–65, *62*
Makgadikgadi Pans Game Reserve 66–70, *67*
Makgadikgadi Pans-Nxai Pan National Park *see* Makgadikgadi Pans Game Reserve; Nxai Pan National Park
Makobo Woods Camp Site 93
Makuri 131
Makurivlei 130, 132
malaria 17, 38, 81, 86, 103, 171, 181, 199
Malatso Camp Site 93
Malealea Lodge 158, 160, 165
Maletsunyane Falls 160
malkoha, green 20
Maloti-Drakensberg Transfrontier Conservation & Development Area 148
Maloti Mountains *146–147*, 148
 see also Mountain Road; Trans-Maloti
mamba, black 119
Mamili (Rupara) National Park 139, 141, 143–144, 145
Manyikeni Open-Air Museum 26

maps
 advice 198
 Botswana 39, *41*, 45, *47*, *51*, *56*, 60, *62*, *66*, *72*, *78*, 82, *84*, *92*, 97
 Lesotho 151, *153*, *159*
 Mozambique 17, *19*, *25*, *31*
 Namibia 103, *105*, *110*, *114*, *121*, 127–128, *130*, 133, *135*, *140*, 145
 South Africa 171, *173*, 176, *178*, 182, *184*, 189, *191*, 193
Maputo Corridor 169
Maputo Elephant Reserve *15*, 17, 18–23, *19*
Maqwee 79
Marakabei Guest House 152, 157
Marienfluss Valley 125
Maseru 153
Mata Mata 43
Mata Mata Tented Camp 43
Matebeng Pass 162, 164
Mboma Island 80
Menoaneng Pass 164
Mercury Island 107
Metisella syrinx 157
Metsimanong 58
Meyer's aloe 185
migrations 52, 57, 67, 73
Milibangalala 21, 22
milkbush 178
minnow, Drakensberg 163
Mohale Dam *149*, 152, 153–154, 156, 157
Mohale Lodge 152, 157
Mohale's Hoek 161
Mokhotlong 165
mokoro 79, 81, 88
Molapo 58, 60
Molopo Canyon 168, 178, 179
Molopo Trail 181–182
Molose waterhole 52, 53
Molumong Guesthouse & Backpackers 158, 165
Monamodi Pans 46, 48
mongoose, water 32, 122
monkey orange, black 18
monkey, samango 28, 32
Mopipi reservoir 70
Moremi Game Reserve 36, 77–82, *78*
Moreswe Pan 52, 53
moringa tree 115
Morromeu Delta 32
Motel do Mar 21, 23
Moteng Pass 156
Mountain Road (Lesotho) 152–157, *153*
Mpaathutlwa Pan 46, 47, 48.49

Muanza 33
Mudumu National Park 139, 141, 143, 145
Muela Dam 152, 154, 156, 157
munondo 24
Myrothamnus flabellifolius 115

N
Nama hut camp 186
Nama people 170, 183
Nambwa 141, 142, 145
Namib Desert 100, *101*
Nata Bird Sanctuary 65
Nata Lodge 63, 69, 70
Nata Sanctuary 63
Naukluft 4x4 Trail 114–119, *115*, *119*
Naukluft camp site 116, 119
Naukluft Hiking Trail 116
neat's foot, coffee 71, 74
Nerine laticoma 45
New Oxbow Lodge 152, 156, 157
N//goabaca camp site 140–141, 145
Njuca Hills 68, 70
Nogatsaa/Tchinga area 85, 89
Nohana 158, 165
Nohana route 161–162
noorsdoring 185
North Camp 73
North-Eastern Parks 139–145, *140*
North Gate Camp Site 79
Nossob Camp 43
Nossob Eco Trail 43
Ntwetwe Pan 61, 66–67
Nuwekloof Pass 193
Nuweveld Mountains 172, 175, 176
Nxai Pan 71, 73, 74, *76*
Nxai Pan National Park 36, 71–76, *72*
Nxamaseri Lodge 93, 97
Nyae Nyae 100, 103, 129–133, *130*
Nyae Nyae Pan 132
nyala 27, 32

O
!O'baha 131,133
Okarohombo camp site 123
Okavango Delta 36
Okavango River Lodge 69, 70, 79, 82
O Lar do Ouro Guest Lodge 21, 23
oldwood 157
Olive Trail 116
omiramba 134
Ondorusu Gorge 124
Ongongo camp site 123

openbill, African 78, 86, 140
oribi 32, 143, 163
Osseberg 4x4 trail 192
ostrich grass 104, 109
Otjikoto Lake 100
otter, Cape clawless 122
owl, pearl-spotted 93
oystercatcher, African black 111

P
Pachydactylus tsodiloensis 92
packing supplies 200–201
Pafuri 28, 29
palm, borassus 31
palm, ilala 31
palm, makalani 66, 121, 125
palm-thrush, collared 32, 123
Palmwag Lodge 123, 127, 128
palm, wild date 31
parrot, Meyer's 136
parrot, Rüppell's 123
Passarge Valley 55, 59
Pass of the Jackals 154
pelican, white 65
penguin, African 107
Perdepoort Trail 177, 181
photography 17
Piper Pans 58, 59
pipit, mountain 164
pipit, yellow-breasted 164
plakkies 185
Planet Baobab 69, 70
Platinum Highway 169
plover, Caspian 68
plover, chestnut-banded 63, 111
plover, grey 111
plover, Kittlitz's 63
Pokkiespram 186–187
Polentswa 43, 44
pomegranate, yellow 173
Ponta Dobela 18, 21, 22
Ponta do Ouro 23
Ponta Malongane Holiday Resort *12–13*, 21, 23
Ponta Mamoli Resort 18, 21, 22, 23
pony treks 158
Popa Falls Rest Camp 140, 141, 145
porkbush 190
porkbush, Namaqua 180, 185
Postberg Nature Reserve 188
pratincole, black-winged 68
pratincole, rock 139
Pseudobarbus quathlambae 163
puku 36, 85
Punda Maria 28–29
Punda Maria rest camp 25
Purros camp site 123
python, Anchieta's dwarf 122–123

Q
quad-bike trips 124
Quithing 162
quiver trees 115, 185, 189

R
rabbit, riverine 174
reedbuck, common 32, 77, 139
reedbuck, mountain 163
resurrection bush 115
rhebok, grey 163
rhinoceros, black 122, 127, 175
rhinoceros, white 20
Richtersberg camp site 187, 188
Richtersveld Arts & Crafts Centre 186
Richtersveld National Park *166–167*, 168, 169, *169*, 183–189, *184*
Riemvasmaak 168, 169, 177–182, *178*, *182*
Riemvasmakers 170, 177–178
roan 27, 78, 82, 86, 136, 137
rock engravings 100–101, 181
rockjumper, orange-breasted 148, 164
rock paintings 36, 89, 93–94, 101, 156, 161, 163, 200
roller, broadbilled 28, 32, 78, 86
roller, European 52
roller, racket-tailed 28, 32
Rolputs camp site 180
Roma 159
Roof of Africa 152–157, *153*
Rooihoek 191, 192
Rooiputs 43
Ruacana 124

S
sable 32, 78, 82, 86
Saddle Hill Guided 4x4 Trail 104–108, *105*
Salsola 63, 68, 104
salt bush 63, 68, 104
Sanddrif 186, 189
sanderling 111
sandpiper, curlew 111
Sandwich Harbour 109, 111, 112, 113
Sangwali village 143
Sani Pass 165
Sani Top Chalet 158, 159, 164–165
Santawani Lodge 79, 82
Sarcocaulon 104
Save River 24
Savute camp site 87
Savute Marsh 83–84, 85, 89
Schwabe, Hans 44
Seaka Bridge 161
secretary bird 164

INDEX

Seforong Gorge 158, 162–163, 165
Sehlabathebe Lodge 158, 165
Sehlabathebe National Park 148, 163
Sekushuwe Pan 52
Semonkong Lodge 158, 160, 161, 165
Sendelingsdrif 186
Senqu River *151*, 164
Senqu River Valley 162, 163
Sesatswe 43, 44
Sesfontein 126–127
Shakawe Fishing Lodge 93, 97
Shandereka village 79, 80
Shark Island camp site 106, 108
shoveller, Cape 131
shrike, lesser grey 68
shrike, white-tailed 116, 123
Sikereti Camp 136, 137
siskin, Drakensberg 164
sitatunga 85, 139, 141
sjambok pod 30
skiing 152, 156
skimmer, African 86
Slogget's rat 155, 165
Solitaire Country Lodge 116, 119
Soncana Waterhole 137
South Camp 73, 76, *76*
Sowa Pan 61, 64, 65
spekboom 190
Sperrgebiet 100, 112
spider, cartwheel 110
spider, white lady 110
spinetail, Böhm's 25, 28
spinetail, mottled 25, 28
Springbokvlakte 184, 188
spring-hare 27
starling, Meves's 28, 123
starling, sharp-tailed 136
star tree 173
Stipagrostis sabulicola 104, 109
stone plants 185
stork, Abdim's 52, 86, 136
stork, marabou 32, 80, 87
stork, open-billed 80
stork, yellow-billed 80
Studtis 193
sunbird, Neergaard's 20
Sunday Pan 58, 59
suni 20
Susuwe 142
Susuwe Island Lodge 145
Sutherlandia frutescens 173
Swamp Stop 93, 97
Swartberg Pass 176
syringa, white 85
syringa, wild 138

T
tampans 60, 199
Tatasberg 185
Tatas River 188
Tchinga 85
teal, Cape 21, 131
Tebellong 163
termitaria islands 144
tern, Caspian 111
tern, Damara 111
tern, Sandwich 111
terrapin, marsh 68
Thaba Bosiu 148, 157
Thabana li-Mele 159
Thabana Ntlenyana 148, 159, 164
Thaba Tseke 154
The Trading Post 158, 159, 165
Third Bridge 79, 80
Thop Fountain 181
thorn, black monkey 24
thorn, sweet 115, 173
thorn, trumpet 42, 57, 71
thorn, umbrella 57
thrush, sentinel rock 164
Thulamela 29
ticks 60, 199
titbabbler, Layard's 116, 118
tit, Carp's 123
tit, rufous-bellied 136
Tjeriktik Camp 116, 118
Tlaeeng Pass 156
toad tree 20
Topnaar community 109
tortoise, leopard 43, 68
transfrontier parks 42
Trans-Kalahari Highway 169
Trans-Kalahari route 54, 58, 59, 60
Trans-Maloti 158–165, *159*
Tsauchab River Camping 116, 119
Ts'ehlanyane National Park 148, 152, 157
tsessebe 85, 141
tsetse fly 199
Tsoana Waterhole 137
Tsodilo Hills 36, 90, 91–97, *92, 97*
Tsoelikane Waterfall 163
Tsonxhwaa Hill 89
Tsumkwe 129
Tsumkwe Lodge 131, 133
turnstone 111
turtles, leatherback 21
Twee Rivieren 43
twinspot, pink-throated 20
Two Rivers 43
Twyfelfontein 100
Tylecodon 185, 189

V
Van Zyl's Pass 125, 128
vehicle requirements
 accessories & equipment 196–197, 201
 Botswana 38
 Mozambique 16
 Namibia 102
 South Africa 170
veterinary regulations 38
Vilankulo camp site 25
Vilankulo to Punda Maria route 24–29, *25*
visas 102
 Botswana 38
 Lesotho 150
 Mozambique 15
 Namibia 102
 South Africa 170
Vubu camp site 143
vulture, Cape 163
vulture, palm-nut 21, 32
vygies 185

W
Walvis Bay 111
warbler, greater swamp 139
Warmquelle 127
waterbuck 32, 77
Waterkloof Trail 116
waxbill, Cinderella 123
weaver, sociable *36*
weaver, southern brown-throated 139
wheatear, capped 52
whimbrel, common 111
white-water rafting 124
whydah, pin-tailed 164
wild dogs 48, 73, 81
wildebeest, blue 48, 52, 57, 67, 73, 85
 Niassa subsp. 27
wood-hoopoe, violet 123
woodpecker, ground 164

X
Xade 55, 58
Xakanaxa 81
Xakanaxa Camp Site 79
Xhumaga Campground 68, 70

Y
Youth with a Mission station 162

Z
Zambezi teak 137
zebra, Burchell's 67, 73, 85
 subsp. Sofala 32
zebra, Cape mountain 175, 191
zebra, Hartmann's mountain 114, 115, 117
Zinave National Park 17, 24, 25, 26–27, 29, *29*
Zygophyllum 104